# GENDER AND PERFORMANCE IN SHAKESPEARE'S PROBLEM COMEDIES

# Drama and Performance Studies

*Timothy Wiles, general editor*

# Gender and Performance in Shakespeare's Problem Comedies

DAVID MCCANDLESS

*Indiana University Press*

BLOOMINGTON AND INDIANAPOLIS

The paper used in this publication meets
the minimum requirements of American
National Standard for Information
Sciences—Permanence of Paper for Printed
Library Materials, ANZI Z39.48-1984.

Manufactured in the United States of
America

**Library of Congress Cataloging-in-Publication Data**

McCandless, David Foley.
    Gender and performance in Shakespeare's problem
comedies / David McCandless.
    p.    cm. — (Drama and performance studies)
    Includes index.
    ISBN 0–253–33306–7 (cloth : alk. paper)
    1. Shakespeare, William, 1564–1616—Comedies. 2.
Shakespeare, William, 1564–1616. All's well that ends
well. 3. Shakespeare, William, 1564–1616. Troilus and
Cressida. 4. Shakespeare, William, 1564–1616.
Measure for measure. 5. Feminism and literature—
England—History—16th century. 6. Feminism and
literature—England—History—17th century. 7. Man-
woman relationships in literature. 8. Sex role in
literature. 9. Comedy. I. Title. II. Series.
PR2981.M39  1997
822.3'3—dc21                    97–3934

1 2 3 4 5 02 01 00 99 98 97

*For my wife Parthy,*
*my mother Elaine,*
*and my daughters Peytie and Lainie*

# ACKNOWLEDGMENTS

Writing this book took me to many brave new worlds and undream'd shores and I was very fortunate to have enjoyed the tutelage and company of so many sagacious guides and stimulating co-travellers. The Shakespeare Association of America offered a wonderful forum for testing out my ideas and for gaining friends and intellectual allies, among whom I would like particularly to acknowledge Evelyn Gajowski, Kay Stanton, Don Foster, Lars Engle, Tony Dawson, Gillian Murray Kendall, and Linda Charnes.

The University of California, Berkeley, provided a wonderfully stimulating environment—as well as a Humanities Research Grant—that made possible the shifts in methodology and perspective crucial to the inception of this book. Of all the students at Berkeley who have enriched and productively challenged my work—both in the classroom and the rehearsal hall—two deserve special mention: Peter Mostkoff, for encouraging me to delve further into Lacan, and Maya Roth, for her insights into *All's Well That Ends Well* and her eleventh-hour bibliographic spade-work, both of which proved very timely.

I was also fortunate to have enjoyed the mentorship of colleagues from Berkeley's Department of English, especially Joel Altman, a supporter of both my scholarly and artistic endeavors, and Don McQuade, who heroically helmed the Department of Dramatic Art at a particularly troubled time. I am additionally indebted to Don for his unerringly insightful commentary on my manuscript.

My manuscript also benefitted from the sensitive and exacting appraisal of a host of other expert readers, including Charles Lyons, Steve Vineberg, Ron Rebholz, Charles Frey, Hugh Richmond, Don Foster, Diana Henderson, and Richard Wheeler.

I am grateful to Timothy Wiles at Indiana University for his enthusiastic reception of my manuscript, and to Robert Sloan, Cindy Ballard, and Sharon Emmons at Indiana University Press for their help in preparing it for publication and circulation.

Finally, there are five people who merit my deepest, most emphatic thanks. I am indebted to my chief mentor at Stanford, Eleanor Prosser, who taught me so much about scholarship in general and Shakespeare in particular. I don't know what Ellie would have thought of this book, which departs markedly from the dissertation I wrote under her, but of one thing I am certain: it would be a better book if she had lived to critique it. Lorne Buchman has been, from our earliest days as fellow graduate students at

Stanford to our (all-too-brief) years as colleagues at Berkeley, my closest friend, biggest fan, and most inexhaustible source of guidance and support, both personal and intellectual.

Barbara Hodgdon, whose pioneering work on Shakespeare and performance  has been an inspiration, read every word of every draft and never failed to provide transformative criticism, invaluable advice, and hearty encouragement. Janet Adelman has been an exceptionally generous mentor, offering penetrating criticism of my work at every turn and, at one truly pivotal moment, giving me precisely the encouragement I needed to leap headlong into psychoanalytic-feminist theory and to draw far more on my practitioner's experience. Janet never failed to offer help when I needed it, despite a workload that would have worn out Hercules—a workload largely owing to her devotion to her students.

Finally, I owe my most heartfelt thanks to my wife, Parthy. "Acknowledgments" quite often end with formidably clever or poetic tributes to spouses or lovers. I'd like very much to say something surpassingly grand or stunning, but perhaps the most powerful tribute I can offer is the simplest: in every conceivable way, this book would not have been possible without her.

# CONTENTS

# Introduction

This study will examine the drama of sexual difference in Shakespeare's problem comedies—*All's Well That Ends Well, Measure for Measure,* and *Troilus and Cressida*—, practice a new mode of performance criticism keyed to a feminist *gestus,* and offer a fresh interpretation of the plays that captures their provocative depth and ambiguity.

Although my investigation submits the problem comedies principally to contemporary theory and theatrical practice, it should be noted that Shakespeare composed the problem comedies at a key moment in England's history: the transition of power from a virgin queen to a sybaritic king, a moment that catalyzed latent tensions in the sex-gender system. Scholars traditionally date *Troilus and Cressida* (1601–02) and *All's Well That Ends Well* (1602–04) in the last years of Elizabeth's reign, *Measure for Measure* (1604) in the first years of James's. As Louis Montrose puts it, "Elizabeth incarnated a contradiction at the very center of the Elizabethan sex/gender system"—the female ruler of a patriarchal society who, as mother to all her male subjects, implicitly imprisoned them in perpetual boyhood.[1] She was both chaste and sexual, "feminine" but dominant. Her self-conscious self-portrayal as Virgin Mother did not preclude a certain amount of sexual adventurism, particularly with Robert Dudley, nor did it, among her male subjects, preclude fantasies of mastery or merger, from the political stratagems of Essex to the erotic dreams of Simon Forman. She was an object of desire as well as fear and reverence—the engulfing mother as monarch.

Elizabeth's successor, James, might plausibly be considered an absent father, given his predilection for reclusiveness and self-mystification. Like Elizabeth, he also unsettled gender distinctions: he was the powerful patriarch as pacifist and epicene courtier, doting on comely male favorites like Somerset and Buckingham. That James himself readily traversed gender boundaries seems clear from a letter he penned to Buckingham, in which he proposes that the two of them make "a new marriage ever to be kept hereafter," lamenting the "widow's life" he has led without Buckingham, and referring to him as "my sweet childe and wife," thus positioning himself not simply as lover but as husband, wife, and father.[2]

In addition, the society over which James presided was much beset by breakdowns in gender codes; especially subversive were the assertive, liberated "city women" of London, who challenged the cultural paradigm of a "closed," passive femininity, and the notorious female transvestites, who challenged the stability of gender itself, demonstrating the constructedness of hierarchical distinctions deemed divinely ordained.[3]

The problem comedies dramatize this crisis in gender. All three plays register a male dread of emasculation and engulfment, a fear of female authority and sexuality, perhaps reflecting the perilous effects on the male psyche of long-standing submission to an indomitable female ruler. In all three plays, central male figures identify desire for a female as dangerous and unmanly. Submission to her power consequently undermines the efficacy of traditional agencies of masculine self-affirmation. In *Measure for Measure*, male authority suffers in the face of a female's disruptive sexual power. Positioning himself as a righteous, omnipotent ruler, Angelo disintegrates once he is beset by lust for the chaste Isabella. In *All's Well That Ends Well* and *Troilus and Cressida*, female sexuality threatens not male authority but male heroism. Both plays depict the deflation of traditional chivalric, militaristic definitions of masculinity.[4] Two overtly sexual women, both named Helen, impeach the integrity of the military enterprise in these plays. Helena of *All's Well* circumscribes Bertram's achievement of military honor, while Helen of *Troilus and Cressida* contaminates the war at its source. The storied Trojan War becomes ripe for mockery precisely because it is fought for the sake of an unabashedly libidinous, emasculating woman. This undermining of a distinctly masculine virtue may well reflect the tensions attending Elizabeth's own circumscription of military exploits and her implicit opposition to the efforts of Essex to revive the chivalric ideal, to create a sphere of male efficacy unobstructed by female authority.

Both *All's Well* and *Measure for Measure* also register anxiety about paternal sufficiency, focusing to a significant degree on the figure of the ailing or absent father. *Measure for Measure*, written in the first year of James's reign, centers on the efforts of an ineffectual ghostly father to recover his potency, to enact a narrative of "the return of the patriarch." The uncertainty of his success perhaps reflects the shakiness of James's own efforts to affirm his paternal authority. The resemblance between the Duke and James has been noted often. Both are withdrawn, enigmatic figures of ambiguous sexuality who undertake surveillance of other people's sexual activities, display a fondness for arranged marriages, and prove themselves capable of both merciless severity and spectacular clemency. If, at one time, the comparison was considered flattering to the king, increased critical uneasiness with the Duke's duplicitous, self-deifying ways suggests that the play may circulate doubt and anxiety about the adequacy of the new king to his paternal function.[5]

These historical circumstances may help account for the main "problem" with the problem comedies: their deviation from Shakespearean comic precedent. Whatever the case, this main problem constitutes the plays' main attraction to critics concerned with issues of gender and sexuality. By resisting comic closure, *All's Well That Ends Well, Measure for Measure,* and *Troilus and Cressida* leave uncontained the subversions of the sex-gender system that the comedies mostly contain. In Northrop Frye's oft-cited formula, Shakespearean comedy depicts the triumph of youthful passion over paternal stricture; young lovers, after a liberating sojourn in an alternative pastoral or holiday world, realize their fugitive love and revitalize a moribund society.[6] More recent criticism has pointed out the essential conservatism of this comic construct and the superficiality of the lovers' triumph: the marriages they make in the end reinforce the sex-gender system so bracingly subverted during the holiday interludes.[7] The anticipated nuptials uphold rather than overthrow the Law of the Father, ratifying the conversion of a male-female difference into a masculine-feminine symbolic opposition that positions the "feminine" as the lacking referent of the "masculine." The comedies enact a carnivalesque purgation of subversive urges: their expansion of "femininity" through instances of transvestite disguise and unfeminine self-assertion and their critique of male callowness and callousness give way to a conventional denouement of "boy gets girl" that restabilizes gender roles. Men who receive correction from cleverer mistresses become their lords and masters; renegade women acquiesce in the femininity they implicitly contested.

In short, the comedies enact an essentially oedipal narrative, a drama of reified masculinity that consigns women to the mythical position of object/obstacle/objective of the male hero's quest, the "Other" out of whom he creates himself. As Teresa de Lauretis puts it,

> [T]o say that narrative is the production of Oedipus is to say that each
> reader—male or female—is constrained and defined within the two positions
> of a sexual difference thus conceived: male-hero-human, on the side of the
> subject; and female-obstacle-boundary-space, on the other. . . . Narrative

endlessly reconstructs [the world] as a two-character drama in which the human person creates and recreates *himself* out of an abstract or purely symbolic other—the womb, the earth, the grave, the woman.[8]

Women, no matter how much they may seem to dominate an individual narrative, are ultimately mere appendages to an underlying master narrative of masculine legitimation.

The problem comedies, though inextricably entangled in oedipal narratives, nevertheless deconstruct these narratives to the point of near rupture, failing to resolve more aggressive subversions of the sex-gender system, effectively breaching or abandoning a conservative comic ending. In particular, all three plays present female figures who contest and confound "feminine Otherness." In *All's Well,* Helena destabilizes femininity by melding unfeminine, erotic aggression with hyperfeminine self-abnegation. In *Measure for Measure,* Isabella tries to resist femininity yet finds herself insistently recruited to perform it in order to serve male interests. In *Troilus and Cressida,* Cressida defamiliarizes femininity by enacting its multiple, seemingly contradictory guises. This unsettling of femininity obstructs the male characters' quests for manhood. Bertram, Angelo, the Duke, and Troilus all unsuccessfully pursue a myth of masculinity that posits woman as object of conquest or vessel of fulfillment.

By suspending the reification of gender norms, *All's Well That Ends Well, Measure for Measure,* and *Troilus and Cressida* become stages for vexed and ungainly impersonations of "man" and "woman" that underline the theatricality of gender, its status as a cultural construct requiring habitual, substantiating enactment. By failing to substantiate it, these characters disclose gender's inadequacy as a signifier, registering dimensions of subjectivity excessive to, or other than, imposed images of masculine power and feminine lack. As Judith Butler puts it,

> This "being a man" and this "being a woman" are internally unstable affairs. They are always beset by ambivalence precisely because there is a cost in every identification, the loss of some other set of identifications, the forcible approximation of a norm one never chooses, a norm that chooses us, but which we occupy, reverse, resignify to the extent that the norm fails to determine us completely.[9]

In the problem comedies, the male characters fail to occupy, and the female figures fail to reverse or resignify, the genders that fail to determine them. The male figures unpersuasively enact and the female characters uncomfortably evade the normative genders they are assigned. Helena, Isabella, and Cressida all seek to circumvent a disempowering, desexualizing consignment to "lack," to negotiate a sexual subjectivity. Female desire thus becomes a key problem in the problem comedies, either repressed, mystified, or perilously—even ruinously—pursued. As complex subjects irreducible to the static role of subservient object, Helena, Isabella, and Cressida become unintelligible within the oedipal plot—and within the phallocentric system of meaning it enforces. They therefore become potential agents of disruption, unwitting saboteurs. In their unassimilability to an oppositionalist gender system, they begin to restore difference to a system that depends upon erasing it.

This study will focus on that potentially subversive unassimilability, assaying the gaps, tensions, and contradictions that arise from the desiring subject's adjustment to—or adjustment of—the phallocentric gender system. Attempting a feminist gestus, it will stage the problem comedies' drama of gender as it unfolds through the play of desire and assists in constituting (or dismantling) the subject.

My critical method weds a theoretically engaged textual analysis to the dynamics of performance. My aim is to think through these plays performatively, to cite or envision performance choices for the sake of integrating text and performance in reciprocally enriching interplay rather than merely corroborating or ornamenting a textual argument. While the performance critic has traditionally positioned herself as expert spectator, I adopt the perspective of the practitioner, bringing directorial modes of inquiry to my critical/theoretical analysis. While I frequently draw on the performance histories of the problem comedies, I more regularly exploit my own experience as a director in dramatizing and theorizing the enactment of gender. I have directed productions of *All's Well That Ends Well* (University of Illinois–Chicago, 1987) and *Measure for Measure* (University of California, Berkeley, 1992), the latter with a specific regard for its examination of gender issues. Therefore, my discussion of *Measure for Measure* is based on a specific production, whereas my analyses of *All's Well* and *Troilus and Cressida* are more speculative and hypothetical.

Because of my focus on gender, the order in which I discuss the plays is keyed not to chronology but to degrees of deviation from the comic oedipal plot. Thus, *Troilus and Cressida*, chronologically the first of the problem comedies, is the last to be discussed, as it deconstructs gender and subjectivity the most radically; the spectral comic ending that tempts resolution in *All's Well That Ends Well* and *Measure for Measure* simply fails to materialize in *Troilus and Cressida*. This earliest problem comedy offers the most extreme instances of male and female subjectivity under erasure. Troilus is but the leading player in a vast spectacle of masculinity degraded by allegiance to an insubstantial ideal, while Cressida's downfall dramatizes the problematic of both female desire (cf. Helena) and female subjugation (cf. Isabella).

The kind of performance criticism I practice in these pages is neither an historicist assessment of "the place of the stage" nor a traditional stage-centered reading. Rather, it aims to align the post-structuralist concerns of the former with the performance-centered approach of the latter. Ironically, Shakespearean performance criticism traditionally has sought to protect the text against the violations of both performance and criticism, positing an authentic text and performance tradition that legislate or at least regulate meaning.[10] In their recent list of the six essential characteristics of Shakespearean performance criticism, Marvin and Ruth Thompson include the effort to establish both a standard of accuracy against which to judge contemporary criticism and a standard of authenticity against which to judge contemporary performance.[11] The first disallows or discredits readings judged insufficiently attentive to the conditions and conventions of performance, and may argue even more peremptorily that Shakespeare's plays can "mean" only in the context of performance. The second, despite celebrating contemporary performance as the ideal forum for understanding Shakespeare, nevertheless sets limits on directorial invention.

This notion of authenticity fails to acknowledge the instability of the Shakespearean text or the unrecoverability of its original performance context. Far from containing an "original writing" that encodes or conveys an "original meaning," the Shakespearean text is itself unoriginal, a document whose relationship to the original performance—not to mention the original script that Shakespeare submitted to his acting company—can only be guessed at. Although some quarto texts proclaimed their fidelity to recent stage representations—"as it hath bene sundry times publiquely acted"—the claims are questionable, to say the least, given the evidence of radically variant quarto versions and the notoriously untidy early modern practice of compiling and transmitting playscripts, a practice over which Shakespeare himself seems to have exercised little control. Indeed, the principal source for half of Shakespeare's plays—the folio—was compiled seven years after his death. In addition, as Stephen Orgel points out, given the evidence of two heavily edited pre-Restoration Shakespearean prompt-books and the probable running time of performances at the Globe, Shakespeare's scripts as we know them were almost certainly cut even for their first performances.[12]

If the Shakespearean text cannot be accorded authentic status, neither can the conditions and conventions of Shakespearean performance. First of all, we cannot reconstruct or recreate them with any certainty. This fact does not diminish the importance of excavatory efforts, both material and scholarly, that extend our understanding. It simply means that one ought not to construct, on their foundation, a prohibitive standard of authenticity.[13] Even if we could somehow physically recreate the original setting and playing style of Shakespeare's plays, we could never recapture their peculiar semiosis, their embeddedness in a distinct, historically conditioned network of corporeal, relational, visual signs. To suggest, therefore, that the best or only way to perform Shakespeare today is on an essentially empty platform stage in an artificial, presentational style, with an actor-audience dynamic emulative of Shakespeare's, seems to me unduly narrow.[14] I have seen productions styled on this aesthetic. Some were vital and illuminating; others were colossally boring. The same holds true for spectacularly conceptual productions that deploy all the technologies of modern stagecraft: some are riveting and some are desultory. The point is that the aesthetic outcome of a particular production depends on the resourcefulness and creativity of the individual artists, not so much on their choice of playing space and still less on their commitment to a specious authenticity.

The Shakespearean text serves not as a legislator but as an enabler of meaning, not as the medium of a discernible truth that performance must animate but as the generator of multiple truths, each of which performance might actualize. Arguments that performance must somehow present "the text itself" construct a false analogy between reading and watching a play. As Barbara Hodgdon points out, watching a play more closely parallels reading an essay about it.[15] The spectator "reads" a performed "reading" of the text, not the text itself. The director facilitates a communal and collaborative writing that parallels that of the critical essayist. Both individuals impart—albeit in radically different languages—a specific vision of the text through the processes of selection, accentuation, parallelism, and framing.

Hodgdon's notion of "parallel practices" supports the post-structuralist concept of interpretation as performance: just as the director and his collaborators interpret the text through performance, the critic "performs" the text through interpretation. Therefore, it is no more appropriate to admonish directors to let the text "speak for itself"[16] than to ask the same of critics. The text must first speak *through* us before it can speak *to* us. As Charles Marowitz asserts, "like it or not, the only voice Shakespeare has is the one through which his interpreters speak."[17] These interpreters—

theatrical, academic, or otherwise—can never give us the whole play, but can only promulgate meanings that are necessarily selective and subjective—and historically conditioned. The history of Shakespearean production—and criticism—is a history of rediscovering and reconfiguring plays according to the consciousness of the times, of bodying forth previously unrealized worlds.[18] Thus *Henry V* may become an anti-war play; *The Merchant of Venice,* an exposé of racial intolerance; and *The Tempest,* a critique of colonialism.

What makes the director (who, after all, did not exist in Shakespeare's day) particularly problematic to traditionalists is her tendency toward intervention and innovation. Whereas the critic may simply suppress scenes or passages irrelevant or even obstructive of his interpretation, the director may actually invent scenes or create images that have no precise textual referent. In order to make their interpretations live on the stage, to give them maximum vitality and cogency—to offer a vision as revelatory and persuasive in theatrical terms as the critic wishes his essay to be in discursive terms—directors take on the status of independent artists that many traditionalists find repugnant. Yet, as Peter Brook asserts, "the only way to find the true path to the speaking of a word is through a process that parallels the original creative one."[19] Extending Hodgdon's notion of "parallel practices," directing parallels the act not only of writing an essay about the play but of writing the play itself anew.

In a highly stimulating essay, Thomas Clayton attempts to establish a standard capable of distinguishing legitimate directorial inventions from self-indulgent distortions.[20] Assessing a production of *Macbeth,* Clayton endorses the decision to make Lady Macduff visibly pregnant because the image complements "dialogue and stage directions." He disapproves, however, of the portrayal of the weird sisters as "three attractive young women in diaphanous robes" because it constitutes a "wholesale reversal of script identities and appearances." "In an adaptation, fine," Clayton concludes. "In a production, distortive."[21]

Yet all productions are necessarily adaptations in the sense that they adapt to the stage a specific interpretation of the text—always a distortion— rather than the text itself. As W. B. Worthen suggests, to the extent that "the text" signifies its full range of performable meanings, performance can only signify the text's absence.[22] Representing the witches as young and attractive is not *ipso facto* a bad choice; its merits as a choice cannot be assessed independently of the production it served (which Clayton does not identify). Perhaps it was merely a baldly gimmicky, meretriciously "theatrical" conceit. Perhaps, however, it was a choice integral to the animation of a governing idea derived from the text, enriching and ramifying an interpretation that, rendered in discursive prose, might seem unobjectionable, even compelling. Certainly recent feminist criticism has paved the way for linking the witches and Lady Macbeth as kindred projections of male sexual dread, a connection arguably obscured by the orthodox presentation of the weird sisters as malevolent, grotesque hags dressed in black.[23] Perhaps the director of the unnamed production to which Clayton alludes wished nothing more than to underline this connection, theatrically corroborating, directly or indirectly, a contemporary critical/theoretical insight. The point is that the production that employed this particular image must be judged according to the totality and integrity of its effects, acknowledged as an independent work of art rather than an imperfect copy dwarfed by a superior original.

The object-relations psychoanalytic model, which will figure prominently in my discussion of subjectivity, offers a way of theorizing this parallel creativity. D. W. Winnicott stresses that, in the "transitional space" of creative play, the individual's relation to objects amounts to inventing what is already there; the object exists both in its own right and as the creation of one's need.[24] This seems to me a highly apposite way of describing the textual object to which the artist/critic relates: it is both an external artifact and a stimulant to the artist/critic's need to represent herself, alien yet assimilable to her inner world. The object submits to subjective use yet retains its essential distinctness; it enriches and deepens the artist/critic with its singularity even as it gives birth to a reconfigured image of itself. Whether the reconfigured images afforded by Shakespearean criticism and performance prove pleasing or irksome to their audiences, the text always survives, awaiting transport into other transitional realms, into other interpretive constructs. This model of creativity offers a more nuanced alternative to the extremes of text-as-nullity (nothing is there but what we project) and text-as-authority (nothing is there but what the text prescribes).

Lurking behind complaints against directorial distortion is the longing for a literary theater, a theater serviceable to a text conceived in literary terms and circumscribed by a set of literary readings. Yet any director who harnesses himself to a text so circumscribed instead of drawing inspiration from a fresh encounter with a living script will surely produce what Brook calls "deadly theater":

> We see [Shakespeare's] plays done by good actors in what seems like the
> proper way—they look lively and colourful, there is music and everyone is all

dressed up, just as they are supposed to be in the best of classical theatres. Yet secretly we find it excruciatingly boring.[25]

Theatrical artists cannot constrict themselves with the impossible ambition of "doing it the way it was written." As Brook asserts, "all the printed word can tell us is what was written on paper, not how it was once brought to life."[26] The director and his collaborators must discover how to bring the text to life in their own unique way.

This argument, in various ways and to varying degrees, has been made by nearly every major director who has bothered to write down his or her thoughts on directing literary masterpieces. Of course, it could be reasonably objected that not every director is Bertolt Brecht, Jerzy Grotowski, or Peter Brook—that this notion of parallel creativity vindicates the efforts of the most self-excited hacks and charlatans to inflict their desecrations of Shakespeare on an unsuspecting public and turns the standard for evaluating Shakespearean performance into some version of Pirandello's "right you are if you think you are." If Shakespeare's plays are to be regarded not as "expressions of intention" but as "material," as stimuli for a satellite artistry, if we must surrender notions of "authenticity" and "fidelity," by what measure are we to rate the success of current performances of Shakespeare?

I would like to adapt Jonathan Miller's notion of "coherent vitality" into a viable standard ("adapt" because Miller himself regards the text as more closed than I do): a production must be alive enough to engage the audience's kinetic, emotional, and mental energies, and coherent enough to give the experience a meaning beyond these sensory and somatic excitations, even if that meaning cannot be precisely captured in language.[27] And who determines whether a Shakespearean performance demonstrates coherent vitality? The same people who always do with any living art form—audiences, critics, trustworthy colleagues.

Of course, in a post-structuralist age, coherence is a highly problematic concept, founded as it is on excluding difference and concealing the conditions of its own production. Before I conclude this introduction, I will do my best to stress the utility of coherence to theatrical experience and to acknowledge the enabling contingencies of my own critical practice, demystifying my own directorial choices by explicitly linking them to a gestic, feminist, psychoanalytic approach.

If my work parts company with some of the assumptions of traditional performance criticism, it shares with historicist inquiries into gender an interest in how the performance of gender inside the theater illuminates its performance outside. It is at least possible that the boy actress did the same thing in the theater that the female transvestite did in society: blurred and denaturalized genders held to be distinct and natural. Indeed, it is tempting to read the boy actress's simulated femininity as a metadramatic index of gender's performative base.[28]

Certainly Shakespeare sometimes calls attention to the convention of the boy actress in ways that underline the theatricality of gender. Cleopatra ruefully anticipates the degrading effects of transvestite impersonation, imagining herself played by an actor who will "boy my greatness / I' th' posture of a whore" (5.2.220–21)—a protest against the very mode of representation that constructs the character speaking it. Shakespeare's use of cross-dressing comic heroines extends this subversive unmasking of convention, presenting a boy who plays a girl who dresses up as a boy but, in so doing, removes the "feminine" markers of his foundational impersonation. This undisguised boy must then pass for a disguised girl. The ploy, however conventional, muddles the clarity of gender identities, particularly in *As You Like It*, which can be taken as a celebration of role-playing and the theatricality of gender.[29] The play presents a boy playing a girl who dresses up as a boy who then acts the part of a girl. In reassuming a "feminine" persona for her tutorings of Orlando, the cross-dressed Rosalind actually plays a hard-headed "masculine" version of herself for the sake of sobering up her besotted lover. One is hard pressed to make nice distinctions between role and self, gender and subject.

In the epilogue, "Rosalind"—the boy actress in women's clothes— addresses the audience, observing that it is customary for the "lady" to give the final speech—invoking a convention reinforcing his status as "lady." Yet, later in the speech, the lady becomes a boy as "Rosalind" remarks, "*if* I were a woman, I would kiss as many of you as had beards" (5.4.18–19, emphasis mine). In the final line, he seemingly returns to the status of woman, "making curtsy"—or at least proposing to—and thus realigning himself with the gestural language of a performative femininity.

"Rosalind's" teasing contemplation of kissing men suggests that the boy actress confounded distinctions not only between masculine and feminine but, to the extent that he attracted a male erotic gaze, between heterosexual and homosexual as well.[30] Even if Shakespeare's society seems less anxious than our own about preserving this distinction,[31] the testimony of Puritan critics such as Phillip Stubbes confirms the boy actress's threat to those who wished to; for Stubbes, the boy actress is monstrously effeminate not simply for donning dresses but for stirring same-sex desire.[32]

Though it is highly profitable to ponder the erotic politics of Shakespeare's plays in the context of their original performance, I would like to examine them from the standpoint of contemporary performance, to consider how the problem comedies' drama of sexual difference has been and could be staged today. I see two advantages to this approach, at least from the perspective of performance criticism. First, it avoids historicist criticism's heavy dependence on a purely speculative recovery of an unrecoverably alien performance tradition. One must be careful, for instance, not to overestimate the subversiveness of the boy actress. It is impossible to know to what extent he was a provocatively evident "construct" and to what extent he was simply an accepted convention—and perhaps even an extremely skilled impersonator. As the exclusive vehicle for representing young women on the public stage, his very familiarity may have mitigated his subversiveness.[33] The vogue of the boy actress and the immense popularity of the boys' companies suggest that Shakespeare's audience, uncorrupted as they were by any tradition of realism, had a far greater tolerance for flagrant theatricality and role-playing than today's spectators. Audiences in Shakespeare's time were prepared to accept a boy not only as Cleopatra but as Malevole and Bussy D'Ambois. So it may be a mistake to make too much out of the "anti-realism" of Shakespeare's theater in general, and of the boy actress in particular, because the very term implies a reaction against a mode of representation that scarcely existed.

Second, however much the boy actress facilitated a critique of the sex-gender system, he also enforced a female "lack" in Shakespeare's theater. If, in contemporary performance, the female body itself offers a source of resistance to phallocentric erasure, that possibility is clearly precluded when the body incarnating Shakespeare's female characters is not female.

Before continuing, I want to make clear the theoretical premises from which my analyses of subjectivity proceed, especially since some of the theorists I cite are not typically on speaking terms. My conception of the subject is derived from a feminist version of the object-relations theory formulated by D. W. Winnicott.[34] In this view, the self is fundamentally social and interactive, capable of intimate, reciprocally transformative relations with others, productively interacting with difference rather than narcissistically subduing it. In the object-relations model, the self is not only aware of its own unique inner world but capable of recognizing and even permeating the other's. Self meets Other in what Winnicott calls the transitional space, manifesting both creativity and adaptability, adjusting external reality as well as adjusting to it.

The feminist revision of this theory places formative interpersonal relations (largely located in the family) within the wider context of the social structures that constitute the external reality with which the core self grapples. It also identifies gender as integral to that external reality—not a fixed and neutral marker of difference but a construct for submitting it to a social organization sustaining male dominance. As gender is derived from an alterable set of social relations, however, it may become a vehicle for restoring difference, for contesting relations of domination and enabling more flexible expressions of self. The transitional space affords not merely personal, psychological renovations of "reality" but collective, political ones as well.

The self that emerges from object-relations theory offers a salubrious alternative to both the Enlightenment essentialist self and the post-modern textually constituted subject. Neither an unchanging, autonomous, trans-historical entity nor an empty site for cultural inscription, the relational self is differentiated, embodied, constituting as well as constituted, produc-tively agentic as well as culturally regulated, richly interior as well as decentered.

Post-modern discourse has tended to dismiss the relational core self by erroneously equating it with the essentialist, thereby precluding agentic subjectivity and, in turn, prohibiting contestation of culturally produced meanings. Once the agentic subject vanishes, so does the transitional space of cultural renovation. External reality becomes synonymous with a closed system of cultural signification; would-be subjects are interpellated into a monolithic ideology or subsumed to a Symbolic Order that makes estrange-ment from interiority the foundation of subjectivity rather than its lamen-table breech. Although post-modernism portrays external reality as utterly contingent and constructed, it also portrays it as indestructible and even undeconstructable—except in esoteric textual terms. If this view of reality produces stasis in the political sphere, the image of the evacuated subject implies madness in the psychological—or at least predicates a subject pathologically incapable of developing a stable interiority or distinguishing between inner and outer experience.[35]

A feminist object-relations theory, by contrast, posits a core self, depict-ing gender as negotiable and phallocentrism as subvertible. Applied to dramatic criticism, it confers agency, uniqueness, and selfhood on Shake-speare's characters. Indeed, the agentic, socially regulated self accords closely with the concept of Shakespearean character recently expounded by Alan Sinfield—a self endowed with agency and interiority yet subject to cultural configuring, occupying the middle ground between the "unitary I" and the post-modern "site."[36] In Sinfield's view, character materializes in the context of a consistently developed interiority. Thus, not every Shakespearean character manifests "character." Female characters, in particular, may seem sketchy and discontinuous. While Macbeth entertains rival subject positions, for instance, Lady Macbeth merely represents "the site upon which they are displayed."[37]

The distinction Sinfield draws is surely accurate, but it ignores the actor's capacity to endow even fragmented characters with depth and continuity. Lady Macbeth, Desdemona, and Cressida may all be imbued with depth in the playing, given an underlying internal continuity that converts their discontinuities into dramatically readable symptoms of a subjectivity disabled by gender ideology. As a consequence of this intelligible discontinuity, these characters become sites for disclosing the dialectic of subject formation, the vexed enactment of cultural imperative. Indeed, the discontinuities reveal what Sinfield calls "faultlines," cracks in the social topography caused by pressure on its constituting structures. The distinction Sinfield draws between a typically masculine integrity and a frequently feminine incoherence may be ramified dramatically to reveal the effects of gender constraints.

The drama of subjectivity in the problem comedies discloses not only female variability but male narcissism, a subjectivity incapable of creative adjustment to external reality, sustained by egocentrically converting the other into a substantiating mirror. I draw on Freud and particularly Lacan to assess this narcissistic subjectivity, which Lacan takes to be normative, and to deconstruct the phallocentrism integral to it, which both take to be incontestable. I adapt these theories not for their prescriptive validity but for their descriptive power, their compelling pertinence to the trajectories of desire and the constraints of gender that the problem comedies dramatize. I read the phallocentrism intrinsic to their theories as a function of alterable patriarchal relations rather than an inevitable consequence of anatomy (Freud) or an impermeable logic of language (Lacan).

For both Freud and Lacan, the human subject forfeits an unmediated instinctual life in return for entry into a mediated realm of signification, forever burdened with a legacy of repressed drives and a condition of estrangement that impels quests for recovered integration, for a coherent identity forged in confrontation with otherness. Freud and Lacan provide immensely useful and powerful accounts of the desire residual to this dislocation: Freud describes its complex circuitry through somatic, psychological, interpersonal, and sociopolitical realms while Lacan describes its pathology, its enactment of an insatiable longing excessive to its object or to any medium that could express or contain it.[38]

So long as one retains a notion of agentic subjectivity, this description of an unadaptive, narcissistic "false" self deranged by its own unmanageable desire proves highly apposite to the world of the problem comedies. These plays especially lend themselves to Lacan's critique of desire as the manifestation of "lack." Helena's obsessive pursuit of the unprepossessing Bertram could be construed as the pursuit of an unattainable, idealized other, a projection of her own need for substantiation. Angelo's brutal pursuit of Isabella offers a more sinister instance of attempting to possess the unpossessable, revealing the ease with which desire turns to violence (against the desired object) and revulsion (against the vulnerability she elicits in him). Both Angelo and the Duke may be understood as attempting to transcend "lack" and impersonate the Symbolic Father, to claim access to the phallus, the symbolic organ whose inaccessibility marks them as lacking.[39] To possess the phallus is to deny "lack" and therefore to deny or resist the desire it generates. Angelo's undeniable desire takes the form of a self-lacerating, sadomasochistic vexation, while the Duke's denied desire expresses itself so covertly and cryptically as to be scarcely there at all.

*Troilus and Cressida* offers perhaps the most concentrated portrayal of an excessive, narcissistic desire: even before his tryst with Cressida, Troilus affirms the insatiability of his overwrought longing—"the desire is boundless and the act a slave to limit" (3.2.82–83)—not so much predicting as predicating Cressida's betrayal in order to validate his positioning of her as unpossessable, idealized other.

Lacanian theory also proves useful in providing a way of linking psychoanalytic thinking and performance issues, for assaying the plight of the narcissistic subject as it strives to represent itself. To enter the Symbolic Order is to enter spectacle, to encounter a repertory of culturally mandated roles. In Lacan's scheme, unlike Winnicott's, the ego does not precede and substantiate its identifications but is constituted by them. As such, these identifications can only be misrecognitions, a mis-taking of the Other as the ground of one's being. Yet, in Lacan's account, there is no recognition to which this misrecognition represents the dysfunctional alternative, no other mode of relating or of constituting the subject. The subject becomes a mimetic effect, constructed in the image of a colonized other.[40] As limited as this view is, it does illuminate a phenomenon recurrent in the problem comedies: the impairing of relatedness due to narcissistic conquest of difference.

If Lacan's notion of subjectivity suggests that "I is an other," then his concept of the gaze implies that "I is one who is seen." The gaze, like the phallus, is not only an (absent) signifier for what constitutes the subject as lacking (in this case within the field of vision) but also the tangible "presence of others as such," a kind of gazing spectacle.[41] In order to become a recipient of the gaze, the subject must fit herself to a "screen" in order to catch the gaze's illuminating projection and thus take on a perceptible (culturally prescribed) identity.[42]

In this book I will discuss the extent to which gender serves, within the problem comedies, as the enactment of misrecognized cultural images. I also will consider how the look may function theatrically to dramatize the play's transactions of desire and constructions of gender. The look, unlike the gaze, is a mechanism of libidinal fixation rather than social surveillance.[43] If the gaze signifies that which determines the subject as lacking, the look manifests the desire that confirms that lack. To look therefore is to lack, to convert the looked-at object into a gaze whose reciprocal look will substantiate the looking subject. The desiring look may itself attempt to become a gaze by transferring lack to the looked-at object and imprisoning him in a fixed image. Kaja Silverman notes that what film theorists have called the male gaze is actually a male look that "transfers its own lack to the female subject and attempts to pass itself off as the gaze."[44] One cannot voluntarily approximate the gaze, no more than one can possess the phallus. One can, however, exploit one's involuntary status as representative (for the Other) of the gaze, turning awareness of specularity into a source of power, practicing an exhibitionism that approximates the gaze by dominating and determining the captives of its allure.[45]

Helena effectively positions her desired object, Bertram, as gaze, turning the reciprocal look for which she longs into a source of signifying light. Yet, in the final scene, by organizing and focusing the spectacle that determines him as lacking, she becomes the gaze for him. In *Measure for Measure,* the failed attempts of the Duke and Angelo to assume Symbolic Fatherhood may be expressed and staged in terms of looking relations. Each attempts to function as dominating gaze, yet each is undone by a look that manifests the desire (the "lack") that he would disavow. *Troilus and Cressida* exposes the "male gaze" as a male look that shifts from fetishistically converting its object into a gaze to positioning itself as gaze by imprisoning its object in a projected "lack."

Let me stress here that what Lacan presents as desire's normative path I take as its pathology—but a pathology startlingly relevant to the erotic extremism the problem comedies dramatize, an extremism that obstructs rather than promotes relatedness. As such, Lacan's theory proves extremely useful in addressing the thematic of desire, in staging the look that fortifies or disables desiring subject and desired object.

Two other theorists whose works figure significantly in my analyses—and who might also be accounted curious participants in a profeminist inquiry into gender—are Gilles Deleuze and Jean Baudrillard, each of whom propounds theories powerfully descriptive of certain facets of the oedipally circumscribed worlds of these plays. Deleuze offers a revision of Freud's formulation of sadomasochism that has crucial pertinence to the psychosexual dynamics of *Measure for Measure:* the sadist punishes a representative of his own desiring ego, mortifying an image of likeness to the mother and fanatically denying lack, while the masochist abases himself before a maternal image of the superego, obliterating likeness to the father and "femininely" coveting lack.[46]

Many of the punishments in *Measure for Measure* could be called sadistic, as the punisher persecutes a representative of an abjected "feminine" self cast off in pursuit of "masculine" omnipotence. Angelo, in publicly shaming Claudio, punishes an image of his own lacking, desiring "feminine" self and then, disabled by his desire for Isabella and the masochistic fantasy it stirs, aims to violate her in the "feminine" image of lacking self to which she recalls him. In turn, Isabella, despite a speech eroticizing sexual renunciation as masochistic fantasy, turns sadist in vituperating Claudio, punishing him in the image of the sexually errant "feminine" self he asks her to embrace in order to gratify Angelo's desire. The Duke, in the play's final scene, treats Angelo as Angelo treated Claudio, subjecting him to a public shaming by sadistically assigning to him the lack that he wishes to disclaim in himself.

Similarly, Jean Baudrillard's notions of hyperreality and seduction are richly illuminative of the world in which *Troilus and Cressida* unfolds, a world of intense superficiality haunted by its distance from a substantiating origin, a world in which the mastery of appearance masks the absence of truth. In Baudrillard's view, seduction is the revenge of substantial appearance against apparent substance, the sirens' summons to the void underlying all signification, a tactic for destabilizing contingent cultural meanings.[47]

Baudrillard's theory may be profitably adapted to *Troilus and Cressida,* so long as one jettisons his perturbingly retrograde pronouncements on gender. Baudrillard genders seduction feminine and asserts that women may exploit their association with appearance in order to unsettle appearance, to disconcert a world in which appearance parades as reality: "woman is but appearance. And it is the feminine as appearance that thwarts masculine depth."[48] In *Troilus and Cressida*, by contrast, Troilus' superficiality thwarts Cressida's depth—not a fiction of depth like his, authenticated by a privileged place in a phallocentric order but a genuine depth, marginal and unassimilable to it. In Shakespeare's play, Troilus seduces Cressida into performing the role of seductress, into enacting an inconstancy that reifies the fiction of his coherence. Troilus' determination to maintain his status as an indisposable sign turns Cressida into a disposable one.

To the extent that the problem comedies are imbricated with oedipal narratives, the theories of Freud and Lacan and, more locally, Deleuze and Baudrillard, are immensely illuminating. But to the extent that the problem comedies deconstruct oedipal narratives, unfolding a drama of gender and subjectivity excessive to and subversive of these theories, they are inadequate, sustaining a phallocentric reading of the sex-gender system that the plays contest and confound.

Certainly Deleuze's discussion of sadomasochism discloses a masculinist bias: women figure in his study only as victims of male sadism or as collaborators in male masochistic fantasy. Moreover, despite the anti-oedipal polemic that informs his other work, Deleuze reads sadomasochism in resolutely oedipal terms, reproducing the binary logic he elsewhere denounces. (Yet even those notorious attacks on the "binary machine" engender surprisingly reactionary images of women: to become a "body-without-organs"—in Deleuze's scheme a desirable metamorphosis—is to "become woman," a construct that both romanticizes and essentializes women's marginal status.)[49]

The same masculinist bias is evident in Baudrillard's theory of seduction, which speciously turns women's historical condition of powerlessness into a source of power. Declaring the phallocratic order unalterable, he suggests that women savor rather than decry their consignment to lack, discovering within it the awesome power of seduction, the ability to negate meaning and disrupt productivity by exposing the arbitrariness of all signs: "[T]he female is nothing," Baudrillard asserts; "this is her strength."[50]

More crucially, both Freud and Lacan reify the foundational illusions of a phallocentric sex-gender system, consigning women to a position of lack, implicitly negating the possibility of female subjectivity. In Freud's system, a woman is imprisoned by biology, unable to transcend her own lacking body; in Lacan's, she is imprisoned by language, unable to transcend a system of meaning that posits the phallus, co-extensive with the male sexual organ, as the symbolic organ of cultural signification. Lacan seems to make up for a "lack" in Freud's theory by reconfiguring castration as symbolic, a lack culturally inscribed on males as well as on females, signifying their estrangement from the real, from the ontological structures of language itself. But Lacan's theory lends male subjects an institutionalized mechanism for disavowing lack by aligning the masculine with the phallus. The male subject becomes the contingent "have" whose fiction of coherence and efficacy the female must sustain by embracing the status of "have-not." If women in Freud's theory are anatomically destined to occupy an inferior position, in Lacan's they are destined to be nonexistent. Even as he amply demonstrates the constructedness of gender, Lacan precludes constructions outside a phallocentric register.

The problem comedies' failure to sustain that phallocentric register opens up a space for feminist critique and intervention, for rescuing the female subject from the positions of inferiority and nonexistence. The French feminists, particularly Luce Irigaray and Julia Kristeva, are invaluable resources for deepening and extending this critique. As Ellen Diamond discerns, their work offers complementary images of performative femininity that assist in staging the problematic of female subjectivity and desire: the mimic (Irigaray) and the hysteric (Kristeva).[51]

In Irigaray's view, the female subject is erased by the phallocentric law of the selfsame, excluded from a signifying economy in which, as Butler puts it, "the masculine constitutes the closed circle of signifier and signified."[52] A woman is thus alien and unassimilable to a system of meaning that predicates her nullity, doomed either to reify it or to retreat into unintelligibility.

Through the notion of mimicry, Irigaray posits a third possibility:

> One must assume the feminine role deliberately. Which means already to convert a form of subordination into an affirmation, and thus to begin to thwart it. . . . To play with mimesis . . . to recover the place of her exploitation by discourse, without allowing herself to be simply reduced to it. It means to resubmit herself—inasmuch as she is on the side of the "perceptible," of "matter"—to "ideas," in particular to ideas about herself, that are elaborated in/by a masculine logic, but so as to make "visible," by an effect of playful repetition, what was supposed to remain invisible: the cover up of a possible operation of the feminine in language.[53]

Irigaray asks the performer of a constructed femininity to expose its constructedness, its theatricality. A woman asserts her essential difference from a feminine ideal by exaggerating or parodying it or—extending the implications of the theory—by exaggerating or parodying its opposite masculine ideal, or even by scrambling the distinct signifiers of each gender. The goal in each instance is, as Diamond asserts, to employ mimicry against mimesis,[54] to destabilize the relation between signifier and signified, feminine and female. The performer consequently becomes unequal to the gender she impersonates, contesting her assigned nullity by confounding the phallocentric scheme of representation that nullifies her, potentially exposing its structures of meaning—and the hierarchical distinctions they enforce—as self-perpetuating fictions. This mimicry or masquerade also intersects significantly with drag: women, too, may play at being feminine—but in order to estrange themselves from the image.[55] Adapted to the material theater, this tactic provides a means of representing the supposedly unrepresentable female subject: to the extent that the performer/character may be perceived as other than her role, she may be perceived as other than other, as something-other-than-lacking.

As Diamond points out, Kristeva's notion of the "True-Real" offers a complementary model of nonmimetic femininity, employing hysteria as a metaphor for a "speaking body" subversively opposed and unassimilable to the phallocentric selfsame, functioning as the source of its own meaning, as the site of proliferating, nonreferential signifiers.[56] Unlike Irigaray's mimic, who asserts difference through the body's imperfect adaptation to a received corporeal image—degrading the gender ideal she cites—Kristeva's hysteric asserts difference through the body's sovereign unadaptability; she asserts difference by embodying it, effectively transcending the phallocentric sex-gender system and its compulsory citations. This notion also has salience to the performance of these plays: the performer's body, consubstantial with that of her character, may be employed against the oedipal narratives marginalizing or abjecting her, may persist to the end as a signifier of unassimilated difference.[57] Both strategies help defamiliarize gender in a performance context, the first by italicizing the performance, the second by refusing it.

Shakespeare's problem comedies present female characters whose engagements with "femininity" may be understood textually and conveyed theatrically in terms of mimicry and hysteria. Helena, Isabella, and Cressida all mimic femininity, with varying degrees of intentionality. Isabella is essentially summoned to perform femininity in an oedipal plot not of her own making. Helena and Cressida, by contrast, voluntarily enact versions of "femininity": Helena puts on a passive, masochistic docility in order to efface her audaciously aggressive desire for Bertram, while Cressida plays a variety of roles—including that of sex-object—in order to survive in a rapaciously phallic world.

All three women may also be understood as ultimately hysteric—that is, nonmimetic: each ends the play as a body awaiting yet escaping signification. Helena wishes to be the "thing" as well as the "name" of wife, yet that category seems too narrow a vessel for her capacious subjectivity. Isabella quite literally opposes an undecipherable speaking body to patriarchal design—the silence with which she greets the Duke's proposal registers a response uncapturable by phallocentric discourse. Cressida also eludes signification: she is unidentical not only to the storied figure she inhabits but to any self that she or Troilus can construct.

Whereas Irigaray and Kristeva conceive mimicry and the speaking body as vehicles for disclosing an essential femininity, I regard them as vehicles for expressing a variable, beleaguered female subjectivity. What is problematic in Irigaray's and Kristeva's theories is precisely the assumption of a distinct female language, an alternative mode of signification and desire derived from an anatomically distinct female body, a body whose multiple, nonphallic sexual capacities render it unrepresentable in phallocentric terms. There are three significant problems with this proposition.

First, it posits a female body free of patriarchal inscription, unblemished by the stigmata of gendered otherness, a nature uncorrupted by culture.

Second, it universalizes the consequences of inhabiting the female body, ordaining a unified experience and discourse of female sexuality: "[W]hatever inequalities exist among women," Irigaray writes, "they all undergo, even without clearly realizing it, the same oppression, the same exploitation of their body, the same denial of their desire."[58] The repressive mechanisms that marginalize or erase women may be the same, but the experience of that repression will surely vary in accordance with race, class, ethnicity, and sexual orientation.

The third problem with the assumption is that it essentializes femininity by deriving it from anatomical difference, upholding an oppositionalist gender system originating in biological ontology, perpetuating a new ideal of anatomy-as-destiny. A subaltern femininity thus becomes institutionalized within the very phallocentric order it means to destabilize. Like Freud and Lacan, Irigaray and Kristeva exaggerate and mystify anatomical differences, deriving totalizing and irreconcilable systems of meaning from them.

In the problem comedies, Helena, Isabella, and Cressida disclose depths of subjectivity unassimilable to the oedipal narratives subsuming them; this unaccommodated depth, however, does not disclose a unifying essential femininity. Each conducts a distinct negotiation with a phallocentric gender system in pursuit of a stable and coherent subject position; their common destiny of subversive indistinction owes more to a common obstacle than to a common essence. If each is caught between the irreconcilable positions of woman and Woman, it is not for the sake of renovating the myth of Woman that they struggle but for adumbrating a subjectivity separable from it. These figures do not represent themselves as authentically female, but release a subjectivity uncapturable by "femininity." Their bodies signify nonconformity to the feminine ideal without necessarily authenticating a femaleness derived from the body.

These strategies of mimicry and hysteria can be adapted to the formulation and enactment of what I would call a *feminist gestus*. The idea of gestus I borrow from Brecht: a *gesture* (broadly defined as any theatrical signifier) that contains the *gist* of a play's sociopolitical import.[59] In Brecht's theater, an individual gestus structures each dramatic episode in accordance with an overall gestus—a kind of directorial concept with an attitude, an attitude of contestation toward the social relations the play records. The gestus is integrally connected with Brecht's notion of the "not, but": dramatizing things as they are in order to evoke the alternative of what they might be— specifically unmasking "reality" as a set of alterable sociopolitical conditions.[60] This unmasking (and the gestus itself) depends to a crucial degree on the *Verfremdungseffekt*, the so-called "alienation effect" (better translated as "defamiliarization effect") designed not to alienate the audience but to estrange the commonplace image they contemplate, to expose its contingency, its complicity in an oppressive power structure, turning it into a "not" that evokes the "but."[61] The gestus assists crucially in uncovering the social/historical determinants of human behavior, contesting the "human" as a cultural fiction masking difference and legitimating relations of dominance.

The idea of feminist gestus I borrow from Diamond—a gestus specifically designed to illuminate the tensions and contradictions intrinsic to phallocentric gender ideology.[62] Because Diamond's discussion of gestus is almost exclusively theoretical, mainly focusing on the hypothetical effects of "alienated" acting, she leaves unanswered the question of how a director conceives and orchestrates gestic effects in the contemporary performance of a canonical text entangled in oedipal narratives. I will try to answer that question with respect to *All's Well That Ends Well*, *Measure for Measure*, and

*Troilus and Cressida.* My aim is not merely to define gestic moments but to practice a gestic criticism, to analyze the plays within a feminist, psychoanalytic context attuned to their complex play of gender.

The gestus I envision aims to underline an unassimilated difference potentially subversive of the fixed definitions of the patriarchal symbolic, upsetting a mimetic structure in which a lacking femininity subjugates the female subject and an omnipotent masculinity deranges the male. To the extent that the phallocentric economy assigns female subjects the status of "not," the "not, but" derived from the feminist gestus may be expressed as "not not, but"—a double negative that, if it does not quite constitute a coherent positive, may at least dissolve phallocentric formulations. The gestus also discloses the cost to male subjects of this female indistinction. Deprived of the "not" to which he must pose as the fully equipped alternative (the "but"), the male subject similarly enters a limbo of indefinition, perilously straying from the path of reified masculinity.

As regards female subjectivity, the strategies of mimicry and hysteria figure crucially in materializing a feminist gestus. In *All's Well That Ends Well,* the gestus centers on the *Verfremdungseffekt* of staging Helena's bed-trick in order to heighten the tension and contradiction surrounding her subjectivity, derived from her paradoxical status of desiring female subject within an oedipal narrative. The staged bed-trick works to unveil a recurrently veiled desire, to confound and estrange a gender system equating femininity with negated libido. This gestic strategy aims to accentuate the tension between Helena's aggressive sexuality and her self-abasing hyperfemininity in order to underscore her status as undecipherable conundrum, a conundrum she embodies in the play's final scene: her visibly pregnant body registers as both reassuringly feminine (maternal) and powerfully sexual, the incontrovertible evidence of a fulfilled, indomitable desire. She presents herself as an unknown body that speaks itself known (and knowing), leaving Bertram groping for more knowledge: "if she, my liege, can make me know this clearly." Helena proves herself unreadable in the play's final scene; she is provocatively other than the safely assimilated feminine other.

In *Measure for Measure,* the gestus derives from a relay of images—most crucially the near-rape of Isabella—that highlight her compulsory objectification as well as her resistance to a normative femininity defined by sexual availability on male terms. The gestus thus works to heighten the strain and incongruity that attend Isabella's status as unwitting and unwilling sexual object. Initially, her status as nun relieves her of the burden of negotiating a sexual subjectivity within a phallocratic order. Once recalled from the convent, however, she becomes entrapped in an oedipal plot in which her body is made to speak the language of sexual availability (a "prone and speechless dialect"). Indeed, her status as nun is assimilated to her object-status; the costume meant to desexualize her body only enhances its sexual allure. Her own sexuality emerges covertly, fitfully, deviantly, underscoring her distance from both the chosen persona of nun and the unchosen role of sexual provocation. In the play's final moments, Isabella is at last released from the oedipal plot and the performance of femininity it has compelled. The Duke, for a second time, requests her hand in marriage and receives no verbal response. Isabella's dialect becomes truly speechless, exclusively bodily, nonreferential, resisting assimilation to the patriarchal symbolic. Though nonmimetic, her body remains inconstestably *there* and, to a crucial extent, more hers than it has been before.

The gestus in *Troilus and Cressida* draws the most directly on the concept of mimicry, literalizing the instability and fragmentation that define Cressida's character by presenting her subjectivity as a series of discrepant masquerades. Inasmuch as she strikes a different pose in virtually every scene in which she appears, she may acquire a new look, put on a new persona in each scene. Far from reducing Cressida to a poseur, this choice enables her subjectivity to cohere in the context of performance. None of the roles she enacts quite fits her; none adequately manifests her complex interiority. She coheres through the consistency of her absence; what she enacts is not-herself. She is always elsewhere; but the elsewhereness evokes an alternative to the disparate guises she assumes. Cressida's elsewhereness derives, to a significant degree, from an inability to stabilize a subject position reconciling her status as both desiring subject and desired object. Her desire ultimately seems as insupportable as Helena's, her desirability as self-imperilling as Isabella's.

Underscoring the gestus of Cressida's masquerade are two staging choices aiming at feminist *Verfremdungseffekt:* first, projecting a huge picture of a glamorously posed Cressida as the backdrop to all her scenes, an allusion to the received image of seductress that constitutes the notorious identity to which she is demonstrably unequal; second, after Cressida's final scene, marooning her among mannequins dressed in the costumes that have marked her multiple self-fashionings. Transferring the trappings of the masquerade to these static proxies, Cressida unveils herself as a kind of unmarked, undecipherable body—the thing itself, unencrusted by mimicry's insignias, a body speaking its own muteness, awaiting yet escaping signification.

Although the feminist gestus focuses particularly on the plight of female subjects contending with subjugating gender myths, it is equally concerned with the travails of male subjects attempting to measure up to a phallocentric masculinity. By following the fraudulent Parolles, Bertram emulates a fiction of constructed masculinity, aiming to authenticate the myth with his military exploits even as his comrades expose Parolles as an impostor. The only alternative to this construct is an image of manhood which, because derived from a nostalgically mythologized absent father, proves equally insubstantial.

Moreover, to the extent that Bertram's masculinity depends on disavowing lack—and resisting effeminizing submission to the lacking Helena—his compulsory submission to her in the play's final scene could be read as self-emasculating. On the other hand, because the bed-trick reconfigures Helena as uncastrating (m)other—neutralizing her threatening difference—the marriage could also be said to affirm Bertram's masculinity, albeit on the shaky foundation of regressive fantasy. Whether Helena radically reverses Bertram's oedipal plot or cunningly refashions herself as agent of its fulfillment, she confounds its reductive teleology and generates questions about precisely what Bertram has (or has not) achieved.

Angelo, unlike Bertram, seems fatally submerged in a failed oedipal plot, unable to sustain a masculinity founded on denied lack. He violently defends himself against the woman whose desirability threatens to afflict him with lack but ultimately suffers the Bertram-like fate of enforced capitulation to a maternal female (Mariana). Although the marriage delivers him from death, it also subjects him to punitive emasculation. Indeed, Angelo's failure to substantiate the image of patriarch proves integral to the Duke's more covert attempt to succeed. Yet the Duke fails because he must stake his own claim for transcendent masculinity not only on Angelo's lacking body but on Isabella's as well. Inasmuch as the Duke must ultimately make Isabella's body the signifier of his phallic sufficiency, its nonmimetic muteness confounds him, or at least obstructs fulfillment of his oedipal quest.

*Troilus and Cressida* essentially deconstructs a phallic masculinity, propping up figures explicitly inferior to their legendary models, who cover their lack with empty displays of macho vaunting. Achilles, the Trojan War's most renowned hero, proves himself a more inflated version of Parolles, a braggart soldier elevated to myth by display and attribution, a legend he sustains through absence from the war and then degrades once compelled to return. The war itself can be seen as a compensatory spectacle of hypermasculine sabre rattling, covering the lack that Helen inflicts on both armies: the Greek generals wage war to redress the collective emasculation caused by Menelaus' cuckolding; the Trojan army fights to substantiate a worth that Helen does not intrinsically possess, to cover the inadequacy of the signifier of their masculine honor.

Within this drama of feverishly disavowed lack, Troilus finds himself effeminized by his desire for Cressida, unable to enact his manhood in the theater of war. When her own performance in that theater seems to negate his masculine sufficiency, he aims at ferociously renovating himself as ruthless warrior, effectively reenacting the war's disreputable origin by attempting to avenge himself on the thief of his love, Diomedes. To the extent that the bellicose Troilus is recurrently called a second Hector, the latter's own disreputable conduct in the final scenes leaves Troilus in the Bertram-like position of embracing an image of masculinity exposed as fraudulent.

The fragility of masculinity within an oedipal drama may be underscored in performance by highlighting the vulnerability of the male performing body, turning it into an object of spectacle, an object of the audience's look. The staged bed-trick that enables the feminist gestus in *All's Well* posits Bertram's body as desired object; the sadomasochistic dynamics of *Measure for Measure* may be dramatized by positioning Claudio's body as degraded object, turning his public humiliation at Angelo's hand into sadistic spectacle. In *Troilus and Cressida,* one could underline the war's status as lacking spectacle by turning the soldiers into preening exhibitionists—and, in particular, turning the parade of returning Trojan warriors into a kind of male beauty pageant. As performance could make clear, Hector's body records the ruination of masculine ideals. His pursuit of the gold armor debases masculinity to a mere ornamental overlay, which, far from protecting him, leaves him vulnerable to the multiple penetrations of the Myrmidons' swords, turning his supposedly integrated masculine body into a feminized mass of "bleeding vents."

The genius of gestus is that it reconciles ideology and drama, creating a politicized drama that, at least potentially, transcends crude didacticism on the one hand and cathartic escapism on the other, imparting a point of the view on the action without draining it of dramatic interest or theatrical vitality. The gestic interventions that I propose aim not to reduce the plays to feminist agitprop but to deepen their complexity and provocation by theatricalizing the critique of gender that they enable. What Brecht celebrated in Shakespeare and sought to preserve in his adaptations was precisely their complexity of action and relativity of character, their refusal to "harmonize their contradictions in accordance with some preconceived idea."[63]

Brecht did not wish to turn Shakespeare's complex dramas into simple-minded Marxist parables but attempted to shape them gestically into vivid investigations of social problems amenable to Marxist solutions. The notion of "not, but" supports this approach: the alternative vision evoked by "but" does not get superimposed on the play but emerges from the dialectical contestation of the "not"—which connotes a set of alterable social relations.

In the case of the problem comedies, the "not" denotes the phallocentric sex-gender system and the "but" an alternative register of difference, desire, and power in which male and female resist conversion into symbolic opposites assimilated to asymmetrical power relations. Admittedly, the "but" in this case evokes an alternative far less concrete than Brecht's Marxist paradigm. Indeed, it is far easier to say what it is not than what it is. If it is not the reigning gender ideology neither is it the untenably utopian ideal of radical ungendering, freeing the body to an utterly natural sexuality uncontaminated by power and cultural influence. Still, even if the body cannot be liberated from cultural regulation, it may be freed from traditional gender constrictions; even if human relations must ultimately unfold within the matrix of power, they need not, as Butler points out, perpetuate relations of dominance.[64] Inasmuch as one's experience of embodiedness—and therefore of sexuality, gender, and subjectivity—is always already mediated by cultural understanding, an expansion of understanding ought to enable a wider range of experience. As a consequence, gender might lose some of its constraining, monolithic inflexibility and become far more dynamically, negotiably open, turning traditional roles into adaptable tools of self-construction rather than ontological determinants of place in the power structure. The feminist gestus I envision does not aim to concretize this more liberal negotiation of difference (the "but") but to make dramatic capital of its conspicuous absence, not to harmonize but to amplify the problem comedies' unharmonized contradictions.

Adapting the Brechtian model to feminist inquiry has the effect of rescuing mimesis from the conservative representational politics with which it is usually aligned. Classical realism, according to many feminist theorists, colludes with phallocentrism by reifying its version of "reality," naturalizing the oppressive mimetic structures that equate the female subject with lack and consign her to the status of fetish, threat, or nonentity.[65] As a consequence many feminist directors seem prepared to abandon the traditional mimetic theater, to turn canonical texts (when assaying them at all) inside out, to rupture narrative, disintegrate character, and keep disbelief resolutely unsuspended in order to deprive the oedipal plot of its seductive trappings.[66]

While such abstention from mimesis has yielded some vital and illuminating theater, it is problematic as a global aesthetic. Certainly it underestimates the subversive potential of some canonical texts (like the problem comedies). Also, by dismissing linearity and referentiality as inevitably phallocentric and practicing a retributive formlessness, it affirms a binarism foundational to the oppositionalist gender system it means to contest, equating masculinity with constricting form, femininity with unruly matter. It also ignores the ways in which realism may be adapted to more contestatory, deconstructive ends; it overlooks the possibility of *exploiting* the scopic desire conditioned and gratified by the traditional mimetic theater. Particularly when adapting classic texts, too insistent a denial of spectatorial pleasure may reduce the spectacle to a mere enactment of negation. As Diamond suggests, realism itself can become a site of intervention, a powerful tool for deconstructing the "reality" it has traditionally reified.[67]

Brecht's theater provides a model for such deconstructive realism, exploiting rather than ceding the satisfactions of narrative, character, referentiality, and scopic and emotional investment. Brecht's major works offer a coherent sequence of actions conducive to legible closure, even if frequently disrupted, sidetracked, or commented upon; characters rounded and believable, even if socially determined, and spectators emotionally engaged, even if discouraged from direct empathy with a benighted protagonist.

The kind of feminist theater that emerges from this Brechtian model works dialectically rather than polemically, confounding rather than annihilating the oedipal plot, accentuating the anxieties and discrepancies that attend the enactment of gender. As Teresa de Lauretis asserts:

> [T]he most exciting work in cinema and in feminism today is not anti-narrative and anti-Oedipal; quite the opposite. It is narrative and Oedipal with a vengeance, for it seeks to stress the duplicity of that scenario and the specific contradiction of the female subject in it, the contradiction by which historical women must work with and against Oedipus.[68]

It is precisely that contradiction between historical women (and men) and oedipal gender constructs that the feminist gestus seeks to underline.

Let me hasten to say that I am not proposing a feminist theater directly emulating Brecht's, although clearly many contemporary feminist theater-makers—most particularly Caryl Churchill—draw inspiration from his work. Nor would I wish to claim that the disruptions of realism I describe are as explicit and pervasive as those theorized and (to a lesser extent) practiced by Brecht. Nor do I share his optimism that theater can directly incite spectators to political activism, to change the world. I do believe, however, that theater can offer a vital, meaningful encounter with the crucial questions of one's social experience and therefore assist in the process of consciousness raising necessary for change.

What I adapt from Brecht is the essential model of a dialectical, gestic theater assimilating realism to a critique of social relations (in this case, the phallocentric sex-gender system) and employing techniques of de-familiarization to expose their reparability, disrupting the spectatorial process that realism customarily provides. To dramatize Cressida's frag-mentation through discrepant masquerades, for instance, obstructs the mimetic apparatus that both sustains realism and substantiates normative gender. This estranging obstruction has the potential to create a Brechtian epiphany of "not, but," evoking alternatives to the constructions of femininity with which Cressida—and the female subjects she provision-ally represents—grapples.

This provisional retention of realism depends upon a provisional reten-tion of the traditional acting techniques necessary to produce the socially regulated core self. The point requires some emphasis because these tech-niques, derived from Stanislavski and dominating actor training in both North America and Great Britain, have so often been used to construct an essentialist, unified subject. Indeed, Worthen contends that the rhetoric of Stanislavski-based acting training explicitly identifies the embodied univer-sal self as its object.[69] It seems a mistake, however, to take the rhetoric of the training as the limit of its effect or to confuse the technique with the mode of subjectivity it has principally supported. Indeed, the mistake parallels that of confusing the core self with the essential, as though any coherent subjectivity connotes transhistorical essence. While the effects of interiority and continuity produced by Stanislavski-derived approaches may be em-ployed to construct an essentialist self, they conduce equally to delineating the adaptive, decentered self. When I speak of Stanislavski-derived ap-proaches, I refer to their common goal of uncovering intentions and motivations so as to produce a distinctly embodied, internally continuous self capable of serving as a plausible surrogate for the audience and creating behavior calculated to appear utterly spontaneous—a series of contrived effects designed to mask their contrivance. While unmasking them for the sake of unfixing character may seem a compelling way to establish the decentered self, it is highly problematic to deconstruct subjectivity at the actorial rather than the directorial level.

The director needs actors capable of constructing character along traditional lines in order to make the problematic of subjectivity comprehensible to an audience that understands character according to those constructions. The utility of character, as conceived and conveyed in traditional techniques, is that it adumbrates a core self even in dramatic transactions that emphasize its constructedness and performativity or threaten it with subjugation or erasure: somewhere beneath the fragmentary, performative manifestations is a self struggling for more coherent representation, a self consubstantial with that of the actor. If, as suggested, Cressida's self is mostly elsewhere during her disparate performances, its coherent manifestation—the conjuring of elsewhere—rests with the actress. The same is true with the contradictory Helena and the relentlessly objectified Isabella: the actress is instrumental in establishing the core self that often registers in opposition to, rather than in consort with, the performance to which it is called. The actor's body need not record a prediscursive, bounded identity but an unbounded social self subject to cultural construction. Character, like subjectivity, is not in-dwelling but in process.

In short, directorial deconstructions of subjectivity require actorial constructions. To deconstruct on the actorial level is to risk estranging the spectator from the actor rather than from the enactment, to deprive the audience of an essential point of entry into the spectacle, to dispense too readily with the benefits of surrogation.

To illustrate this point, I'd like to offer two contrasting examples, one confirming the utility of conventional characterization to a critique of subjectivity and the other illustrating the difficulty of a more iconoclastic approach. A renowned Shakespearean deconstructor recently opined that Kenneth Branagh's careening performance of Hamlet—seemingly a series of isolated, discontinuous gestures unhinging character—corroborated her theory that Hamlet's search for a self fails because he has no self to find.[70] In fact, Branagh's own commentary indicates a persistent effort to project a core self and to characterize along conventional lines: "I was determined to be correct and proper in mourning for my father. . . . Hamlet wants to be an example of what he believes is correct behavior. . . . I wanted to be clear that this Hamlet puts on his antic disposition."[71] Branagh's performance would almost certainly not have gratified this critic's bias—would not have conveyed the image of a negated self—if he had not created such a vivid and engaging self in the first place. Hamlet's struggle to cohere as a subject would be incoherent without a Hamlet who wishes to cohere, without an actor capable of registering the internal continuity that unifies his externally discontinuous gestures of self-reification. Actorial logic and interpretive closure are not essentializing, simplistic practices but tools for constructing intelligible characters capable of manifesting complex and unessentializing subjective crises. Criticisms of Stanislavski-based acting seem to assume that such devices as motivation, objective, subtext, and superobjective are discernible signifiers fixing and flattening character rather than the invisible mechanisms of a character's signifying power.

By contrast, Neil Bartlett's recent performance-art *Twelfth Night* at the Goodman Theatre in Chicago disdained not only conventional character drawing but also "good acting," in an apparent effort to depict the post-modern, textually constituted subject.[72] In order to emphasize the perform-ativity of gender, Bartlett cast virtually all the roles across gender lines and then highlighted the resulting discrepancies. In particular, the actress playing Orsino deliberately botched her male impersonation.[73] The audi-ence presumably was meant to read her hapless performance as a disclosure of the arbitrariness of theatrical signs—and of cultural constructs in general. The reaction of audiences and critics suggests, however, that many regarded her failed mimicry merely as bad acting, confirming the difficulty of deciphering unfamiliar—or, in this case, contentiously alien—modes of character drawing.[74] Such modes run the risk of reducing the entire production to a bewildering void, a studied frustration of mimetic desire apt to be more exasperating than enlightening. Inasmuch as today's spectator does not think of herself as a blank slate for cultural inscription, she is unlikely to recognize herself in the image of the post-modern subject-as-cipher. As a theory, deconstruction has the healthful effect of disclosing the underlying conditions and enabling exclusions of a specific discursive practice. As a strategy for performance, it risks becoming a parasitical harpy, devouring the production's content and disabling the audience with a nostalgia for absent orientations. To the extent that character enables such orientation, directors of Shakespeare are ill-advised to dispense with it entirely. More-over, to the extent that the actor is not simply expressive but instrumental, a signifier in the director's conceptual scheme, the effect of traditional techniques will have more to do with the directorial intention they serve than with any intrinsic ideology they might be thought to possess.

Once more Brecht's example is highly instructive. Although reputedly hostile to traditional techniques, Brechtian acting depends to a surprising extent on Stanislavskian imperatives. Although his theoretical writings harp repeatedly on the actor's separability from the character, Brecht required his actors to identify emotionally with their characters before configuring them gestically, undergoing a naturalistic phase of character development.[75] As Brecht himself said, "we shall get empty, superficial, formalistic, mechanical acting if in our technical training we forget for a moment that it is the actor's duty to portray living people."[76] Brechtian acting does not radically displace Stanislavskian principles but assimilates them to a political purpose.

Moreover, as Herbert Blau points out, the gestic configuring Brecht required was less a function of a coherent theory than the product of a rehearsal environment animated by inquiry into social relations and buoyed by a spirit of stylistic experimentation.[77] Thus, the actor's role as gestic exhibitor is, to a large extent, an inevitable consequence of his place in a gestic exhibition, his collusion with a director intent on dialectical theater. The unified self is a necessary effect not of a particular acting style but of a particular directorial strategy—conscious or otherwise—to elide the sociopolitical dimensions of the drama.

Although the actor possesses the capacity to shape the gestus she executes as well as a power to signify on her own terms, I want to retain some notion of the actor as instrument of a directorial author-ity. Such author-ity does not derive from mystically divining an undiscoverable authorial intention. Indeed, the director's authority becomes acceptable only if she readily admits that her interpretation is partial, selective, subjective, derived not from a fixed and final meaning intrinsic to the text but from the mediating agency of her own philosophical and ideological predispositions. Directorial choice arises from an encounter not with manifest intention but with malleable material, the residue of an unrecoverable original performance that necessitates, as Brook asserts, a parallel creative endeavor on the part of the director and her collaborators, generating a new performance that is derived from and inspired by the text but never coincident with it (or, in Worthen's terms, opposite to it).

This positioning of the director as author-ity requires other qualifications. First, it turns performance into something it fundamentally is not: a text—a tangible thing to be scrutinized and analyzed. Still, without this conversion of performance into performance text, there could be no performance criticism of any sort. As a primarily visceral and affective *experience,* performance must remain forever impenetrable by criticism of any kind.[78] Second, it turns directorial activity into something it usually is not: the unilateral theatrical translation of a preset, unchanging, scrupulously detailed "reading." The directorial concept often springs from a far more intuitive, visionary (though never prediscursive) experience. Far from being static and monolithic, the concept evolves and sometimes even changes in the course of consultations with designers, rehearsals with actors, and performance. The current demand for a decentered director seems redundant in light of the inescapably collaborative nature of theatrical performance. Good directors are always already decentered conduits of a collaboratively authored performance.

Third, the director-as-author construct seems to collapse performed meaning with directorial intention. In fact, directorial intention at best can only limit the range of a script's meanings—and even then imperfectly and incompletely, given the spectator's ultimately unruly imagination. Moreover, even those spectators who submit to the prescribed range may discover a host of discrepant meanings. The director's job is not to orchestrate a single performed meaning—clearly an impossibility—but to structure a meaningful experience, to control a performance's chain of signifiers, to compose a kind of aural/visual poem through manipulation of the *mise-en-scène* in order to elicit a spectator response provisionally congruent with his vision, so that, on some (possibly subconscious) level and to an extent necessarily limited by the vagaries of audience response, the spectator grasps something of the director's concept (or gestus).

Even so, the audience may not be able to articulate that "grasp" with anything resembling the director's own expression. Indeed, the audience's experience is ultimately irreducible to any sort of verbal articulation, residing in somatic, psychic, and spiritual zones uncapturable by discursive language. This is not to suggest that these inarticulate responses cannot be productive or transmitted into the language of critique. Brecht, though a staunch opponent of empathy (sympathetic identification with a suffering protagonist), proclaimed emotional response an essential ingredient of productive spectating.[79] It is not only permissible but desirable to be moved, if one is moved *to* a more enlightened engagement with sociopolitical "reality."

So, while my discussion implicitly constructs a quasi-Brechtian audience—passionately detached and critically engaged—capable of reading my directorial choices in a manner congruent with my intentions, I readily admit that it is pure construction. The audience's ultimate intractability to directorial control is one of several reasons that I do not attempt an extensive semiotic analysis of the *mise-en-scène* of these plays. Inevitably, such analyses rest on abstract theorizing about theatrical signification that turns the audience into a static receptor of unidirectional stimuli, ignoring its unruly diversity and its creative function in completing and reciprocally shaping the performance's meaning, a signifying agency not easily measured in semiotic terms. Semiotics' principal value lies in depicting performance as encoded rather than neutrally referential, a dispersal of signifiers enmeshed in deeper cultural and social structures. Its principal liability lies in promulgating a universal system of theatrical meaning, ignoring the crucial distinctions between performance and language, and failing to capture theater's more wide, varied, and phenomenological mode of communication.

Ultimately, whether one addresses performance pragmatically or semiotically, it is impossible to characterize audience response without recourse to unverifiable generalizations. The audience that emerges from either account must be a hypothetical construct, an enabling fiction. Thus, while I do read my choices semiotically in the sense of fitting them to a specific conceptual aspiration, I do not situate them within a universal language of the stage in order to explain precisely how they would achieve the effects I propose for them. Whether they would achieve such effects can only be determined in performance—and even then not definitely, given the diversity of audience response and the impossibility of measuring it. The audience to whom these choices are truly addressed is my audience of readers, who must assess their persuasiveness in relation to the gestic critical performance they serve, not to the absent theatrical performance they can only faintly evoke.

The problem comedies represent a fascinating subgenre in Shakespearean criticism, principally by virtue of resisting absorption into other genres.[80] My analysis, by defying chronology and ending with *Troilus and Cressida*, orders the plays in relation to a movement from comedy to tragedy. Certainly *All's Well That Ends Well* bears the closest kinship to the comedies, centering as it does on an enterprising heroine's rehabilitation of a defective mate. That the rehabilitation may fall short, that the mate's defects may exceed those of his predecessors, that the marriage the heroine makes may fail to ease anxieties about his worth, only underscore the play's crucial deviations from comic precedent. Helena greatly surpasses Portia or Rosalind as a desiring subject because she lacks what they have: a reciprocally desiring suitor. At the same time, she does far more than either to position herself as object, frequently assuming an incongruous, abject "femininity." While their usurpation of male attire furthers their correction of future husbands—and signifies their power—Helena's assumption of a penitent pilgrim's garb accentuates her powerlessness, her temporary renouncing of a transgressive, unfeminine desire. Helena's vacillation between ("masculine") dominance and ("feminine") abjection leaves her gender and subjectivity suspended and unsearchable.

*Measure for Measure,* while retaining a comic structure (at least insofar as it ends in multiple marriages), takes a step closer to tragedy, not simply in presenting a vision of experience encompassing death and degradation but also in afflicting a disempowered woman with the burden of an unbearable difference, aligning Isabella's fate with those of Ophelia and Desdemona. In a sense, *Measure for Measure* resituates the story of an early comedy—*The Taming of the Shrew*—within a potentially tragic context, in which threatening female difference is figured not as belligerence but as corruption. Like Hamlet, Angelo genders perfidy female—so much so that he describes the sin growing within him as a kind of pregnancy: "the strong and swelling evil / Of my conception" (2.4.6–7). Angelo's brutal propositioning of Isabella yields to the Duke's more cunning effort to tame her: whatever his motives (or our judgment of them), the Duke's plot has the effect of manipulating Isabella into a position of helplessness from which she is most likely to accept him as husband.

*Troilus and Cressida* surpasses *Measure for Measure* in its images—unameliorated by comic structures—of death and betrayal, approaching *Hamlet* in presenting a diseased, diminished world inhospitable to heroic gestures, a world contaminated at its source by a sexually corrupt woman. Just as Ophelia unwittingly inherits the legacy of female treachery Hamlet first perceives in Gertrude, so Cressida is made to reenact Helen's original humiliation of her man. Troilus most resembles Othello in the degree to which he invests his subjectivity in an Other. The difference is that Othello founds his selfhood on his beloved's constancy, Troilus on her inconstancy. His pose as true requires her exposure as false. The burden of inherited female perfidy is even heavier for Cressida than for Desdemona, inscribed as it is in classical legend.

Helena, the Duke, and Troilus each tries but fails to cohere through a culturally appointed role (wife, prince, and exemplar of truth), which, in turn, constricts the subjectivities of the one each must position as other: Bertram, Isabella, Angelo, and Cressida. This focus on an unachievable subjectivity makes *Hamlet*, written just before the problem comedies, the intertext for all three.[81] Although the search for a coherent self is less overtly sustained in the problem comedies and dispersed through several characters rather than concentrated in a single, dominant protagonist (who insistently divulges his psychic fractures while rehearsing different subject positions), it is nevertheless a recurrent concern of all three plays. Moreover, the problem comedies hold greater focus on the complex play of difference, as Hamlet's obsessive crisis of identity tends to divert attention from the casualties of his misogynistic ranting.

The problem comedies are also more open to gender critique than are the romances, the Shakespearean subgenre to which they are most frequently compared, on the basis of what appears to be a comparable wedding of quasi-tragic experience to quasi-comic idealization (an admissible comparison only if one excludes *Troilus and Cressida*). Although the jealous fulminations of Posthumous and Leontes, in particular, underscore the violent dislocations to male identity of perceived female inconstancy, the idealized conclusions of *Cymbeline* and *The Winter's Tale* tend to exorcize magically the provocations of difference, as the offending women, Imogen and Hermione, are safely returned to male favor at the cost of desexualization. *Pericles* and *The Tempest* focus on father-daughter relationships that subsume difference to the redemptive mission of restoring the patriarch. In the problem comedies, the project of self-integration through subduing difference is much less successful. This lack of success is precisely the point of entry for the present study.

# 1

## All's Well That Ends Well

The starting point for my discussion is Susan Snyder's recent character-ization of *All's Well* as a "deconstructed fairy tale":[1] lurking beneath the folkloric narrative of the poor physician's daughter who deploys magic and cunning in order to overcome a dashing Count's disdainful resistance are the unrepresentable spectres of female sexual desire and male sexual dread. Indeed, the play invests the fairy tale motifs that W. W. Lawrence believes undergird *All's Well*—"The Healing of the King" and "The Fulfillment of the Tasks"—with potent erotic subtexts.[2] In adapting "The Healing of the King," Shakespeare, like his model Boccaccio, departs from tradition in making the King's healer a woman. Lawrence barely mentions this innova-tion, but it seems highly significant, especially since Shakespeare, unlike Boccaccio, makes Helena's gender—more particularly, her sexual ardor and allure—indispensable to the cure.

Integral to the narrative of "The Fulfillment of the Tasks" is the bed-trick, an explicitly sexual event in which a disprized wife wins back her husband by making love to him incognito, taking the place of another woman (in some versions the wife herself in disguise) whom he has wooed. *All's Well* deconstructs this folkloric device by wedding it to genuine sexual perturba-tion. The bed-trick is not simply the consummation of a marriage, in which Helena cleverly satisfies Bertram's seemingly impossible conditions, but an act of prostitution, in which Helena services Bertram's lust and submits to humiliating anonymous "use," and a kind of rape, in which Helena coerces Bertram into having sex with her against his will.

Yet, as many critics have noted, the play seems to suppress its own erotic subdrama.[3] Certainly Shakespeare idealizes and mystifies the sexual arousal that empowers Helena's cure of the King. He lends Helena magical and hieratic powers, giving her the capacity to effect a supernatural cure. He similarly desexualizes her erotic agency in the bed-trick, allowing Diana to serve as Helena's sexualized double. Diana also suffers Bertram's degrading slander in the play's final scene, allowing Helena to reenter the play as a saintly, resurrected figure whose visible pregnancy sanctifies her sexuality and who elicits an instantaneous reformation from Bertram. The bed-trick becomes a transcendent event, vastly removed from groping bodies in the dark, from the kind of event imaged as "defil[ing] the pitchy night" (4.4.24).[4]

I propose in this piece to stage the play's erotic subdrama, to push it further to the surface, for the purposes of tracing the play's provocative interrogation of gender. Helena and Bertram are both inextricably entangled in gender's constrictive myths. Helena performs and seeks to reify a normative femininity that her aggressive desire contradicts, while Bertram enacts a normative masculinity that his model, the meretricious Parolles, radically destabilizes. The reading I wish to stage adumbrates a theatrical staging that I will extend by citing and imagining corroborative directorial choices. I will consider, in particular, how the circulation of the look reinforces or disrupts gender roles. My investigation of performance will focus most heavily on the implications of performing the unperformed bed-trick. In performance, the bed-trick constitutes a "lack" in the play's narrative because it is unperformed, not part of the play's visceral, theatrical life, a plot mechanism scarcely capable of disconcerting spectators to the degree that it has critics. I want to examine the extent to which staging the bed-trick can assist in dramatizing the "deconstructed fairy tale" that lies at the heart of *All's Well*—can assist, that is, in bringing to the surface the erotic subdrama that the play represses, and, in so doing, deepen the play's deconstruction of gender. Indeed, a staged bed-trick demystifies and substantiates a female sexuality that the play elsewhere mystifies and evades, and thus begins to redress the "lack" not only in the play's performed life but in a representational economy in which woman figures only as absence.

## HELENA'S FEMININITY: Subject vs. Object

Helena has been such a puzzle and provocation to critics because she occupies the "masculine" position of desiring subject, even as she apologizes fulsomely for her unfeminine forwardness and works desperately to situate herself within the "feminine" position of desired object.[5] At the same time, Bertram poses problems because he occupies the "feminine" space of the objectified Other, even as he struggles to define himself as a man by becoming a military and sexual conqueror. He is the desired object, the end of the hero's (or, in this case, heroine's) gendered journey of self-fulfillment.

Helena's opening soliloquy conveys the plight of a woman trapped between active ("masculine") and passive ("feminine") modes of desire. She clearly expresses her desire to consummate a sexual love, calling herself a "hind" who wishes to be "mated by the lion" (1.1.85–92). At the same time, she adopts a "feminine" posture: she cannot mate but only be "mated." Furthermore, as a hind desiring a lion, she cannot mate at all. Helena thus naturalizes the culturally established distinctions of gender and class that make Bertram a forbidden object. In addition, Helena trains a desiring look on Bertram, submitting her "curled darling" to rapturous objectification, only to affirm a "feminine" helplessness, lamenting the impossibility of eliciting his returned look.[6]

> 'Twas pretty though a plague,
> To see him every hour, to sit and draw
> His arched brows, his hawking eye, his curls,
> In our heart's table—heart too capable
> Of every line and trick of his sweet favour.
> (1.1.92–96)

Her look manifests lack and insufficiency, conveying a masochistic fixation: it was pleasurable torment—"pretty though a plague"—to survey his beauteous, unattainable form "every hour" (1.1.79–98).

Once galvanized by Parolles' bracing anti-virginity jape, however, Helena resolves to "feed" her desirous look, to make the object of worship an object of consumption:

> What power is it which mounts my love so high,
> That makes me see and cannot feed mine eye?
> The mightiest space in fortune nature brings
> To join like likes, and kiss like native things.
> (1.1.220–23)

That Helena imagines a sexual feeding here seems plausible, given the imagery of "joining" and "kissing," not to mention the suggestive phraseology of "mount[ing] my love." The "space" separating her and Bertram she portrays as a product not of nature, which favors their "joining," but of "fortune," which seems here to mean "standing in life" (*OED* 5) and thus to represent culture.

The language Helena employs is characteristically elliptical, stemming from her guarded, coded, sexually charged dialogue with Parolles. The obscurity of her discourse perhaps reflects the unspeakability of her desire. Her exchange with Parolles begins as a theatrical "turn," with Helena playing "straight man" for the swaggering poseur. As straight *man,*

Helena translates her unspeakable desire into the discourse of male bawdry, seeking a kind of release through the sublimated pleasures of naughty talk, even if her lines serve principally as cues for Parolles' ribaldry.

Helena's salacious banter with Parolles marks her first explicit deviation from normative femininity, marks her as provocatively "open" in a social spectacle that, in Shakespeare's time, demanded female "closedness."[7] Lisa Jardine asserts that Helena reveals herself as "too [sexually] knowing for the innocent virgin she professes to be."[8] Yet Helena does not profess to be anything at all in the play's opening scene. Rather, she challenges the spectator's attempt to hold her to a stable identity. She appears a grieving daughter, reveals herself a despairing lover, and finally emerges a resolute wooer, signaling a subjectivity that eludes a coherent singleness.

Certainly Parolles regards Helena as sexually knowing and therefore "open" to ravishment. Performance could make clear that Parolles not only jests with Helena but cheekily flirts with her, launching, behind the cover of licentious badinage, an assault against her own virginity. The two of them may actually engage in some version of the erotic combat they describe: Helena "blows up" (arouses) Parolles, and Parolles seeks an opportunity to "blow up" Helena (make her pregnant). Although Parolles casts Helena as desired object, she maintains her status as desiring subject, rejecting subjection to his controlling look. Her objection to his greeting—"save you, fair queen" (106)—registers a protest against being treated like a "quean." She claims the right to control her own sexual destiny, resisting Parolles' injunction to "answer the time of request," and thus rejecting the notion that a woman must not exercise choice but must make herself the object of a man's. If Helena initially agrees to play the role of imperiled virgin, she ends the scene by emasculating Parolles, not simply by declining to gratify his desire but by mocking his cowardice and thereby undermining his masculine honor, provoking his retributive threat to return in order to "naturalize" (i.e., debauch) Helena.

Helena's query, "how might one do, sir, to lose [virginity] to her own liking?" (150–51) conveys something more than a rebuff of Parolles' lecherous overtures. By invoking the possibility of fulfilling her own desire, Helena begins to take seriously Parolles' aspersion of virginity—or, more specifically, his vision of the naturalness and regenerativeness of sexuality. She steps outside the scene's theatrical frame and trades the role of "straight man" for that of surprised convert. She disregards his censure of her wish to choose rather than be chosen and answers his challenge, "will you anything with it?" decisively if obscurely:

> Not my virginity yet:
> There shall your master have a thousand loves,
> A mother, and a mistress, and a friend,
> A phoenix, captain, and an enemy,
> A guide, a goddess, and a sovereign,
> A counsellor, a traitress, and a dear.
> His humble ambition, proud humility;
> His jarring concord, and his discord dulcet;
> His faith, his sweet disaster; with a world
> Of pretty, fond, adoptious christendoms
> That blinking cupid gossips.
>
> (165–75)

Modern editors have been inclined to assume a missing line between Helena's terse defense of virginity and her expansive list of lovers' endearments. "There" is usually taken to mean "at the court," and the speech is explained as Helena's anxious contemplation of courtly rivals whose enchantments may well stir Bertram's desire. The speech might be better understood, however, as a coded disclosure of Helena's own erotic stirrings. Her need to speak cryptically and elliptically not only betrays a compulsion to conceal her sexual passion but also reflects the difficulty of representing female sexuality within an oedipal plot that typically idealizes or erases it. If one gives up the idea of a missing line, the sense of Helena's response is captured in G. Wilson Knight's paraphrase, "I shall not part with my virginity to anyone yet, because therein your master has an infinite love."[9] Knight, however, backs away from the aggressively sexual connotations of this decoding, asserting, "I do not think, at this early stage in her story, it can mean 'in giving your master my virginity I shall give him a thousand loves,' since she has no good reason at this stage to expect such an event."[10] Helena's lacking a reason to expect "such an event" is surely beside the point; she clearly desires to "mate" with Bertram and, stoked by Parolles' libidinous exhortations, she presumably builds on the tantalizing possibility of losing her virginity to her own liking—that is, to Bertram. The speech becomes the link between this heretofore unthinkable idea and the conception of her bold plan for winning him.

She wishes Bertram well, she tells Parolles, but would rather *do* him well—"show what we alone must think." She would like to give her well-wishing (that is, her love) a "body" which "might be felt" (180–81). Her wish that Bertram feel the body of her love foreshadows the offering of her body in the bed-trick and in marriage. Perhaps "at the court" has seemed the best candidate for Helena's imagined "there" because virginity—or rather the unpenetrated female territory it predicates—has been perceived, within a phallocentric register of meaning, not as a "there" but as a "nowhere," a "nothing-to-be-seen" in Irigaray's striking phrase.[11] In a Shakespearean sense, the virgin "knot" connotes a "not."[12]

Thus the key to the speech may lie not in a missing line but in a missing language—one that embodies a woman's "thereness" and enables the expression of female desire. Helena appears trapped within the phallocentric linguistic system that Lacan describes, in which female desire is literally unspeakable, always already reconfigured as the desire for male desire.[13] The unspeakability of Helena's passion compels her to speak it evasively and mystically. She thus characterizes her "virginity" as a kind of philosopher's stone (5.3.102), a "tinct and multiplying medicine" that blesses Bertram with a supernally expansive love and allows her, for his sake, to assume all the guises of the courtier's beloved—to become a kind of shape-shifting superwoman. "I am his anything," Helena seems to say, as though embracing the status of possession that Petruchio prescribes for Kate when he calls her "my any thing" (3.2.332).

In addition, Helena continues to believe that she must be "mated": she cannot unleash this mystical female power, cannot become Bertram's idealized courtly lover, until Bertram "has" her maidenhead, discovers her wonders "there." Bertram will, in effect, give birth to her as a woman, becoming the fount of signification, a father as well as husband, confirming a transference implied in Helena's earlier assertion that his image had supplanted her father's (79–83). Once more the play seems to dramatize the contradiction of female subjectivity: Helena expresses an active ("masculine") longing to consummate her passion but in terms that betray a "feminine" urge to empower and sustain Bertram, to fit herself to his fantasies—or at least to his received images of femininity. Helena's feminine hope that Bertram might love her once he knows her (sexually) eventually impels her "masculine" orchestration of the bed-trick.

Helena continues to feminize her desire throughout her campaign to win Bertram, offering compensatory performances of exemplary chastity to atone for the unchaste boldness of her plan.[14] Her urge to simulate a normative femininity furthers an oedipal narrative that depends upon muting her sexual provocation. Forced by the Countess to confess her love for Bertram, Helena disclaims the desire to win him that we know she harbors, reviving the self-abasing hopelessness of her first soliloquy, once more portraying Bertram as an unattainable heavenly body that she worships (1.3.204–207). In a conversation with the King, she betrays a similar compulsion to appear normatively chaste. After Lafew does his best to mark their meeting as a sexual tryst, Helena precipitously withdraws her suit when the King taints her proffered cure with imputations of prostitution, "humbly entreat[ing]" a "modest thought"—requesting his belief in her chastity—as she prepares to take her leave (2.1.127–28). Her willingness to suffer a prostitute's punishment if her cure fails (2.1.170–73) seems designed to dispel any lingering suspicions of unchastity, to distance her holy magic from wanton witchery.[15]

In 2.3, the scene in which Helena is to choose a husband, her status as desiring subject becomes public. The King, submitting a batch of eligible wards for her inspection, formally confers "looking power" upon her: "fair maid, send forth thine eye. . . . peruse them well" (52, 61). He also lends her the masculine privilege of choice: "Thou hast power to choose, and they none to forsake" (56). Her public position as dominant woman is so unprecedented that Lafew mistakenly believes that the young lords have rejected her rather than vice versa: as a woman, she cannot be the chooser but only the object of choice.[16] Helena's singular ascent requires another compensatory performance of "femininity." Although she has, in fact, "command[ed]" the King to grant the fulfillment of her desire (2.1.194), she protests her chastity to the assembled suitors and blushingly retires before the King ratifies her authority and compels her to continue.

Helena has come a long way from her earlier masochistic fixation on Bertram. In surveying the undesired suitors, her look frees itself from libidinal investment and so emulates the gaze by marking them as signifiers of her power (over the King), as participants in her spectacle. At the same time, Helena also derives power from being looked at, from being the center of attention, the belle of the ball. Her "to-be-looked-at-ness"—in cinema a signifier of female "lack," according to Laura Mulvey[17]—becomes in the theater an attribute of power, a specularity that approximates the gaze rather than marking her as its object. As Lacan puts it,

> At the level of the phenomenal experience of contemplation, this all-seeing aspect [of the gaze] is to be found in the satisfaction of a woman who knows that she is being looked at, on condition that one does not show her that one knows that she knows.[18]

Within the theatrical frame, the looked-upon central performer and her observers do indeed collude in the kind of disavowal of specularity that Lacan describes. Of course, Helena (or the actress performing her) is looked at not simply by the other figures on stage but by the play's spectators as well. Yet here, too, she may escape a fetishizing look by availing herself of a strategy inaccessible to the film actress: returning the look. In this particular scene, such an effect could be achieved by placing the prospective suitors within the audience, so that when Helena sends forth her eye, she surveys "us" as well as them, bringing us into spectacle by breaking the fourth wall—by determining us, the audience, as lacking by linking us with those desiring suitors whom she rejects. Even in relation to the audience, then, Helena may represent not "to-be-looked-at-ness" but "looking at to-be-looked-at-ness."

When she finally claims Bertram, as Snyder observes, "she does her best to deny her role as aggressive desiring subject and to recast herself properly as object":[19] "I dare not say I take you, but I give / Me and my service, ever whilst I live, / Into your guiding power" (102–104). Bertram, however, discerns and resists this implicit emasculation, dismissing her protestations of vassalage and reclaiming the masculine privilege of looking: "I shall beseech your highness, / In such a business give me leave to use / The help of mine own eyes" (106–108). Bertram refuses to let Helena function as gaze for him. He breaks the stage picture of the happy affianced couple that Helena, in collusion with the King, has created. Indeed, if Bertram takes his protest to a King enthroned upstage right, and the humiliated Helena drifts downstage left, her stage observers shift accordingly, "facing out" in order to look at her. Helena takes a vulnerable position and accepts the status of "to-be-looked-at" as the audience no longer looks at her but looks at her being looked at. She is now clearly the object of the male look, the pawn in a male power struggle, standing by mutely as the King and Bertram proceed to debate her worth. If Helena is born to femininity and at certain moments compelled to achieve it, here it seems thrust upon her.

To call attention to Helena's "performative" femininity is not to accuse her of hypocrisy or willful deception. To point out that her self-effacements are self-serving is not to rehearse the tired, limited characterization of her as a two-faced, manipulative man hunter.[20] It seems to me more helpful to understand Helena's hyperfemininity as a kind of *misrecognition* that she persists in enacting. Helena can perform femininity with such conviction because she has successfully internalized a culturally imposed image of Woman. When Helena seems to affect femininity for the sake of covering her unfeminine, predatory tracks, she may not be crudely dissembling but, like a good method actress who loses herself in the role, truthfully simulating, thereby authenticating the role demanded of her. As Butler suggests, gender is . . . a construction that regularly conceals its genesis; the tacit collective agreement to perform, produce, and sustain discrete and polar genders as cultural fictions is obscured by the credibility of those productions.[21]

Helena challenges a restrictive standard of feminine chastity but, while doing so, she must answer to the chaste self-image shaped by patriarchal society. As John Berger puts it, a woman is "almost continually accompanied by her own image of herself."[22] One reason, no doubt, that Helena has elicited such contradictory critical assessment is that she so vividly embodies the contradiction foundational to female subjectivity in a phallocentric system of meaning—that between self and cultural mirror, woman and Woman.[23]

In performance, one way to call attention to that contradiction would be to assign two actors to the role of Helena: a woman accompanied by a man in drag who would step in whenever Helena "acts feminine." These two Helenas would then take turns, sometimes within the same scene (Helena's interview with the King in 2.1, for instance) or even the same speech (for example, the first soliloquy), while at other times a single Helena would dominate (the female for Helena's combative exchanges with Parolles, the cross-dressed male for her doleful evasions of the Countess). In a modern-dress production of *All's Well,* costuming could accentuate this duality, with the cross-dressed male (as cultural mirror) far more unerringly "feminine" in appearance than the female, whose attire could be freer and more individualized, even androgynous. This prettified, feminine, male-constructed Helena then becomes kin to the lavishly festooned Parolles, a culturally constructed gender image compelling imitation. Such a choice dramatizes the process of misrecognition, exposing the performativity of gender in a manner congruent with much of feminist theater theory.[24] Director/theorist Jill Dolan took a similarly deconstructive approach to her staging of *A Midsummer Night's Dream:*

> [W]hen Helena prostrated herself and pleaded with Demetrius to "beat me," Puck halted the action, directing "ACT-UP" fairies to reconfigure Helena's masochistic desires by taking over for her and Demetrius. The male and female actors moved in and out of the Balinese-derived masks which indicated these two roles, suggesting the construction of gender and the representational constraints placed on women.[25]

In addition, Dolan underlined the theatricality of gender by cross-dressing Theseus and Hippolyta in the final scene and by "cross-casting"

Oberon and Titania: the fairy king was a mustachioed woman in suit and hat, the queen a man in high heels, leather miniskirt, and rhinestone-studded bra.

The two-actor approach I describe might, however, have the regrettable effect of collapsing Helena's core self with a "masculine" desire as symptomatic of cultural influence as her "feminine" self-abjection. The director may therefore prefer to capture Helena's doubleness not through double-casting but through the concentration of its contradictory effects in a single actress—an actress capable of projecting a core self that dramatizes the contradiction as a symptom, preventing the role from sliding into static incoherence. Helena thus becomes as self-possessed and unself-consciously sensual in her active moments as she is self-effacing and studiously chaste in her passive ones. Traditional criticism has tended to portray Helena as either long-suffering Griselda or cunning vixen (thinly veiled versions of "madonna" and "whore"), either glossing over her audacious desire and celebrating her virtue or reading her virtue as a mask for audacity and regretting or deploring her duplicity. A characterization keyed to Helena's doubleness invalidates these reductive caricatures, underscoring the inadequacy of phallocentric constructs to an understanding of Helena's complex subjectivity. This approach challenges audiences to reconcile Helena's indomitable sexuality with her obsequious femininity, to account somehow for a nice girl who seeks and obtains what has traditionally been considered the bad girl's pleasure.

Helena's doubleness manifests itself unmistakably in her one scene with Bertram (prior to the play's final moments). In one sense, she savors "feminine" subservience as the reward for her "masculine" boldness, embracing wifely subjugation with a fervor that mortifies Bertram. "Come, come, no more of that," he protests when she pronounces herself "his most obedient servant" (72). She seems to accept—even to flaunt—a neutered passivity for the sake of eliciting male love.[26] At the same time, her lavish self-effacements seem designed to compensate for her irrepressible, potentially transgressive desire. In asking Bertram for a kiss, she offers a muted sexual overture and claims some measure of her conjugal rights—yet in language so elliptical that it virtually negates the desire it manifests. When Bertram demands, "what would you have," she answers,

> Something, and scarce so much; nothing indeed.
> I would not tell you what I would, my lord.
> Faith, yes:
> Strangers and foes do sunder, and not kiss.
>
> (2.5.83–86)

Once more Helena struggles with the unspeakability of her desire, managing to speak it only indirectly and negatively. It is "something" which quickly becomes "nothing," something she would *not* tell. Although she shifts back into affirming it ("yes") she quickly subsides into a pause, manifesting her search for a language expressive of her desire. As though confirming the impossibility of finding it, she proceeds to describe the desired kiss as something strangers and foes do *not* do.[27]

As noted, Helena's "masculinity" is as much a construct as her "femininity" for, as Foucault has argued, sexual desire is as much culturally engendered as naturally derived.[28] Accordingly, Helena's desire is directed toward the culturally approved end of marriage, an institution that, at least according to the puritan propaganda of Shakespeare's time, confirms a woman in femininity by delivering her to permanent chastity and subservience.[29] Helena herself seems to affirm her belief in this ideal of redemptive marriage when, in an attempt to enlist the Countess' sympathies, she assesses the impossible alternatives imposed by a marriageless life:

> if yourself,
> Whose aged honour cites a virtuous youth,
> Did ever in so true a flame of liking
> Wish chastely, and love dearly, that your Dian
> Was both herself and Love, O then give pity
> To her whose state is such that cannot choose
> But lend and give where she is sure to lose;
> That seeks not to find that her search implies,
> But riddle-like lives sweetly where she dies.
> (1.3.209–17)

Helena presents the "feminine" alternative to marriage as the "sweet death" of terminal sexual pining, the "masculine" as the "loss" of chastity that attends "lending" and "giving" her body. She implies that she must choose between fruitlessly preserving her virginity or fruitlessly expending it. Marriage, by contrast, offers the fruitful option of expending *and* preserving her virginity—or at least preserving the virginal purity that chastity commends. In marriage, Dian is both herself, the goddess of chastity, and Love (or Venus), the goddess of desire. In marriage, that is, a woman may be both sexual and chaste, "living sweetly where she dies" in quite a different sense. This speech suggests that Helena wishes to channel her sexual desire into culturally idealized marital chastity.

Yet Bertram annuls the marriage that Helena takes such pains to make, and in terms that aim at quashing her desire, imprisoning her in the female negative, in the land of "not" and "never." "I have wedded her, not bedded her," he informs his mother, "and have sworn to make the 'not' eternal." In his letter to Helena, he does indeed afflict Helena with an "eternal not": "in such a then I write a never." In so doing, Bertram swears to make Helena's virgin knot eternal, demanding that she remain lacking, accepting her status as the negative signifier of his masculine positive. Indeed, the "dreadful sentence" that Bertram hands Helena demands the very sexual renunciation that she undertakes in her pilgrimage. She embraces a monastical chastity, reconfiguring herself as a penitent whore getting herself to a nunnery, disavowing her desire and receding into iconicity, inspiring the Countess to compare her to the Virgin Mary (3.4.25–29).

From this perspective, Helena's pilgrimage becomes the ultimate compensatory performance of femininity. Some commentators have regarded the pilgrimage as a ruse for renewed pursuit of Bertram.[30] While it is tempting to read her farewell sonnet as yet another coded disclosure of desire, its tone and content accord exactly with the masochistic, grief-stricken, guilt-ridden soliloquy in which Helena announces her intention of fleeing France in order to secure Bertram's return. Shakespeare transforms what had been, in Boccaccio's story, a relentless pursuit into a pilgrimage converted to pursuit by virtue of a miraculous coincidence. Once more Shakespeare seems to mystify Helena's sexuality, portraying her as the prodigious recipient of another heavenly favor that works to validate her desire.

Helena's sexual renunciation ends when she locates another mirror of misrecognition: Diana, who defines femininity for Helena by virtue of her attractiveness to Bertram. As Catharine MacKinnon asserts, "socially, femaleness means femininity, which means attractiveness to men, which means sexual attractiveness, which means sexual availability on male terms."[31] In order to win Bertram, Helena, the devoted would-be wife, must refashion herself as sexual object. Her goal shifts from the fulfillment of desire to the achievement of desirability.[32] Her desire is no longer simply the desire to wed but the desire to be desired. She thus identifies with, and acts through, the woman whom Bertram covets. Helena says not "I wish to become a woman" but, rather, "I wish to be like her whom I recognize as a woman," mimetically replicating a gender ideal.[33] Helena's deputization of Diana offers an extreme instance of her need to conceal her desire. Only when Helena secures the services of a surrogate who agrees to embody that desire and risk the "tax of impudence" that Helena herself carefully dodges does she manage to secure Bertram.

Helena's employment of Diana allows her to remain on a kind of pilgrimage—away from patriarchy's center (represented by the King) to a position on its margins where she can operate more daringly. She gets herself to a kind of secular nunnery, joining a confederacy of women who assist her in an intrigue that leads to her rebirth into patriarchal culture as wife and mother. Yet she must still take pains to prove her femininity, assuring the Widow of the lawfulness of her seemingly unchaste plot. She also continues to refer her power to the King ("That you may well perceive I have not wrong'd you / One of the greatest in the Christian world / Shall be my surety" [4.4.1–3]) and to invoke Heaven, mystifying her bribery of the Countess as an implement of divine providence ("Doubt not that heaven / Hath brought me up to be your daughter's dower" [4.4.18–19]). Having, in effect, pimped Diana by exposing her to censure as a whore (a censure she actually suffers in the final scene) Helena undertakes to redeem Diana by reversing the mirroring process and turning her into an image of herself, a virgin positioned for advantageous marriage, a status the King ratifies in the final scene by extending to Diana the same privilege of choosing a husband that he once conferred upon Helena (5.3.327–28)—a position seemingly contrary to her wishes to "live and die a maid" (4.2.74).

## BERTRAM'S MASCULINITY: Rite of Passage

One must understand Bertram's treatment of Helena in light of his quest for normative masculinity. He begins the play as a liminal figure, an "unseason'ed," uninitiated male caught in the limbo between boyhood and manhood. In the play's opening lines, his mother, the Countess, not only heralds but laments his passage into manhood—"in delivering my son from me, I bury a second husband"—registering his birth as a man as the death of a husband-surrogate, as though regretting her powerlessness to hold him in perpetual boyhood. The incest she evokes may be metaphorical but, within the oedipal plot enveloping Bertram's development, it raises the specter of maternal engulfment threatening to his masculinity. His quest for manhood meets with two principal obstructions: an absence of men willing and able to help him achieve it and the continued presence of Helena, who, in consort with his mother, launches a campaign to marry him and (at least from his perspective) return him to maternal dominance.

Bertram seems adrift in a world of strong women and weak men, men who fail him as father figures. His own father is dead and cannot instruct him in courtly or military arts. Lafew, despite an explicit promise to the Countess to advise Bertram (1.1.71–73), makes little attempt to do so, and on occasion even evinces scorn for his charge (2.3.99–101). The King, a surrogate father, seems rather to block Bertram's passage into manhood, shaming him with marriage to Helena and excluding him from the wars.

The histrionic Parolles happily fills the void, embodying a fiction of masculine grandeur that Bertram attempts to actualize, a mirror of misrecognition in which Bertram insists on seeing himself, a narcissistic reflection of an idealized self that confers an illusion of wholeness. In particular, the supposedly battle-tested, sumptuously plumed Parolles offers Bertram an image of military glamor and promotes participation in the Italian war as a rite of passage into manhood. Thus he praises Bertram's determination to fight as evidence of potency: "Why, these balls bound, there's noise in it. 'Tis hard!" (2.3.279–83).

Yet the Countess and King both define manhood for Bertram as an imitation of his father, the true "perfect courtier" (1.1.60–61, 1.2.19–22). They admonish him to live up to his father's memory. Parolles becomes a rival father figure whom Bertram's own father, speaking through the King, indirectly disparages with his criticism of meretricious fashion-mongers who beget nothing but clothes ("whose judgments are / Mere fathers of their garments"). Later, Lafew implies that Parolles was begot *as* clothes, that he was not born but made by a tailor (2.5.16–19). These images impute to Parolles and his like sterility, unmanliness, and—through the emphasis on costume—imposture and barren theatricality. Indeed, by Lafew's reckoning, Parolles constructs a persona that displays attributes of a social rank and gender to which he has no legitimate claim. By insisting on calling Parolles a "servant," Lafew disputes his nobility (2.3.186–95, 242–51), and by referring to him as a "hen" (213), denies his masculinity. Indeed, Lafew tells Parolles, "I write man, to which title age cannot bring thee" (198–99) and casts similar aspersions when the King summons Parolles to testify against Bertram: "I saw the man today, if man he be" (5.3.203). Yet Parolles' histrionics problematize the notion of a masculine essence implicit in Lafew's disparagements. He functions as a symptom of the tailoredness of gender, performing a masculinity that seems as much a caricature of the cultural norm as the performed femininity of Helena. In following this counterfeit soldier-courtier, Bertram appears to be doing what Helena has already done: internalizing and authenticating a culturally inscribed myth of gender, saying not "I'm a man" but, rather, "I'm like him whom I recognize to be a man."

His father's masculinity, such as Bertram confronts it, may be no more authentic than that of Parolles, for it is also derived from a performance, from the King's dramatic death-bed celebration of the Count. The King constructs an exceptional figure, a hero/courtier of fabulous proportions, who seems partly a product of the King's intense nostalgia for a lost youth. The King not only draws the Count's character for Bertram to emulate but, at one key moment, speaks for him ("'Let me not live,' quoth he"). In a sense, the King impersonates Bertram's father, giving the Count's melancholic reflection on mortality a particularly dramatic recitation by turning it into his own death-bed speech—his own enactment of a father's dying advice to his son. Indeed, with one foot in the grave, the King becomes a virtual medium for the deceased Count's spirit. His line, "methinks I hear him now," could refer not only to a recollected worldly voice but to a newly audible, other-worldly one. The King functions as the ghost of Bertram's father, whose underlying message is, "remember me." Yet the "me" that Bertram is asked to remember is so mystified and glorified that he appears to be left with a choice between two equally fantastical images of manhood: the inaccessibly legendary and the insidiously fashionable.

Despite exhorting Bertram to emulate his father, the King denies him the opportunity to do so by forbidding his soldiership, rendering him unable to prove himself "the son of a worthy Frenchman" (2.1.11–12). Bertram implicitly equates exclusion from the war with emasculation:

> I shall stay here the forehorse to a smock,
> Creaking my shoes on the plain masonry,
> Till honor be bought up, and no sword worn
> But one to dance with.
>
> (2.1.30–33)

Bertram accuses the King, who ought to have initiated him into manhood, of prolonging his boyhood by consigning him to the company of women, precluding his purchase of masculine honor, leaving him with a permanently sheathed, ornamental sword rather than a phallic weapon. His affected farewell to the departing soldiers also conveys his sense of emasculation: "I grow to you, and our parting is a tortur'd body" (2.1.36–37)—an image highly suggestive of castration.

Moreover, in imagining himself the "forehorse to a smock," Bertram imagines himself a woman's beast of burden, an animal she drives and whips. He thus protests the emasculating reversal of the roles of man/woman, rider/horse, master/slave that had become homologous in Shakespeare's England.[34] Bertram's paranoid fantasy seems to be almost instantly fulfilled. Upon choosing Bertram as husband, Helena offers her "service," but, by coercing him into being her sexual partner, she implicitly commands Bertram to do her "service." Rather than being allowed to "woo" and "wed" honor, as the King commands the departing soldiers, Bertram becomes an object of a woman's wooing and wedding. The King, at Helena's behest, subjects Bertram to the very calamity he had urged his soldiers to avoid— bondage to female sexuality:

> Those girls of Italy, take heed of them.
> They say our French lack language to deny
> If they demand. Beware of being captives
> Before you serve.
>
> (2.1.19–22)

Bertram is "captive before he serves," in thrall not to one of "those girls of Italy" whom the King stigmatizes, but to the girl from Rossillion, the girl next door, with whom he grew up. While he is primed to resent any imposed responsibility that keeps him from going a-soldiering, marriage to Helena is, from his perspective, the very worst of fates, regressing him even further into boyhood by returning him to the maternal domination he presumably escaped when ending his constrictive "marriage" to the Countess.[35]

Perhaps the best demonstration of the distance between Bertram and Helena comes when Parolles, urging Bertram to "steal away" to the wars in order to avoid the emasculation of marriage, characterizes Helena's virginity in terms radically different from her own:

> He wears his honor in a box unseen
> That hugs his kicky-wicky here at home,
> Spending his manly marrow in her arms,
> Which should sustain the bound and high curvet
> Of Mars' fiery steed.
>
> (2.3.279–83)

The site of Helena's miraculously generative sexual love becomes a lack, an unseen box, a black hole that consumes Bertram's manly essence, an effeminizing, contemptible "kicky-wicky." The opportunity to mount Mars' fiery steed in manly combat rescues Bertram from his emasculating role as forehorse to a smock.

That Bertram's rejection of Helena stems more from sexual dread than class prejudice seems borne out by his dismissal of the King's promise to endow her with title and dowry. If Bertram were concerned solely with social status, marriage to the King's favorite would seem distinctly advanta-geous. The King, after his lengthy lecture equating honor with virtue, puts the matter quite plainly: "if thou canst like this creature as a maid, / I can create the rest." Bertram's response is equally unambiguous: "I cannot love her, nor will strive to do't" (2.3.142–43, 145).

Bertram "cannot" love Helena. She cannot be an object of his sexual desire, cannot be a "real girl" in Havelock Ellis's terms.[36] This fact is striking, as she so easily achieves that status with the other men in the play, sexually provoking Parolles, Lafew, and the King alike. Lafew considers Helena so much a "real girl" that he would like to consign those seemingly standoffish suitors to the fate of castration (2.3.86–88). From Lafew's perspective, anyone who would not consider Helena a "real girl" is not a real man.

From a psychoanalytic perspective, Bertram cannot love Helena because she is a forbidden object. The Count's responsibility for "breeding" Helena (2.3.114) reinforces her status as a sister figure. The Countess's sponsorship of her matrimonial campaign makes her a kind of mother-surrogate as well. The Countess sees in the passionate Helena an image of her younger self (1.3.128–31). By colluding in Helena's plot, the Countess aims to help Helena secure her son as husband, to revive by proxy the relationship she herself has lost.[37] Helena also may be considered a maternal figure by virtue of her status as partner to the King, Bertram's surrogate father. In an apparent reversal of the oedipal plot, in which the son sacrifices the mother as the price of masculine autonomy, the King blocks Bertram's achievement of manhood by forcing upon him the object of his own sexual interest ("follows it, my lord," Bertram protests, "to bring me down / Must answer for your raising?" [111–13]).[38]

In addition, the first of the identities Helena hopes to derive from marriage to Bertram is the one conspicuously removed from the realm of courtly love that engenders them: mother ("There shall your master have a thousand loves, / A mother, a mistress, and a friend").[39] On one level, of course, Helena simply invokes a biological fact: she may become pregnant as a consequence of intercourse with Bertram. Indeed, motherhood is an essential requirement of Bertram's impossible conditions for marrying her ("when thou canst . . . show me a child begotten of thy body that I am father to"). On another, she explicitly identifies with the very maternal image that repels Bertram and, by raising the spectre of castration, drives him to the wars. Within an oedipal framework, Helena's maternal associations make her a forbidden object, a mystified (m)other both attractive and repellant to Bertram. In one sense, then, his military campaign represents a retreat: like

Parolles, he "runs away for advantage when fear [in this case fear of Helena's sexuality] proposes the safety" (1.1.201–203).

Lavatch later characterizes Bertram's campaign in precisely the same terms. Bertram will not be "killed"—his manhood will not be "lost"—because he runs away from Helena: "The danger is in standing to't; that's the loss of men, though it be the getting of children" (3.2.37–42). If the swaggering, ornamental Parolles mirrors the glamorous masculinity for which Bertram strives, the wisecracking, enigmatic Clown voices the sexual anxiety that underlies it.[40] His first jest portrays female sexuality as a force that deflates male sexuality in its insatiable demand for "service," hence the Clown's preposterously cheerful acceptance of cuckoldry: "the knaves come to do that for me which I am a-weary of. He that ears my land spares my team, and gives me leave to inn the crop" (1.3.43–45). Thus Lavatch celebrates his nonsexual servitude to the Countess: "that man should be at woman's command and yet no hurt done!" (1.3.92–93).

In addition, the Clown parallels Bertram's course by presenting himself as a man recoiling from marriage and female sexuality ("I have no mind to Isbel since I was at court . . . the brains of my Cupid's knock'd out, and I begin to love, as an old man loves money, with no stomach" [3.2.12, 14–16]). When Bertram returns from the wars, having embraced the sexual experience that Lavatch eschews, the Clown suggests that the patch upon his cheek conceals syphilitic scars, reading the patch as a signifier of Bertram's corruption by female sexuality ("it is your carbodano'd face" [4.5.101]).

Lavatch seems to function as Bertram's secret sharer in a second sense: his scant commentary on Helena indicates a comparable need to construct her as a sexless madonna. Late in the play, thinking Helena dead, Lavatch affectionately eulogizes her as "the sweet marjoram of the sallet or rather the herb of grace" (4.5.16–17). This remark suggests that his earlier misogynistic ditty decrying female turpitude and seemingly linking Helena with Helen of Troy might actually mark her as the unnamed "one good woman" exempt from his slanders, dissociated from her notorious namesake and the corrupting female sexuality she epitomizes (1.3.70–79). Lavatch's need to desexualize Helena provides a subtext for his only direct speech to her, in which he offers the seemingly arbitrary anti-joke about the Countess's "wellness." In locating "wellness" in the other world, Lavatch may be admonishing Helena for her excessively worldly (that is, sexual) conduct, urging her to a monastical chastity, implicitly scolding her unchaste entrapment of Bertram. His later eulogy celebrates her seeming compliance, her expiration at the end of her penitential trek to a holy shrine, her ascension to saintly martyrdom.

Bertram so distinguishes himself in the Florentine wars that he ascends to the position of "general of our horse" and wins the masculine honor he had so craved. The scene of his ascension (3.3) often has been cut in performance but it affords an opportunity for staging a grandiose military ceremony dramatizing Bertram's ritual birth as a man, as young warrior-god. The ceremony could center on Bertram's reception of a sword, symbolizing his supposed acquisition of the phallus. In such a staging, the Duke unfurls the sword, raises it high, executes some histrionic sword salute—collectively seconded by a troop of sword-wielding soldiers—then lowers it to a kneeling Bertram, who takes hold of it, kisses it, then rises to receive it. Perhaps a pounding of drums accompanies the ceremony, which climaxes in multiple gun shots. As the thunderous volleys cease, Bertram steps forward and declares, "Great Mars, I put myself in thy file; / Make me but like my thoughts, and I shall prove / A lover of thy drum, hater of love" (9–11).

Bertram occupies the same position that Helena did in 2.3: the center of attention, the object of an admiring, even fetishizing, male look. Like Helena, Bertram functions as both spectacle (to be looked at) and simulated gaze (determining through looking). He is the glittering, glamorous presence who constitutes the others as lacking, as needing to be seen by him. Like Helena, Bertram may function as gaze for the play's spectators as well, if they are joined by soldiers extending the lacking army beyond the proscenium arch.

If the ceremony seems sufficiently overwrought and theatrical, it may begin to convey the extent to which Bertram delivers himself to a role, embracing a mythical masculinity and effectively becoming his own Parolles, who ought to be exiled to the periphery during this scene. Bertram's birth as a man coincides with his willing entrance into spectacle, his assumption of the image of ruthless warrior after rejecting that of domesticated husband.

If Bertram, contrary to the Clown's insinuations about his patch, sustains a bleeding wound—either in battle or in ritual—his ascent to manhood can include a ceremonial purgation of femininity familiar to tribal rites of passage: the bleeding wound symbolizes a male vulva that enables a masculine rebirth superseding his original birth through woman. By spilling blood and voicing rage (declaring himself a lover of Mars' drum and a hater of love), Bertram "gets the woman" out of himself and achieves manhood.[41]

At the mid-point of the play, Bertram and Helena appear to have achieved the extremes of emblematic masculinity and femininity. One could underscore this polarity in performance by creating a tableau at the end of 3.4. (invariably the end of "Act One" in performance), presenting Bertram as gilded, sword-brandishing military hero and Helena as supplicating, saintly madonna. Barbara Dameshek's 1993 production for Shakespeare Santa Cruz extended this idea, counterpointing a soldiers' chorus chanting in rap style "lover of thy drum, hater of love" with the ethereal singing of women dressed in white who assisted Helena in a highly stylized donning of her pilgrim's costume: as the Countess read her letter, Helena walked down a path of white gauze fabric while wrapping around her waist a banner that contained the first line of her sonnet ("I am Saint Jacques' pilgrim, thither gone" [4]).

Some critics have attempted to justify Bertram's rejection of Helena, or at least to present it sympathetically, as an understandable rebellion against a degrading forced marriage.[42] This laudable championing of Bertram's cause ignores the fact that a character must first become a subject before an audience can take offense at his or her being treated as an object. Theatrically speaking, Bertram has not yet become enough of a subject for the spectator to perceive his injury when the play's sympathetic heroine chooses him as husband. His first two scenes are public, dominated by his elders, allowing him little opportunity to display an individuated character. In the first, eager to leave for Paris, he struggles to play the dutiful, respectful son. In the second, he strives to make a favorable impression on the King. Only in his third appearance, free of his elders and petulantly protesting his exclusion from the war, does he exhibit a discernible subjectivity. Yet this effusion of personality is unlikely to win him many admirers. Nobody likes a whiner.

Most critics have found Bertram manifestly unworthy of Helena's devotion.[43] Certainly his conduct alienates the play's other characters, each of whom defames him at one time or another. He humiliates and abandons Helena, defies and enrages the King, and so offends his mother that she resolves to disown him and later endorses the King's threat to punish him— possibly even to execute him. His callous treatment of Diana repulses his comrades-in-arms. Offered an unearned second chance to regain the favor of his benefactors, he instead renews their ire—particularly the King's—and to save himself from censure and disgrace, he contemptuously scorns the woman to whom he had sworn eternal love. An unremittingly unsympathetic Bertram poses considerable problems for performance, however: Helena appears hopelessly foolish and deluded if the object of her pursuit is a thoroughly disagreeable clod who unequivocally disdains her. Since the play clearly derives dramatic interest from the discrepancy between Helena's unquestioning desire and Bertram's questionable desirability, the crucial question for the director to address is this: just how bad is Bertram? To what extent should he be seen as "worth it?" To what extent should one mitigate his defects in performance? Should the audience perceive something potentially redemptive in his character or potentially receptive in his attitude toward Helena? A performance that predicates Bertram's unequivocal inadequacy generates less tension and conflict—ingredients essential to dramatic interest—than one that leaves the question of Bertram's worth unresolved. Who wants to watch a play about a terminally besotted girl pursuing an insufferably churlish boy? In such a production, the play's ending becomes an unambiguous anti-climax, confirming what the audience could be presumed to have known all along: that Bertram is a boor, Helena a masochist, and their marriage an almost certain catastrophe. Such an approach does not so much deconstruct the comic love story as decisively preempt it. Indeed, the play's notorious open-endedness depends upon preserving the possibility of a comic resolution—which in turn requires the possibility of Bertram's reformation, which requires presenting him as reformable, or at least worth reforming, and therefore worth attending to as the play progresses.

Directors have employed various means to mitigate Bertram's obnoxiousness. Some have cast a physically striking, charismatic actor (such as Mike Gwilym, who played the part for Trevor Nunn) in order to make Helena's attraction credible, while others have opted to accent Bertram's youthfulness in order to make his trespasses tolerable. Paul Venables, for instance, who played the part in Barry Kyle's 1989 RSC production, was "baby-faced," "guileless," and "slightly goofy": "the sense that his errors and offenses were committed in a blissfully naive thoughtlessness . . . made him ultimately forgivable at the play's end."[44]

Directors have also aimed to redeem Bertram by lending him a subtextual complexity that qualifies and complicates his mistreatment of Helena. In Peter Hall's recent RSC production, for instance, Toby Stephens's callow, self-involved Bertram begins to mature in the second act when tested by the ravages of war and the first confused stirrings of sexual passion. The actor's subtext registered strongly with one critic who wrote, "[Bertram] doesn't seem to know what to feel, but it's clear he's feeling *something* deeply, for the first time."[45] Helena thus became the jewel in the crown of his hard-won maturation.

Trevor Nunn devised a different subtext for Bertram in his 1981 production, drawing on a psychoanalytic reading of repressed desire. According to Harriet Walter, who played Helena,

In Trevor's scenario, Bertram had funny dreams about Helena. She's someone who's been raised in the household but is only the daughter of a family retainer. So he's somehow disturbed by her because he *mustn't* love her. He doesn't like the effect she has on him so he cuts her out.[46]

In Nunn's view, according to Walter, "Bertram had loved Helena all along but discovered it too late."[47] Yet Gwylim, Nunn's Bertram, objected to this interpretation and consequently keyed his performance to the dismissive gestures on the surface rather than the messier emotions underlying them.[48]

Nunn's choice offers the actor playing Bertram an emotional investment in Helena that adds drama and intrigue to his mistreatment of her, creating and heightening the conflict on which drama depends. Such a subtext could establish that Bertram struggles against feelings for Helena that confuse and unnerve him, that he rejects her not out of contempt but out of fear. Some directors have flirted with this interpretation, in particular turning Helena's request for a kiss into a stimulus for feelings that belie Bertram's apparent disdain for her. In Noel Willman's (1953) and Tyrone Guthrie's productions (1959), Bertram seemed ready to grant the kiss until, reminded of Parolles' presence, he recoiled and brusquely dismissed Helena, as though admonished by Parolles' image of uncompromised masculinity.[49] In John Houseman's production, as well as in Kyle's, Bertram willed himself to reject Helena and then remorsefully sought to make amends, turning to her as if to speak a kind word in Houseman's show, seeming tempted to hug her in Kyle's.[50] In all four cases, an agitated and uncertain Bertram evinces feelings that undermine the genuineness of his rejection. He seems motivated by a need to defend himself, not only against the force of her passion but also against the unseemliness, the unmanliness, of his own.

These choices illustrate the directorial necessity of planting in earlier scenes effects necessary to those in later ones. A bitter and hateful Bertram in 2.5 may so alienate the audience as to foreordain an unambiguously dissatisfying ending instead of a provocatively ambiguous one. In Elijah Moshinsky's BBC production, for instance, Ian Charleson's Bertram dismissed Helena harshly and disdainfully, as though her request for a kiss mortally offended him. Indeed, Charleson, normally a resourceful actor, was so narrowly sulky and conceited as Bertram, and Angela Down so relentlessly downcast as Helena, that long before their final pairing off, which Moshinsky seemingly wished to portray as a touching reconciliation, I had lost interest in them. A reconciliation of such antithetical forces can only be untenably miraculous or preposterous rather than intriguingly, even irritatingly tenable. A Bertram with some measure of merit or appeal or mitigating "unseasonedness" not only keeps the ending open but also helps ensure that Helena will appear uncomfortably obsessed rather than fool-ishly deluded.

## DRAMA OF DIFFERENCE: Old and New Tales

Bertram constructs a narrative of initiation that essentially subsumes the oedipal plot in which woman functions as both figure of obstruction (Helena) and figure of closure (Diana). Bertram's ascension to manhood requires that he prove himself a sexual as well as military conqueror. So he sets his sights on Diana, a "real girl," a sexual object safely removed from the maternal realm. Bertram's oedipal plot intersects with what feminist critic Susan Griffin considers the quintessential pornographic plot: despoiling an idolized virgin.[51] For Bertram, who worships and supplicates Diana as a goddess but means to use her as a whore, the bed-trick becomes a mostly auto-erotic exercise. His lust reduces Helena and Diana to interchangeable embodiments of *Woman*, functioning as passive, anonymous receptacles. Of course, Helena's plot *requires* her willingness to become *Woman*, to enter the bed-trick having assimilated the fantasy image of Diana that Bertram projects. Through the bed-trick, Helena does not so much negate as revise Bertram's oedipal narrative, substituting herself as both bed-mate and figure of closure.

In appointing Helena her impossible tasks, Bertram sets up a fairy tale framework only for the sake of demolishing it. While the tasks themselves present a fairy tale challenge—do these things and "then call me hus-band"—his decoding of them precludes a fairy tale solution: "But in such a 'then' I write a 'never'" (2.4.57–61). Helena, however, insists on the fairy tale framework, reading his metaphor of rejection as a scenario of acceptance and orchestrating the bed-trick, a folkloric convention, in order to secure him as husband. Helena, however, describes the actual event in anything but fantastical terms:

> O strange men,
> That can such sweet use make of what they hate,
> When saucy trusting of the cozen'd thoughts
> Defiles the pitchy night; so lust doth play
> With what it loathes for that which is away.
> (4.4.21–25)

Helena's language is again elliptical: her assertion that strange men make sweet use of *what* rather than *whom* they hate evokes once more her hidden, forbidden sexuality, the "there" of her previous conjurings. Her disillusioned look transforms Bertram from curled darling to lustful debaucher. Just as she had predicted, his incontinent passion impels him to surrender his ancestral ring ("in his idle fire, / To buy his will, it would not seem too dear" [4.1.26–27]). Her recent trials seem to have curbed her rapt idealizations. Helena temporarily releases Bertram from his position as substantiating mirror, the Prince Charming who enables her fantasy of ascent to love and esteem. She now configures him as Other, as personification of difference, a creature from whom she is *estranged*. She redirects her energies to overcoming this estrangement, straining against her disillusioning knowledge to reconfigure Bertram as curled darling. If, in the play's first half, Helena follows a fantasy image of Bertram, in the second half she undertakes to subdue the real Bertram to it—to facilitate or fabricate his transformation back into the creature of her fancy and so solidify her preferred image of herself.

In addition to the folkloric tropes that Lawrence identifies, *All's Well* also discloses affinities with other "old tales" that more directly address this problem of "strangeness." I am thinking, in particular, of The Loathly Lady, which deals with male fear of female sexuality, and Beauty and the Beast, which dramatizes the female's struggle with male sexuality. In each story, the protagonist's love—acceptance of the loathliness or beastliness (that is, sexual difference) of his or her opposite—converts ugliness into beauty. Beauty and the Beast depicts a young woman's transference of love from father to Beast, the sexually menacing male Other. According to Bruno Bettelheim, "only after Beauty decides to leave her father's house to be reunited with the Beast—that is, after she has resolved her oedipal ties to her father—does sex, which before was repugnant, become beautiful."[52]

At the start of the play, Helena has already made this transference. "What was [my father] like?" Helena muses. "I have forgot him. My imagination / Carries no favor in't but Bertram's" (1.1.81–83). Moreover, far from fearing male sexuality, Helena initially embraces Bertram's beastliness, portraying him as a lion with whom she wishes to mate. Indeed, by portraying herself as a hind, Helena both affirms her own sexuality and evokes a fundamental difference in "kind" that divides them. The bed-trick forces Helena to confront the un-kind Beast within Bertram and to undertake his taming. Bertram, by contrast, recoils from Helena's loathliness, her menacing sexual difference ("what [he] hate[s]"), seeing in her an image of the old crone or castrating mother.

Helena's story—and, by implication, *All's Well* itself—also sports intriguing parallels to what Jane Yolen identifies as the common incidents of the traditional tale of Cinderella: "an ill-treated through rich and worthy heroine in Cinders-disguise; the aid of a magical gift or advice by a beast/bird/mother; the dance/festival/church scene where the heroine comes in radiant display; recognition through a token."[53] Helena fits this profile to a significant degree: a worthy yet socially undesirable young woman who finds herself, thanks to a magical gift, miraculously conveyed to, and radiantly displayed at, a royal public ceremony. ("Mort du vinaigre!" exclaims Parolles, apparently stunned by her glamorous appearance, "is not this Helena?" [2.3.44].) It is surely no accident that both Tyrone Guthrie and Trevor Nunn, directors of two celebrated modern productions of *All's Well*, staged this scene as a lavish ball and costumed the poor physician's daughter in an elegant gown, effectively portraying her as Cinderella-turned-princess. And, while she fails to enchant the prince at first, she does become the object of his desire at another clandestine encounter, which she proves publicly by means of a token that seals their marriage. The token in this instance is a ring, as it is in several versions of the traditional tale.[54]

In psychoanalytic terms, the traditional tale presents a heroine who comes to terms with her own sexuality. Her cinders-guise externalizes her dread of the dirtiness of her own sexual drives. Her awareness of the underlying dirtiness impels her to exit the dance prematurely three times, unable to yield to her sexual longing for the reciprocally desirous prince (the midnight deadline that impels her departure is not part of the traditional tale but, rather, the invention of Charles Perrault, whose seventeenth-century version provides the source for the well-known Disney movie). In the climactic scene, she affirms her sexuality by meeting the prince in her cinders-guise and, in an overtly "phallic" gesture, triumphantly inserting her foot into the slipper.[55] In *All's Well*, by contrast, the prince runs from the heroine, whose active sexuality begrimes her chastely feminine persona. She wins the prince by catching him and taking him into the cinders with her.

Traces of Beauty and the Beast and Cinderella may be found in the romance novel, a kind of contemporary fairy tale that also sports parallels to *All's Well*. The "new heroine" of those novels

> is no longer split between two archetypal female characters: the plain-naive-domestic-selfless-passive-chaste heroine and the beautiful-sophisticated-worldly-selfish-assertive-sexually active Other Woman. Instead, the New Heroine is both good and sexual.[56]

Helena holds in unresolved tension the roles of good girl and sexual adventuress that the "new heroine" has apparently successfully assimilated. A motif of taming the beast figures prominently in these contemporary tales:

a seemingly beastly (i.e., hard and unyielding man) loses his heart to the worthy heroine and becomes a sensitive lover. As though ruled by this fantasy, Helena endeavors, through the power of her love, to transform the beastly Bertram into the Prince Charming of her fantasy. Helena's own narrative of self-fulfillment—and a narrative pressure of the play itself— resembles a romance novel in which the cruel hero's callous disregard of the desirous heroine masks a depth of adoration he ultimately avows.[57] The romance novel—and possibly *All's Well* as well—predicates a retributive fantasy of benign dominance-and-submission. As Tania Modleski puts it,

> A great deal of our satisfaction in reading these novels comes, I am convinced, from the elements of a revenge fantasy, from our conviction that the woman is bringing the man to his knees and that all the while he is being so hateful, he is internally groveling, groveling, groveling.[58]

One may say that Helena seeks to transform Bertram's fantasy by enabling it, replacing the pornographic narrative of violating an idealized virgin with the romance-novel plot of eliciting a redemptive kindness from an unyielding male.[59]

## STAGING THE BED-TRICK

Indeed, if the bed-trick were dramatized, it would literally dislocate the narrative of Bertram's debauchery: "I will tell you a thing," the Second Lord confides to this brother, "but you shall let it dwell darkly with you" (4.3.10– 11). This report of one woman's degradation would then give way to the dramatization of another woman's desire. Within the oedipal plot, says de Lauretis, "the place and time of feminine desire" are "nowhere" and "now," which are representable only from an "elsewhere of vision" and within "a different narrative temporality."[60] In virtually every performance of *All's Well,* the place of the bed-trick is precisely "nowhere" or "elsewhere." Its narrative temporality is *other* than the play's—parallel but not precisely coincident with that of the French Captains' gossip. Indeed, the literal death they ascribe to Helena becomes the only means of registering the metaphorical "death" of sexual pleasure she experiences during the bed-trick (4.3.47–59).[61] Through the bed-trick, Helena arrests Bertram's teleological quest for manhood and forces it into the atemporal "now" of her desire, replacing the march of "masculine" time with the occupation of "feminine" space. This hitherto unrepresented space of the bed-trick emblematizes a female difference unrepresentable within a phallocentric framework that associates that space with a "nothing-to-be-seen." If Helena's goal in the bed-trick is to undo the "knot" that Bertram vowed to make eternal, a staged bed-trick can begin to undo her "not," to deliver her from the constraints of a "lacking" femininity.

The staged bed-trick serves as a powerful gestus by creating an alternative space (not but) of female erotic agency, defamiliarizing Helena by unveiling her persistently veiled desire, enabling her to embrace unapologetically the status of sexual subject. Far from resolving her baffling doubleness, the staged bed-trick exacerbates it, intensifying the aggressiveness that belies Helena's habitual self-abjection, stressing not only her contradictory status within the play's narrative but the contradictory status of women assimilated to a phallocentric construct of idealized femininity to which they are always already unassimilable. This effect of heightened contradiction is precisely what de Lauretis identifies as the hallmark of the most effective feminist art:

> [I]t should be possible to work through [narrative] codes in order to shift or redirect identification toward the two positionalities of desire that define the female's oedipal situation; and if the alternation between them is protracted enough . . . the viewer may come to suspect that such duplicity, such contradiction cannot and perhaps even need not be resolved.[62]

By accentuating Helena's doubleness, the staged bed-trick underscores her nonmimetic subversiveness, her assertion of a difference ultimately unconforming to oedipal femininity. It brings her closer to hysteria, to a realm outside the oedipal plot where she must serve as the source of her own signification.

This outside realm, this elsewhere, substitutes unscripted body language for sanctioned verbal text, allowing Helena to replace the passive silent body Bertram expects with her own powerful "speaking body." She controls "elsewhere" by controlling its speechless discourse, effectively inscribing a condition of lack on Bertram's body. The circumstances that she stipulates— silence and darkness—deprive him of the operations that define him as masculine subject: speech and dominating look. Helena positions Bertram so that he lacks language to deny what she commands, transforming him into precisely what he sought in Diana: a masterable body.

An often overlooked marker of Helena's mastery is her curious postcoital detention of Bertram. "When you have conquer'd my yet maiden bed," Diana says on Helena's behalf, "remain there but an hour, nor speak to me" (4.2.57–58). What, one must ask, is the point of this detention? What takes place during that hour? Surely the two lovers do not simply lie there together, not seeing, not speaking, not touching. It seems that Bertram is being set up for something—but that something is never explicitly revealed. Does the dilation of the trick express a desire on Helena's part for a more sustained intimacy, for an extension of "now," for satisfaction on *her* terms? Does it aim beyond mere sexual intercourse for the "something more" of *jouissance*? Does it portend Bertram's unknowing immersion in the space he sought to penetrate and withdraw from, his submergence in the neverland of "there"? In arranging the assignation with Diana, Bertram wishes for nothing more than the performance of sex, a "trick" in another sense of the word. Helena not only offers him a different kind of trick but attempts to elicit a different kind of performance, one that transcends a merely performative sexuality. This curious ellipsis not only offers another veiled glimpse of Helena's erotic agency but also evokes her need to tame the beast, to transform a one-night stand into a foretaste of conjugal love.

The moments preceding Bertram's entrance could parallel those of Helena's aborted wedding night, which one could dramatize by cutting the Clown from 2.4. and setting the scene in a bedchamber, showing Helena readying herself for Bertram's arrival, attended by women who hasten away upon hearing a knock at the door. Helena then walks to the door and opens it, admitting not the longed-for Bertram but his leering emissary Parolles, who reports that Bertram must postpone "the great prerogative and rite of love" (2.4.41). One could then repeat this staging for the later scene: once more Helena readies herself, attended by women (this time her coconspirators Diana, the Widow, and Mariana), but this time she too flees upon hearing the knock, leaving Diana to welcome her wayward husband.

The trick itself could begin with Diana's placing a blindfold on Bertram and yielding her place to Helena. The blindfold not only provides a realistic explanation for Bertram's inability to distinguish her from Diana but also visually links him with his double, Parolles, who is likewise blindfolded and tricked in the very next scene. The blindfold would both deprive Bertram of the look and signify his blindness to the threat of castration that originally drove him from Helena. Diana could plausibly place the blindfold on Bertram if the first part of the scene were staged as a playful chase, a physicalization of the verbal cat-and-mouse game that characterized their last meeting. At some point, Helena could literally emerge from the shadows and replace Diana as the object of Bertram's pursuit.

Extending the implications of Bertram's post-coital detention, Helena could then initiate a kind of suspended foreplay, deflecting Bertram's lust-driven energies into more dilatory, sensual rhythms, indicating a desire for "something more" and ultimately turning his hasty act of undressing into a sustained performance for her benefit. If one positions Helena upstage of Bertram, the audience perceives her as looking subject and Bertram as looked-upon object. Helena emulates the gaze by making a spectacle of Bertram, constituting him as lacking through the projection and control of her desiring look. One could underline this powerful "gaze" by visually contrasting it with her earlier powerless look: during her woebegone first soliloquy she could actually watch Bertram watch himself in a mirror as he finishes dressing for his journey to Paris. In the bed-trick, by contrast, he undresses in the mirror of Helena's preemptive look. Here, as in the husband-choosing ceremony, Helena signifies not "to-be-looked-at-ness" but "determining-through-looking." In both scenes, she elicits and manages male desire, drawing a look that manifests lack. But now she looks back, unaided by the King's authority, desiring the man who desires her despite himself, functioning as the gaze for him as he previously did for her.

The play provides other possibilities for reinforcing this look. In 3.5, for instance, Diana, her mother, and Mariana all position themselves as spectators to the triumphal procession of soldiers. Diana "sends forth her eye" over these glistening combatants and lights on Bertram as desired object. The previously all-male military world admits female spectators who watch a display of macho glamor that once more positions Bertram as "to-be-looked-at" male.

Similarly, one could turn Bertram's attempted seduction of Diana (4.2) into a spectacle by positioning Helena, the Widow, and Mariana as spectators, concretizing the female frame of reference that contains the scene. Within this play-within-a-play, Diana acts the part of sexual tease, defamiliarizing the role of "the girl-who-says-no-but-means-yes" by exposing it as performative, presenting herself instead as "girl-who-says-yes-but-means-no." The concealed female audience also marks Bertram's incipient masculinity as performative. "My mother told me just how he would woo," exclaims Diana, "As if she sate in 's heart. She says all men / Have the like oaths" (4.2.69–71). Like Helena in her hyperfeminine mode, Bertram enacts a culturally inscribed script without knowing it, affirming his kinship with "all men" by venting unctuous oaths and fulsome endearments in order to arrange a one-night stand. Because the play's audience watches not only Bertram's performance but also the women watching it, the scene parallels that of Parolles' capture, in which concealed pranksters also watch their victim walk into a trap. One could extend this staging of the female look in the bed-trick, with Diana, the Widow, and Mariana joining Helena as spectators to Bertram's striptease.

In addition, Helena's reanimation of the King provides a parallel opportunity to accent her sexual power and to stage the unstaged. The cure, like the bed-trick, constitutes a significant "lack" in the play's narrative, its absence similarly serving to mask Helena's sexuality—at least insofar as the play strongly hints that the cure is sexual in nature, that Helena revives the King by arousing him.

Indeed, Helena's interview with the King functions as a kind of antecedent bed-trick. Often set in a bedchamber, it is an erotically charged, intimate meeting that forges the contract that the bed-trick ultimately fulfills. Calling himself Cressida's uncle, Lafew insinuates that Helena's medicinal powers derive from her sexual allure and later attributes the King's revival to an increase in lustiness, an interpretation Bertram seems to share in calling it a "raising" (2.1.72–78, 97–98; 2.3.41). The King suggests that entertaining Helena's cure would be tantamount to prostitution and ultimately yields to her in terms that connote an assent to sexual union: "sweet practicer, thy physic I will try, / That ministers thy own death if I die" and "thy will by my performance shall be serv'd" (2.1.185–86, 201). In addition, while the King claims his "heart owes the malady," the association of "fistula" with the anus makes Helena's attempted cure a particularly intimate act and connects All's Well's stricken monarch with the Fisher King, whose wound "between the thighs" (suggesting emasculation) seems similarly sexual in origin.[63] The sexual symbolism of the King's ailment, combined with the sexual language surrounding its proposed cure, give the impression of a sexually contracted or sexually disabling disease. If the King is so afflicted, poised to die because infected by a woman, his warning to departing soldiers to avoid Italian girls, combined with the Clown's suggestions that Bertram's patch conceals a syphilitic scar, circulates even more widely the fear of female sexuality that shadows Helena's pursuit of Bertram.

More to the point, it burdens Helena with the weight of male sexual dread, necessitating the vindication of her chastity. Although this scene comes the closest of any in the play to affirming Helena's erotic agency, it nevertheless shrouds that agency in mystical incantation and miraculous faith healing. The director may therefore extend the feminist gestus simply by judiciously demystifying Helena's hieratic ministrations to the King, making clear in performance the extent to which she not only persuades and inspires but sexually excites him, inducing appreciable gains in vigor as the scene progresses. This preliminary rejuvenation both anticipates and initiates the actual healing. It could even be said to substitute for it.

Some directors have attempted, with varying results, to bring the scene's sexual undercurrents to the surface, to suggest that Helena secures Bertram as bed-mate by, figuratively speaking, going to bed with the King. In John Barton's 1967 production, Helena was reduced to a "tease of a girl" who titillated the King by sitting on his bed and fluffing up his pillows,[64] and in Moshinsky's BBC version she was a proper young woman whose erotic effect on the King—culminating in a lingering kiss—seemed both incongruous and unintentional. Closer to the mark perhaps was Barry Kyle, who, in his 1989 RSC production, attempted to preserve the scene's mysticism as well as accent its eroticism: his Helena "kick[ed] off her shoes to perform a circling, energetic, sexually assertive, slightly fey dance," exuding an aura of "white witchery."[65]

My own choice would be to extend the erotics of Helena's encounter with the King into a staging of the cure itself, first by eroticizing the gesture of "laying on hands" suggestive of faith healing.[66] At the half-line, "my art is not past power," Helena could pause, reach under the King's nightshirt, and place her hand on his chest, a gesture at once sensual and clinical, disclosing Helena's mode of diagnosis: "nor you past cure." Given that more intimate areas of the King's anatomy might require a healing touch, one could also capture the scene's peculiar mixture of sex and witchery by having Helena perform a kind of mystical sensual massage, moving her hands soothingly and rhythmically around the stricken parts of his body without actually touching him, an image that extends the conflation of faith healing with sexual stimulation. If one dispenses with the arguably dispensable interview between the Countess and the Clown (2.2), one could extend this mystical therapy into a dramatization of the cure itself. Having regained full vigor at Helena's hands, the King could rise from his sickbed and continue to respond to Helena's gestural stimulations, initiating a pattern of rhythmic movement that could slowly shift into a celebratory, intimate dance, setting the stage for their dancing entrance in the next scene.

Of course, these displays of female erotic power have their limitations. The dominating, objectifying look afforded Helena by the staged bed-trick reverses rather than replaces a masculine-feminine polarity, supporting asymmetrical power relations. Moreover, to the extent that Helena secures control of the King and Bertram by withholding satisfaction of the desire she elicits, she claims the only kind of power seemingly available to women in a phallocentric economy: the power derived from the excitation and frustration of male desire, from "blowing up" men and thereby inducing surrender to their will.

Nevertheless, the powerful position of speaking body/looking subject that Helena achieves through a staged bed-trick has the subversive effect of freeing her desire from "feminine" constraint, defamiliarizing the disabling gender roles with and against which Bertram and Helena struggle. By decisively (if only temporarily) giving up the "feminine," Helena establishes the limits of gender-typing and thus evokes a more nuanced enactment of gender than the oedipal polarity permits. In addition, by releasing Helena's repressed erotic energies and suggesting her longing for the "something more" of *jouissance,* by accentuating the anxiety and incongruity that attain to her pursuit of Bertram, the staged bed-trick potentially restores the female difference that Bertram—and the play—so fretfully elides.

### FINAL SCENES: Unresolved Tension

The drum-trick parallels the bed-trick in several key respects and so functions as an ironic substitution scene: both Bertram and Parolles lack language to deny their captors' schemes; both transgress in intention but not in fact; both mistake the familiar for the strange; and both succumb to primitive drives (fear in Parolles' case, lust in Bertram's).[67] In addition, by subjecting Parolles to humiliating exposure, the drum-trick also forecasts Bertram's own humiliation in the final scene. Parolles' discasing functions as a warning that Bertram fails to heed, an emasculation that fails to threaten his masculinity because he has already actualized the image of military and sexual conqueror that Parolles merely projected. Bertram perceives no threat in the wreckage of a discarded model.

One could stage the moments following the removal of Parolles' blind-fold as a court-martial, a ritual emasculation, in which Bertram and the French Captains, before contemptuously dismissing him, ceremoniously strip Parolles of his sword, his insignias, and his extravagant military costume, leaving him virtually naked. To the accompaniment of a drum roll—ironically underscoring the agency of his demise—Parolles suffers the destruction of his carefully constructed masculine facade. Like Bertram in the staged bed-trick, Parolles submits to the feminization and specular-ization of his body, but as object of shame rather than desire. Parolles also takes Bertram's place as center of attention in a military pageant whose staging could parallel that of the general-of-our-horse ceremony. The collective male look strips Parolles of manhood even as it had conferred it on Bertram.

Parolles' near-nakedness lends his final speech added significance:

> Simply the thing I am
> Shall make me live. . . .

Rust sword, cool blushes, and, Parolles, live
Safest in shame! Being fool'd, by fool'ry thrive!
There's place and means for every man alive.
(4.3.333–39)

The "thing" that Parolles is becomes the "place" that he fills. His resolution to thrive by foolery may thus be read as a wish to find employment as a professional jester. The human actor requires a role—a Lacanian "screen"— in order to enter into the spectacle of the world.[68] Stripped of his macho soldier's garb, Parolles seeks a fool's motley, aiming to reconstitute himself by recostuming himself. Lafew seems to have been right all along: the soul of this man *is* his clothes.

Before reentering the Symbolic Order at the play's end, Parolles passes through an (undramatized) limbo of statuslessness and genderlessness in which, as Lavatch had predicted, he signifies nothing (2.4.23–27). One might stage this liminal phase by arranging for Parolles to cross paths with Helena and her women as they journey home to France. If, like Kyle, the director portrays Helena's group as a "little female army behind their wooden cart,"[69] the hungry, outcast Parolles—perhaps transformed by his derelict wanderings into the semblance of a bare, forked animal—could join their army, gratefully donning a dress that one of the women extracts from a trunk in order to cover his bare limbs. Such cross-dressing could underline Parolles' genderless status, his consignment to ranks of not-men, confirming Lafew's disparagements of him as a "hen," one who cannot "write man."

Parolles' feminine attire could also sharpen the additional shaming he receives from the Clown and the old Lord, each of whom had earlier seen through his macho impostures (2.4.23–37; 2.5.45–46). Parolles acquiesces in his own humiliation for the sake of gaining entry into the Symbolic Order. Since he can no longer be a soldier or courtier or even a man, he becomes a "tame" one to be kept (2.5.45–46), accepting a permanently liminal, "lacking" status. His appearance in the final scene in full fool's regalia marks his debut as professional jester. Indeed, his equivocating testimony at Bertram's trial may easily take the form of a fool's quibbling word games. Ultimately, Parolles demonstrates the constructedness not only of gender but of subjectivity, the cultural regulation to which a core self is subject. The audience discerns that role-playing is foundational to Parolles' subjectivity even as, thanks to the actor, it grasps a "Parolles" separable from the roles he plays. His descent to the status of fool may therefore be read as an act of self-preservation rather than self-evacuation, a survival artist's anti-heroic adaptation to a cultural order that would otherwise erase him.

In the final scene, Bertram, despite disowning his disgraced double, suffers a comparable shaming, a comparable assault on his constructed masculinity and capitulation to those he formerly scorned. Helena avenges her earlier humiliation at Bertram's hands by orchestrating his utter ruination: he is censured, disgraced, and threatened with execution. The drama that she oversees virtually reenacts the earlier scene. Once more the King tries and fails to make a match for Bertram (Lafew's daughter Maudlin). Once more Bertram scorns and humiliates a prospective wife (Diana), a threateningly desirous stand-in for Helena who claims him as husband. Once more the would-be wife suffers transformation from subject to disprized object. Indeed, Bertram might repeat his earlier beseeching move upstage to the enthroned King in an attempt to make a spectacle of Diana, reinforcing his efforts to put her on trial, to portray himself as her victim, a helpless male preyed upon by female cunning (5.3.210–19).

Bertram tries to align himself with the King, whose royal look approximates a gaze. In fact, Helena functions as gaze in this final scene. She establishes and orchestrates the spectacle. Hers is the all-seeing unseen eye for whose sake the others perform. One might even position Helena as concealed spectator to the play's final scene in order to foreground this function. When Helena herself enters the spectacle, she decisively resumes the position she previously secured in the husband-choosing scene, the all-observing observed of all observers. Helena-as-gaze thus makes a spectacle of Bertram, turning his triumphant homecoming into a trial, foiling his attempt to act the part of prodigal son, the reformed rake reconciling with a forgiving father (the King). She also prevents the fatherless Bertram from gaining Lafew as father-in-law by ruining his hopes of marrying Maudlin. Helena dominates the play's final scene but, characteristically, she is not physically present—not "there"—until its final moments.

She embodies herself—and her desire—through two rings which, once introduced, turn the tide quickly and overwhelming against Bertram. The first ring, which Helena places on Bertram's finger during the bed-trick, functions both as a wedding ring, signifying her consummation of the marriage, and as a symbol of Bertram's bondage to the female sexuality he had previously abhorred. The ring around his finger signifies the (k)not that Helena has tied around his body, the "there" in which Bertram seemingly loses himself during the bed-trick and from which he cannot escape. The ring, a gift from the King, also represents Helena's power to "command" patriarchal authority, to enlist the King's assistance once more in winning Bertram as husband (5.3.83–86). Its introduction thus induces the King to turn violently against Bertram, leaving him vulnerable to Helena's further manipulations. The second ring, which Bertram surrenders to Diana in exchange for (he thinks) her sexual favors, also signifies Helena's dominance, her success in securing Bertram as permanent sexual partner by fulfilling his conditions for marriage. By surrendering the token of his masculine honor, Bertram further binds himself to a dominant female sexuality.

These rings restore Helena's dominance not only covertly but, as tokens of her unrepresentable sexuality, nonmimetically as well. Certainly they play havoc with the King's attempt to conduct an orderly investigation into their origins and meanings. Although a careful reader can keep track of them, the rings' dizzying trajectories in performance render them virtually nonreferential, or at least unstable and ungraspable, signifiers without a clear signified. The King goes so far as to suggest that Helena's ring possesses alchemical properties, conjuring multiple owners just as its elusive referent ("there") generated multiple identities for Helena (5.3.101–106).

Diana's evasions and equivocations concerning the rings further destabilize meaning, transporting the King to the realm of "Not": "It was not given me, nor I did not buy it. . . . It was not lent me neither. . . . I found it not. . . . I never gave it him" (5.3.272–76). Diana diverts the King's investigation into the unraveling of a riddle, initiating the kind of representational shell game imagined by Irigaray in her description of a nonmimetic "hystera theater": "[Y]ou will always already have lost your bearings as soon as you set foot in [it]."[70] Trying to explain her acquittal of Bertram, Diana makes the riddle explicit, evoking the hidden secrets of the nonmimetic bed-trick:

> he's guilty and not guilty.
> He knows I am no maid, and he'll swear to't;
> I'll swear I am a maid, and he knows not. . . .
> He knows himself my bed he defil'd,
> And at that time he got his wife with child.
> Dead though she be, she feels her young one kick.
> So there's my riddle: one that's dead is quick.
> And now behold the meaning.
> (5.3.189–91, 300–304)

Diana's "hysterical" discourse confounds distinction, deranging the binary logic on which language—and mimesis—depends. Her words insist on an impossible two-in-oneness, a meaning capable of unifying opposites, of reconciling positive to negative. This assertion of the "not-one" proves an "abuse" to the King's ears until Helena steps forward and offers herself as unambiguous signified, the answer to the riddle, the "meaning" of the spectacle, the "one" who dissolves contradiction.

Yet Helena herself continues to be impenetrably contradictory. For one thing, she continues to mystify her power and desire, staging her return as a miraculous resurrection that once more casts her as necromancer—or, in this case, "exorcist" (5.3.304). To ensure her reception as savior, she positions Bertram as redeemed sinner, masking the elements of revenge and erotic conquest that also mark her homecoming.[71] Like Duke Vincentio, who resolves to make Isabella "heavenly comforts of despair," Helena sanctifies her scheme to rescue Bertram from the calamity she herself has created—presumably in order to elicit feelings of indebtedness conducive to capitulation.

Moreover, Helena reaffirms doubleness in calling herself, essentially, a wife and no-wife ("the shadow of a wife, . . . / The name, and *not* the thing" [5.3.307–308, emphasis mine]), thereby perpetuating rather than dissolving contradiction. Bertram affirms that she is both "name" and "thing" and begs her pardon, as though ready to accept her as wife and end her riddling self-division. Yet he follows his seemingly unequivocal affirmation with a more conditional one: "[I]f she, my liege, can make me know this clearly, / I'll love her dearly, ever, ever dearly" (315–16). Characteristically, Helena affirms her claim to have met his conditions in negative terms: "[I]f it appear not plain and prove untrue, / Deadly divorce step between me and you"— once more raising the spectre of a permanent "not," the "never" of Bertram's original formulation. If Helena does indeed succeed in securing Bertram as husband, the marriage she makes can represent, at best, a double negative: she successfully negates Bertram's negation of their wedding. She proves herself not a not-wife. Whether she can truly achieve the status of wife remains provocatively questionable.

Equally questionable is precisely what it would mean to achieve it. What does "the thing" signify? The suspicion that "wife" connotes "safely nullified female" haunts the play's final scene. On one hand, Helena no longer feels compelled to simulate normative femininity. She does not disclaim dominance of Bertram by fulsomely protesting subservience. She does not hesitate to call the Countess "mother" (5.3.119). At the same time, given her previous displays of obsequiousness, given the wife's submissive status in marriages of Shakespeare's time, to become "the thing" of wife may mean to erase permanently those aspects of herself at odds with normative femininity, to end doubleness at the expense of self-erasure. From this perspective, her dominance of Bertram ultimately enables her to submit to him in marriage. Ever in thrall to Bertram, she wins him only by putting him temporarily in her thrall so that she can put herself permanently in his. Although Helena's narrative dominates Bertram's, allowing her to construct him as the Other out of whom she creates herself, at the same time her fundamental, culturally prescribed desire is to become the object of his desire, the Other out of whom he creates himself:

> The end of the little girl's journey, if successful, will bring her to the place where the boy will find her, like Sleeping Beauty, awaiting him, Prince Charming. For the boy has been promised, by the social contract he has entered into at his Oedipal phase, that he will find woman waiting at the end of *his* journey.[72]

The fulfillment of Helena's quest for womanhood depends upon fulfilling Bertram's quest for manhood, functioning as figure of closure for his oedipal plot. Despite persistently demonstrating her divergence from lacking femininity, Helena ultimately appears to embrace it, to read her worth and constitute her identity in the returned look of her Prince Charming, to resolve her doubleness by submitting to his "one."

Helena aims to deliver both herself and Bertram to a fairy tale denouement that safely reinscribes a masculine-feminine polarity, submitting difference to a symbolic opposition that turns Bertram into her substantiating mirror. In the immediate aftermath of the bed-trick, Helena recoiled from male lust and affirmed Bertram's difference ("O strange men, / That can such sweet use make of what they hate" [4.4.21–22]). In the play's final scene, however, she emphasizes his likeness to her, his "kindness" ("O my good lord, when I was like this maid, / I found you wondrous kind" [5.3.309–10])—a word that connotes kindredness as well as gentleness or generosity.[73] Helena needs to claim Bertram as one of her own kind, to create him in her own image—the same image she has sought doggedly to impose despite all his obstinate assertions of alienness. In the final scene, Helena tries to confirm Bertram in kind-ness by "crush[ing] him with a plot." She replaces his prodigal-son narrative with a version of the romance-novel retributive fantasy, aiming to bring him to his knees (a posture he has assumed literally in more than one production), abusing him in order please him, positioning him to savor the bondage he initially abhorred.[74] She succeeds only to the extent that she elicits an apology and a capitulation that approximate and promote the kindredness she covets. The play, however, offers no assurances that Bertram has truly accepted transformation from Beast to Prince Charming or that he can ever hope to match Helena's idealized vision of him.

Critics have long lamented the paltriness of Bertram's conversion speech, but the problems with the play's final scene run much deeper.[75] Because

Bertram has twice before falsely professed admiration for Helena (2.3.167–73; 5.3.44–55), no words of his, no matter how eloquently or torrentially penitential, could ever suffice to confirm his sincerity. Nor, for that matter, could his actions. Even the most extravagant, self-abasing gestures may be symptoms simply of feverish gratitude rather than of genuine conversion. Helena may be able to work up feelings in Bertram that simulate and even enable love but do not actually generate it. And, of course, Bertram may simply cunningly simulate a penitential swoon. In either case, Helena manipulates Bertram into affecting a kind-ness that he may quickly discontinue upon resuming his male prerogatives in marriage. Perhaps Bertram functions here as a male Kate—a seemingly tamed lout who performs the submissive part his dominant spouse has taught him but who may, after all, only be performing. Because, in the play's second half, Helena's aim seems to shift from wedding Bertram to eliciting his desire—from being the "name" to being the "thing"—it may be that, for the second time in the play, her goal eludes her even as she appears to achieve it.[76]

Moreover, Helena's attempt to embrace femininity is scuttled not simply by Bertram's uncertain response but by her own unfeminine excess, her embodiment of a doubleness that resists reduction to a legible unity. Even as she attempts to accommodate herself to the oedipal plot, she remains elsewhere. Even as her pregnant body allows her to inscribe herself as "wife" and "mother" within the patriarchal order, it also projects the nonmimetic *jouissance* of the bed-trick.[77] On one hand, that is, Helena's pregnant body assimilates her sexuality to a reassuringly feminine, maternal image that evidences Bertram's potency and paternity. On the other, it manifests her sexual dominance, serving as the text of Bertram's fulfilled conditions—and thus as the cause of his capitulation. It also speaks of her own desire and pleasure, reaffirming the active sexuality transgressively alien to the oedipal plot.

Let's look at this double effect in greater detail: on one level, Bertram's apparent readiness to accept Helena's satisfaction of his conditions invites a revisionist reading of them as coded desire, embedding a fantasy of merger with the dreaded but desired female other.[78] The conditions are themselves provocatively contradictory, both prescribing and prohibiting sexual intercourse with Helena. Indeed, assuming that Bertram harbors a hidden desire for Helena, the conditions themselves constitute a riddle: how can I have sex with you without suffering shame or emasculation? How can you have sex with me without contaminating yourself or surrendering maternal purity? Helena's answer is the bed-trick, which allows Bertram not only to fulfill his forbidden desire for her involuntarily but to overcome a disabling, contradictory apprehension of female difference: through the bed-trick Helena assimilates for Bertram's sake the seemingly unassimilable roles of wife and lover, (m)other and "real girl" and, in so doing, appears to become "one" with the oedipal plot.

The finale of *All's Well* could therefore be said to dramatize (at least on one level) the amelioration of castration anxiety—the dread of loss and lack that attends Bertram's aversion to Helena. Helena presents herself as uncastrating, one who has already "had" Bertram sexually without damaging him. She steps forward as the eroticized mother figure of his dreams. Her "resurrection" at the play's end represents the final mystification of her own sexuality, an unthreatening eroticizing of the saintly guise she assumed for the pilgrimage. She replaces her own degraded double, sanitizing the wayward desiring self that the beleaguered Diana personifies. Her visible pregnancy—her status as mother—purifies the sexuality it affirms. It also ratifies Bertram's manhood, signaling his conquest of her, his success in "blowing her up." Moreover, given the belief circulating in Shakespeare's day that a woman could conceive only if she experienced an orgasm,[79] Helena's pregnancy serves as proof not simply of his sexual potency but of her satisfaction by him. Also, by helping him to become a father, Helena promotes Bertram's resemblance to the father he was urged to emulate from the outset.

The bed-trick becomes Bertram's initiation into manhood, with Helena serving as his initiator, the womb or matrix through which he is reborn, negating his attempt to "get the woman out," to undergo a rite of passage symbolically affirming his separation from woman. His "second birth" repeats rather than replaces the first, affirming his maternal origin. In this world of absent fathers, no viable model of manhood exists for Bertram. Helena essentially takes the place of Bertram's father, as her possession of his ancestral ring suggests. Bertram becomes her creation rather than the Count's. In marrying Helena, Bertram finds his masculinity affirmed through a reassuring maternal presence, getting what he may have wanted all along: a wife/lover/ mother who allows him to become a man by remaining a boy.

On another level, Helena's difference is not so easily assimilated, and the impossible conditions represent not a fantasy to fulfill but a law to countermand. By consigning Helena to the realm of Not, Bertram reinscribes the Law of the Father, dismissing her body as nothing-to-be seen, erasing her by textualizing her, subduing her to the patriarchal symbolic. By seeming to return from death—the realm of permanent "not"—Helena underscores her resistance to symbolic erasure, her subversive unassimilability to the lack culturally assigned her. The body Bertram used and disposed of proves itself indisposable; the invisible object of the bed-trick becomes formidably subjective and visible, returning in the person of a would-be wife, a once and future lover, who claims him like an avenging spirit.

Helena defeats the phallocentric negation embedded in Bertram's text by offering the text of her own pregnant body as proof of her in-disposability, a text whose meaning exceeds the limits of the conditions it fulfills and the symbolic categories (wife, mother) to which it is subject. By bearing material traces of the nonmimetic bed-trick, by textualizing her own aspiration to *jouissance,* Helena records a difference irreducible to anatomy. Her body becomes not the source of a prediscursive, universal female meaning in which she shares but a signifier of her own elusive subjectivity, the text of her own persistent riddle. Helena brings Bertram, however obscurely, new knowledge of herself, offering allusions to their time in bed and visible proof of their mutual gratification—allusions both tantalizing and confounding. Her body claims knowledge of Bertram and attributes to him a knowledge of her that contradicts and challenges his lack of knowledge, sparking the desire to know more. When Bertram declares, "if she, my liege, can make me know this clearly," the "this" he wishes to know surely encompasses a good deal more than the details of Helena's fulfillment of his conditions: it must include the mystery of female difference, of an otherness he may now perceive as other than "nothing-to-be-seen," other than Other, distinct from the culturally prom-ised Woman awaiting him at his oedipal journey's end. To desire to know more of Helena is to desire *her,* to regard her as a riddle worth solving. The "this" that Bertram's wishes to know becomes homologous with Helena's "there," suggesting that the performance of sex has solved his problem with sexuality, that he loves her and loves her knot—to rework Parolles' definition of a gentleman's love for a woman. Yet this solution, and the desire for knowledge it predicates, are simply intriguing possibilities. As the play ends, Helena remains elsewhere, suspended somewhere between known and not known. By recurrently transcending the lacking feminin-ity she seemingly strives to embrace, Helena moves beyond the realm of "not" to the elsewhere of "not, but," paradoxically inserting herself into the oedipal plot as the source of her own meaning, hysterically coexisting with her own negation.

The play's refusal to dissipate its tensions or substantiate its tentative resolutions leaves its drama of sexual difference suspended, arrested in an unresolved but provocative, even poignant, tension. Helena remains a mystery to be solved by the reader and spectator as well. So, too, does Bertram. Both characters aim to ground themselves in genders that the play suggests are groundless—or at least unstable, fluid, performative. Neither manages to forge a stable identity or secure a clear destiny. Modern performance could underline Helena's and Bertram's status as subjects-in-process, active agents inextricably engaged with subjugating myths of gender. In particular, a staged bed-trick, by fetishizing the male body and empowering a female gaze, could underline the instability of those genders they seek to stabilize, taking the play's provocative dramatization of difference to startling and invigorating lengths.

The play itself also remains a riddle to be solved. It interrogates the happy ending it provisionally enacts by refusing to exorcise the doubts that have clouded Helena's pursuit of Bertram from the outset. It seems almost deliberately designed to force the audience to confront the implications of its need for a comic love story in which imperiled protagonists happily transcend all conceivable obstacles and vexations. Even as Helena finally secures Bertram as husband, the play stokes doubts about the sincerity of his conversion and the seemliness of their union. Does their reconciliation evidence the flourishing of mutual love and desire or the wedding of delusion and opportunism?

The play gestures toward comic closure while refusing to harmonize its anti-comic discordances. For this reason, the director may wish to insert Lavatch into the final scene as a signifier of that anti-comic spirit. The Clown's strained and dissociated jesting manifests not only sexual but metaphysical anxiety. His jokes "keep touching religion like a sore tooth."[80] On at least three occasions he addresses issues of salvation and damnation (1.3.28–37; 2.4.1–13; 4.5.36–55). When Lafew, unnerved by such apocalyptic raillery, calls Lavatch "a shrewd knave and an unhappy," the Countess concurs, "So 'a is. My lord that's gone made himself much sport out of him; by his authority he remains here, which he thinks is a patent for his sauciness" (4.5.60–63). In this brief exchange, one not only hears of Lavatch's bitter and melancholic disposition but deduces their probable source: the death of the Count, to whom the Clown was evidently much attached. Lavatch is a walking symptom—of the fear of female sexuality, of the dread of mortality, of the instability surrounding the death of the father. In the midst of a narrative straining to resolve itself comically, he personifies that principle in experience that resists comic idealization.

Lavatch might be placed as brooding, skeptical spectator to the play's final events, signaling the stubborn persistence of his personified question. Can dread of female sexuality be so easily exorcised? Can the unruliness of male sexuality be so safely assimilated to a redemptive marriage of the very sort that Lavatch mocked in his opening scene? Can any of these characters achieve "wellness"? Can the play itself achieve it, mired as it is in a truculently realistic anxiety? The melancholy jester/scourge sticks like a burr to this play. One could close the play with the King's summoning his subjects offstage, leaving Bertram and Helena alone at last, sealing their marriage with a kiss. Upstage of them, standing in the shadows but perturbingly visible and intensely observant, is Lavatch, an unanswered, perhaps unanswerable question mark. The play ends by directing focus to a doubting look that disrupts Bertram's and Helena's attempt to signify "happily married couple" in the spectacle of the world.

In the play's epilogue, the actor/King declares, "The king's a beggar, now the play is done; / All is ended well if this suit be won, / That you express content" (Epi. 1–3). The play ends well if we say that it does. Remembering Lavatch's definition of "wellness" as a state of grace beyond human experience, one must perhaps admit that, given the play's engagement with that often unlovely and dispiriting experience, it ends as well as it can.

# 2

# *Measure for Measure*

*Measure for Measure* invests the traditional tales from which it is derived, "The Corrupt Magistrate" and "The Disguised Ruler," with a degree of sexual perturbation greater than that of *All's Well That Ends Well.*[1] Shakespeare departs from all previous versions of the first tale by making the magistrate's victim a would-be nun—a novice of the notoriously strict order of St. Clare—who refuses to gratify the magistrate's wish for sexual favors in exchange for her condemned brother's life. The bed-trick Shakespeare invents to resolve this dilemma—and to adhere to the outline of the original narrative—further problematizes the play's sexual dynamics, introducing a character resembling Helena in her masochistically "feminine" mode, a desirous woman hopelessly pining for a truculently resistant man. Shakespeare then envelopes this story within a revisionist treatment of the "Disguised Ruler," replacing the traditional figure of the beneficent monarch who dispenses justice incognito with an enigmatic Duke who, while pursuing uncertain ends for undisclosed reasons, indulges in sexual intrigue and deceives and humiliates two different women.

While *Measure for Measure* goes further than *All's Well* in foregrounding the sexual dynamics embedded in its sources, it shares with *All's Well* a tendency to suppress or mystify the psychodrama it enacts, principally by fitting two of its key characters to ecclesiastical personae. The Duke's friar's disguise mystifies whatever sexual motives or feelings underlie his intrigues, while Isabella similarly cloaks a sexual vexation in a novitiate's robes, striking a ferociously chaste pose that simplifies and neutralizes her complex sexuality.

As in the previous chapter, my principal task will be to frame the play's provocative interrogations of gender within a feminist gestus by teasing out its erotic subdrama. The Duke, Angelo, and Isabella are (albeit in distinctly different ways) as entangled in gender's constrictive myths as Helena and Bertram. Like Bertram, Angelo erects a masculine facade partly in defense against a fear of engulfment and effeminization. Like Helena, Isabella performs femininity for much of the play, with the crucial difference that she is specifically directed to do so. The Duke pursues his own version of the oedipal plot which, though vastly different from Bertram's in some respects, discloses a common goal: actualizing a myth of masculinity that positions a woman as figure of closure.

In *Measure for Measure*, however, gender becomes far more imbricated with power, expressing itself in essentially sadomasochistic transactions.[2] According to Deleuze, sadomasochism externalizes an internal rupture in libidinal governance: the ego, rather than negotiate between the forces of repression and desire, cedes victory to the former, identifying itself exclusively either with punitive paternal authority or with the transgressive, guilt-ridden self it punishes. The sadist punishes an image of his or her desiring self, mortifying the flesh of a feminized surrogate. The masochist covets punishment in expiation of desire, savoring the mortifications that confirm her or his feminized status.[3] In relation to gender, sadism and masochism take "masculinity" and "femininity" to extremes. Sadism entails not simply disavowing but transferring "lack" to a degraded substitute, while masochism requires not only accepting but coveting the reception of "lack" from an exalted fantasy figure.

My central claim is that *Measure for Measure* can be most profitably fitted to a feminist gestus if read and staged in terms of its sadomasochistic dynamics.[4] The Duke, Isabella, and Angelo are all reclusive ascetics who deploy extreme defenses against eruptive sexual drives. Angelo resists likeness to the libidinous Claudio by sadistically punishing him. He then finds himself moved by his passion for Isabella to a masochistic longing for degradation. He tries to save himself by punishing her in the image of his own degraded sexuality. Isabella similarly oscillates between masochistic and sadistic positions, savoring feminine "lack" in her erotic beating fantasy but embracing "masculine" potency in excoriating her brother, transforming him into a figure of her own repressed desire. In the final scene, the Duke's intended exhibition of "masculine" power takes shape as a sadomasochistic spectacle: he punishes Angelo as the personification of his disavowed "lack" and attempts to manipulate Isabella into a "lacking" femininity.

Many of the staging choices I discuss are designed to underline these sadomasochistic dynamics: opening the show with a piece of sadomasochistic ritual, repeating the imagery of kneeling and supplicating throughout the play, accentuating the sadism of Angelo's public shaming of Claudio, and underlining the mortifications to which the Duke subjects Angelo, Isabella, and Mariana in the play's final scene. These choices are integral to the kind of feminist *gestus* I envision for the play, which depends most particularly on the characterization of Isabella. Her choice of chastity over her brother's life is as much a problem to be worked out in performance as Bertram's rejection of Helena. I examine the extent to which two particular gestic stagings can assist in illuminating her dilemma and redefining her chastity in more intelligible, contemporary terms: depicting Angelo's violent propositioning of her as an attempted rape, which Claudio inadvertently reenacts when desperately imploring her to comply. I also discuss the importance of defamiliarizing Isabella's image as maniacal prude. Because I have so recently staged the play, I use examples from my own work more often than in the previous chapter. In particular, my consideration of the play's final scene includes a detailed description of my own staging.

## THE DUKE AS GHOSTLY FATHER

If the central figure of *All's Well* is a desirous young woman unreconciled to powerlessness, the protagonist of *Measure for Measure* is an ascetic older man unreconciled to power. Although the Duke's age is not given, he professes to shun the assemblies of "burning youth," claims a "grave and wrinkled" purpose for his friarly masquerade (1.3.5–6), and is described by Lucio as "past it"—past the youthful whoremongering that Lucio mischievously ascribes to him (3.2.182). Certainly many directors choose to place his age in a generation removed from that of Angelo and Isabella, underlining his status as nominal father of the land. *Measure for Measure* thus transfers principal interest to a figure of only secondary importance within the world of *All's Well:* the stricken monarch in need of revival. Although the Duke is not dangerously ill, his own metaphors mark him as infirm and impotent: he claims that his "rod" is "mocked" rather than "feared" (1.3.26–27), speaks of handing over the "organs / Of our own power" to Angelo (1.1.20–21), and calls love a "dribbling dart" (1.3.2). He also evokes (and possibly identifies with) an impotent, imperiled paternity while lecturing Claudio on the vanity of human wishes ("thine own bowels, which do call thee sire, . . . / Do curse the gout, sapego, and the rheum / For ending thee no sooner" [3.1.28–32]). In so hastily departing and disappearing, the Duke comes to resemble not only the King but the deceased Count, an absent rather than ailing father.

In an important sense, the Duke is absent not only from his citizens but from the audience as well. For almost the entire play, he impersonates a friar, wearing monastic rather than ducal garb, tempting spectators to forget his identity as Duke—a temptation far less present to readers guided by the text's consistent assignment of his lines to "Duke." The Duke's prolonged masquerade complicates one's efforts to construct a stable subjectivity for him. For instance, when he instructs Claudio on the wretchedness of life or blasts Pompey for his "beastly" trade, one wonders if he is sincerely venting personal convictions or merely simulating a friar's righteousness. Even the core self the actor projects cannot lend the Duke an identity unambiguously separate from the friar's. Whatever the Duke's level of investment in his friarly persona, it remains his principal medium of self-presentation. When he briefly drops it for two speeches in 3.2, he does little to disclose an accessible self: in the first he elevates his wounded vanity to the status of slandered "greatness" (3.2.185–89), and in the second he adopts his most god-like tones in portentously denouncing Angelo's crimes (3.2.261–82).

Not only does the spectator have little access to a Duke unmediated by his friar's role but "the Duke" is itself a role that the man called the Duke must play. Indeed, the man called the Duke is actually named Vincentio but is never so called by the play's characters and seldom if ever by the play's commentators, suggesting a further difficulty in discerning his subjectivity. One must hesitate to credit even Escalus' characterization of the Duke as "a gentleman of all temperance" (3.2.237). The Duke essentially elicits from Escalus a validation of his preferred self-image as a salve for the wounds inflicted by Lucio's prankish slander. While for much of the play one watches the friar at work, one may be fitfully and fretfully aware of the Duke who represents him, of the enigmatic Vincentio, who represents the Duke, and of the actor who represents Vincentio. "The Duke," one might say, exists under erasure. He seems simply an effect of theatricality, constituting himself solely through performance. Even more than Parolles, the Duke depends on role-playing to cohere as a subject, making difficult the separation of person from persona. Having judged his performance in the role of "Duke" a failure, Vincentio takes on a new role, as though its enactment will better prepare him for a return engagement as Duke—as though this more overt impersonation will enable him to achieve embeddedness in the role required of him by the social spectacle. At the very least, his masquerade as friar allows him to orchestrate the circumstances optimal for his re-presentation of Duke.

Whatever the cause of the Duke's withdrawal, its effect is one of displayed potency. His friarly masquerade conduces to—and perhaps aims at—an effect of rejuvenation, a recovery and legitimation of patriarchal authority.[5] Like Helena's, however, the Duke's reinsertion into the Symbolic Order requires a descent into liminality. He takes off his breeches and dons a friar's dress, aligns himself with women, circulates reports that he has died or entered a monastery, and sends letters whose "uneven and distracted manner" and contradictory contents provoke Angelo to wonder if the Duke has lost his mind (4.4.1–5). These images of desexualization, death, anti-worldly withdrawal, and witlessness are all aspects of a liminality that register the Duke's structural absence. The father of the land has become a ghost—or at least "a ghostly father"—undergoing a temporary "death" ("lack" writ large) in order to give birth to himself as a man.[6]

In performance, the Duke's liminal phase need not entail self-negation. It may serve instead as a transitional space of productive make-believe in which the Duke's "play" both enriches his core self and encourages adaptation to external reality. Many Dukes, most prominently Michael Pennington's, have used the masquerade as a vehicle of personal growth, finding rather than losing themselves in the friar's robes.[7] While "the Duke" is structurally absent, in other words, "Vincentio" may become more present, working toward the subjectivity he signally lacks at the beginning, submerging himself in experience rather than distantly contemplating it.

The problem is that, whatever the positive effects for the Duke of his liminal phase, it extends rather than limits his power and allows him to indulge in some distressingly high-handed machinations. Moreover, the reality to which the Duke ultimately adjusts is a patriarchal myth sanctioning the power he wields so imperfectly. It is a fiction likelier to constrict than expand his subjectivity. The same could be said of the friar disguise. If it enables a journey toward self-awareness it may also support a retreat from it, allowing the Duke to mystify his own inaccessibility, to turn his "lack" into an aspect of otherworldliness. Even during his masquerade, in other words, the Duke may be bent on turning himself into an emblem, borrowing ecclesiastical garments, speaking in sometimes gnomic and oracular tones (3.2.216–31, 261–82; 4.2.203–206), manipulating people and events in an affectation of divine providence.[8]

The Duke's interiority ultimately seems more indeterminate than Helena's, even more dependent upon performance, even more unsettled by an effort to transcend lack. As Lacan would have it, the Duke's lack founds and defines his subjectivity; his emptiness vividly illustrates the self-estrangement attending entrance into the Symbolic Order. Like Bertram, the Duke misrecognizes himself in the image of an external fiction of supermasculinity. Whereas Bertram falls initially under Parolles' spell, the Duke falls under the spell of his own idealized vision of himself (fleetingly personified, I will argue, by Angelo) as omnipotent ruler. The Duke wishes to do more than wield a sword in martial combat; he wishes to wield the phallus, to actualize the myth of Symbolic Fatherhood. To the extent that the phallus is the absent organ whose inaccessibility marks its subjects as lacking, the Duke attempts to transcend lack by identifying with a lacking signifier. "There is ultimately no affirmation more central to our present Symbolic Order," asserts Kaja Silverman, "yet at the same time more precariously maintained, than the fiction that the exemplary male subject is adequate to the paternal function."[9] *Measure for Measure* interrogates this precarious affirmation, as the Duke strives to be adequate to the paternal function, negating the "lack" that haunts his governance.

If the Duke's liminal status as ghostly friar reinforces his paternal "lack," his paternal self-substantiation requires transferring "lack" to Angelo and Isabella, humiliating the former and possessing the latter. Like Helena's, the Duke's liminality takes the form of a desexualization that leads to an attempted resexualization: specifically an attempt to sexualize his desexualized relationship with Isabella. Yet the Duke never directly affirms desire for Isabella. Indeed, his quest to be Symbolic Father forbids his doing so; to desire is to lack, to lack is to discredit his pose (or the pose he wishes, ultimately, to strike) as omnipotent. From a narrative standpoint, the Duke's desire for her—indeed, his sexuality—is "lacking." Like Helena, he must fulfill his desire covertly. His proposal to Isabella consummates a covert campaign to bind her to him, to acquire a feminine signifier of his paternal sufficiency without having once betrayed the lack that desire installs.

The text provides several hints of the Duke's covert desire. When first arresting Isabella's exit from Claudio's cell, he speaks of "the satisfaction I would require," and later in the same speech uses the word in its explicitly sexual sense, urging Isabella to give Angelo "promise of satisfaction" (3.1.154–56, 264). In addition, the Duke secretly (and, as performance could make clear, voyeuristically) witnesses Isabella's excoriation of Claudio and appears to find the sensual fervor of her "speechless dialect" as provocative in rage as Angelo finds it in supplication. Left alone with her, he extols the same chaste allure that exercises Angelo:

> The hand that hath made you fair hath made you good.
> The goodness that is cheap in beauty makes beauty brief
> in goodness; but grace, being the soul of your
> complexion, shall keep the body of it ever fair.
> (3.1.180–84)

The speech counters Hamlet's words to Ophelia:

> the power of beauty will
> sooner transform honesty from what it is to a bawd than
> the force of honesty can translate beauty into his
> likeness.
>
> (3.1.110–13)

In Hamlet's mind, Ophelia's chastity falls prey to beauty's corruptive influence. The Duke says precisely the opposite of Isabella: she will retain both chastity and beauty, exercising a sexuality free of corruption. The Duke essentially configures Isabella as a sexualized madonna. He might well say "get thee from a nunnery," especially since his later proposal of marriage requires such a displacement.

The Duke's desexualization may therefore be more apparent than real, a function of his friarly disguise. "My mind promises with my habit no loss shall touch her by my company," the Duke assures the Provost when requesting a private interview with Isabella (3.1.177–78). The disclaimer is disingenuous, however, based as it is on a congruence between intention and appearance—"mind" and "habit"—that the Duke cannot legitimately claim. The Duke's neutered persona sanctions a series of covert intimate meetings with young women and a potentially titillating management of their sexual lives.

These meetings turn almost exclusively on sexual matters and take the form, both literally and figuratively, of confessions. The Duke's formal confession of Juliet necessarily highlights her transgressive sexuality; Mariana's description of the Duke as "a man of comfort whose advice / Hath often still'd my brawling discontent" (4.1.8–9) corroborates his own claim to have confessed her (5.1.527), to have elicited intimate disclosures presumably centering on her obsessive desire. Isabella too confesses a secret to the Duke—albeit involuntarily—venting her sexual dread and sense of violation to Claudio as the secluded Duke looks on, unobserved.

In all three instances, the Duke's role as father-confessor gives him access to young women's private lives, licensing the disclosure of potentially tantalizing secrets. Confession, as Sade seems to have grasped, is an inherently sadomasochistic exercise. The confessing sinner takes the role of corrupt flesh, the confessor that of chastening law. To repent is to affirm lack to an unlacking, unseen figure (in effect, a veiled phallus). As Foucault points out, the heavy emphasis (in the new pastoral of the Counter-Reformation) on reporting and repenting even the flimsiest, most fleeting sexual intimations produced quasi-pornographic effects, converting transgressive sexuality into substantiating discourse.[10] That such discourse could stir the prurient interests of the confessor seems clear from the case of Cornelius Adriasen, who erotically flagellated a host of female penitents for ten years in the sixteenth century.[11] Certainly Sade exploits the erotics of confession in his orgiastic scenes, presenting corrupt father-confessors peering up the skirts of unsuspecting confessors or sitting with half-naked whores between their legs.[12]

Contemporary productions have endeavored in various ways to convey the Duke's covert sexuality. Some, in fact, have elected to make it overt. Keith Hack's 1974 RSC production seems almost to have had Sade in mind, characterizing the Duke as a lecher who fondles Isabella while pretending to comfort her, "lustfully encompassing her in the folds of his cloak."[13] In Robin Phillips's 1975 production at Stratford, Ontario, the Duke was a more circumspect roue, keeping Mariana as mistress and casting a fond eye at attractive specimens of both sexes.[14]

Other productions have sought to reveal the Duke's sexuality more subtly, in particular planting hints of an attraction to Isabella or at least an investment in her beyond the pontifical. In some ways, the dynamics of performance make this approach almost inevitable. The Duke enjoys two covert meetings with Isabella in a "dark corner" of Vienna's prison, and one hardly requires Pompey's direct linking of prison and brothel (4.3.1–4) to discern in these meetings a kind of sublimated tryst or to grasp the stimulating effects on the Duke of his seclusion with a young, sexually provoked woman. Many recent productions have marked the three meetings between the Duke and Isabella (3.1, 4.1, 4.3) with such intimate gestures as touching, hand-holding, hugging, and chaste kissing. In Noble's production, for instance, the Duke and Isabella shared a spontaneous, triumphant embrace when they concluded their plot in 3.1, and then, "remembering their status as novice and friar, they nervously disentangled themselves."[15] A similar nervous disentanglement took place in 4.3 of Bogdanov's production, as a leering Lucio discovered the two in a compromising embrace, discommoding the Duke and setting up Lucio's later insinuating line, "But yesternight, my lord, she and that friar, / I saw them at the prison. A saucy friar, / A very scurvy fellow" (5.1.134–36).[16]

Like Helena's, the Duke's "lacking" sexuality gets expressed primarily through surrogates and secret sharers. Angelo enacts the desire for Isabella that one can trace only retroactively to the Duke.[17] The Duke essentially punishes Angelo for overtly coveting the woman he covertly desires. Angelo assumes the status of lack, embodying the feminine, sexually erring ego that the Duke, functioning as personified superego, must sadistically mortify.

At the outset of the play, Angelo seems to occupy quite a different status, assuming the image of the all-mighty phallic authority that the Duke wishes to substantiate—in effect, playing Parolles to his Bertram. The imagery of the play's opening scene marks Angelo not simply as a double but as a son: "What figure of us think you he will bear?" the Duke asks Escalus. Angelo, protesting his unworthiness, exclaims, "let there be some more test made of my mettle / Before so noble and so great a figure / Be stamp'd upon it" (1.1.16, 48–50). The imagery of stamping suggests not only duplication but procreation; Angelo becomes the Duke's progeny through an act of male parthenogenesis. Reversing the oedipal agon, the father gives way to the son, accepting castration, offering Angelo "all the organs / Of our own pow'r" (1.1.20–21). The Duke-as-infirm-father stays on in the figure of "Old Escalus," an ineffectual subordinate to Angelo, one who is either overruled (failing to obtain a pardon for Claudio) or misrules (acquitting the obviously guilty Pompey and Froth despite Angelo's advice to whip them, issuing a stern warning that the gleefully unrepentant Pompey privately scorns [2.1.244–56]).[18]

More provocative still is the fact that Angelo functions not simply as son but as father, or at least as paternal *imago,* taking on the roles of both ego-ideal and superego.[19] In appointing Angelo to be a more perfect version of himself, filling his vacated place and negating his "lack" by wielding the phallus more powerfully and authoritatively, the Duke effectively positions Angelo as ego-ideal, an idealized mirror of masculinity conferring an illusion of wholeness.

At the same time, Angelo functions as a personified superego, manifesting an exacting rectitude that indirectly shames and constrains the Duke. Angelo undertakes, in the Duke's allusive phrase, to "weed *my* vice" (emphasis mine), suggesting that the exclusively sexual crimes that Angelo punishes may be regarded as symptoms not simply of the Duke's lax governance but of his own corrupt sexuality. In that sense, Claudio too becomes the Duke's stand-in, both a creature of his lax governance ("we bid this be done, / When evil deeds have their permissive pass / And not the punishment" [1.3.37–39]) and an extension of his own sinning flesh. Angelo not only "weeds" the Duke's "vice" but "lets his [own] grow"—a growth that can refer to the phallic swelling that Angelo registers once aroused by Isabella ("what's this, what's this" . . . "the strong and swelling evil / Of my conception" [2.2.162; 2.4.6–7]). Angelo affirms his own sexuality while implicitly disciplining the Duke's, just as the superego forbids the male subject's emulation of the father's sexual life: "[Y]ou may not do all that [the father] does; some things are his prerogative."[20] What the male subject may not do, in particular, is desire the same woman. Yet the Duke's discovery of Angelo's desire for Isabella initiates his own involvement with her, eventuating in a marriage proposal that, if accepted, would confirm the Duke's oedipal victory over Angelo.

If Angelo resembles Parolles in modeling phallic masculinity, the Duke, unlike Bertram, seems to know or suspect from the outset that his idol is a fraud. Indeed, it could be legitimately inferred that the Duke deliberately sets Angelo up for a fall. Already aware of his shoddy treatment of Mariana, branding him a "seemer" from the beginning (1.3.54), the Duke nevertheless lends Angelo the reins of authority, as though expecting him to betray his image of righteous severity—as though wishing to discredit Angelo's claim to paternal adequacy in order to bolster his own. Once discovering Angelo's aggressions against Isabella, the Duke orchestrates his downfall and takes pains to distance himself from him. Angelo becomes his scapegoat, the discredited recipient of the Duke's own disavowed lack.

Thus, like Bertram, the Duke seemingly wishes to actualize the image that his double reveals himself to be merely performing, to enact the misrecognition that his shattered mirror betrays. When Lucio attempts to dissociate him from Angelo, the Duke objects not to the dissociation itself but to what he clearly perceives as Lucio's mischaracterization of it: *he* is the prodigious celibate and Angelo the predatory lecher (3.2.104–85).

Lucio shares Angelo's function of personifying the sexual self that the Duke wishes to disclaim and sadistically discipline. If Lavatch represents a voice for saying the unsayable, articulating the sexual dread that underlies Bertram's flight from Helena, Lucio becomes an instrument for exaggerating the unsayable, grossly amplifying whatever sexual feeling informs the Duke's friarly masquerade. Lucio not only constructs an image of the Duke as a disreputable rake but embodies it, mirroring the corrupt sexuality that he projects onto the Duke. Yet the Duke resists this identification and, by exposing and mortifying Lucio in the end, turns him, like Angelo, into a target for transferred "lack." He is a thing of darkness—or of dark corners—that the Duke refuses to acknowledge his.[21]

Like Helena, the Duke must cope with private drives at odds with the cultural myth he is expected—and expects himself—to internalize. The difference is that he does not (like Helena of the play's first half) openly divulge those drives, but (like Helena of the second half)  channels them into eroticized scheming and surrogation. While Helena's conflict emerges with relative clarity, the Duke's does not: undivulged drives collide with an unsolidified self. Like Helena, the Duke embodies a confounding double-ness, striving to uphold a cultural myth while manifesting subjectivity inadequate to it. The Duke of Dark Corners and the Symbolic Father are caricatures of the conflicting subject positions derived from this collision of self and symbolic paternity, of private anxiety and spectacular sufficiency.

In performance, one could dramatize the Duke's doubleness by staging the libidinous look that subverts the affected transcendental gaze. Hastily leaving Angelo and Escalus in the play's opening scene, the Duke avows an aversion to specularity:

> I'll privily away. I love the people,
> But do not like to stage me to their eyes;
> Though it do well, I do not relish well
> Their loud applause and aves vehement.
> (1.1.67–70)

The Duke affirms a preference for invisibility, a mode of governance that requires visible manifestations of power—spectacles of punishment in which the all-powerful sovereign, while keeping his body out of sight, nonetheless em-bodies himself by punitively impressing his authority onto the vulnerable bodies of transgressors.[22] By declining to enforce the laws, by declining to stage these sadomasochistic spectacles, the Duke makes him-self utterly invisible. In so doing, he gives up his cultural function as surrogate-gaze, founder and focus of the social spectacle. One may therefore regard his masquerade as an attempt to reconstitute himself in that func-tion, to become a mechanism of surveillance, to make his look the locus of power (i.e., the gaze). The Duke oversees and controls a spectacle that culminates in his own decisive assumption of visibility.

My own production endeavored to identify the Duke's would-be gaze as a voyeuristic look. It opened in a decadent sex club presenting two succes-sive spectacles: a young man flagellating himself before his mistress and a fantasy auction overseen by Mistress Overdone, in which riotous patrons bid on prostitutes clad in outfits catering to specific male fantasies. The Duke sat in a second-level balcony, his back to the action, gazing through a telescope at the stars. As the proceedings became more frenzied, he pivoted in his chair and trained the telescope on the action below, an act of looking that precipitated a descent from his elevated, god-like perch.

The Duke's progress through the production was subsequently marked by other moments of voyeurism: in 2.3, he placed himself in a secluded nook of the prison and watched, undetected, the disrobing and strip-search of a female convict, carried out in silhouette behind a scrim. He placed himself in a similar position in order to watch Isabella's intimate scene with Claudio, framing as spectacle her intimate confessions and passionate outbursts. This act of coercive looking forecasts his control of Isabella's sexual life and his manipulation of her into a performance of helpless femininity.

These instances of voyeurism undercut the Duke's attempts in the final scene to impersonate the gaze as both temporal power and center of attention. The Duke tries to stage himself to his people's eyes, embracing specularity as a means of reconstituting his power. "O, my dread lord," confesses Angelo,

> I should be guiltier than my guiltiness,
> To think I can be undiscernible,
> When I perceive your Grace, like pow'r divine,
> Hath looked upon my passes.
>
> (5.1.366–70)

The Duke's triumphant visibility in the play's final scene elevates his previous invisibility to a signifier of divinity, bolstering his claim to god-like, gaze-like authority. He both makes himself visible and stages spectacles of punishment made possible by invisible divinations. He embodies himself both directly and, through the specularization of subordinate bodies, indirectly.

As with all attempts to identify an individual look with the gaze, however, the Duke ultimately reaches for a degree of control and libidinal satisfaction beyond his grasp, ironically confirming his "lack."[23] His attempt to authenticate transcendental authority founders on his own human fallibility. His governance at play's end seems no more effectual than at the beginning, no more capable of regulating wayward desire. Having previously failed to enforce the law, the Duke now enforces marriage to arrest destructive passions—but with conspicuously little support from the parties involved. The Duke's triumphant spectacle is a decidedly strained *coup de theatre* in which the players (most especially Isabella), by failing to heed their cues, fail to effect his miraculous transformation to potent ruler. By exposing the essentially theatrical nature of the Duke's subjectivity, *Measure for Measure* exposes the theatricality of political authority, the insubstantiality of the Symbolic Father.

### ANGELO'S SADISM: Punishing Claudio

Angelo, unlike the Duke, makes visible his power—and his sadistic tendencies—from the outset, bodying forth his sovereignty by shaming the body of a transgressive subject. He stages Claudio's arrest as a piece of sadomasochistic street theater. At Angelo's command, Claudio is publicly disgraced, enchained, and paraded through the streets to prison. "Why dost thou show me thus to th' world?" he protests to the Provost (1.2.116). My production aimed to accentuate the sadomasochistic dynamics of this punishment by clearly marking it as a ritual of humiliation: Claudio was not only in chains but very nearly naked, wearing the bloody welts from a whipping he had received. The Provost placed Claudio on a slip-stage (which was used throughout to underline a character's specularity), subjecting him to the collective look of the assembled citizenry, who approximated the gaze by functioning as a mechanism for shaming his sexual drives.

Angelo completed the *mise-en-scène* by standing alone on a second-level balcony, watching the proceedings with discernible satisfaction, a solitary, privileged, gratified viewer, projecting onto Claudio's body the "lack" that he himself disavows. Claudio became the feminized image of Angelo's persecuted ego, the abjected sexual self. Angelo feminized Claudio not simply by subjecting his body to humiliating display but by eroticizing and dephallicizing it, positioning him as a consumable (sexual) object. While Claudio is not, strictly speaking, a masochist, he does play the role of dutifully self-reproaching penitent in the sadomasochistic theatrics of punishment: by asserting that his heedless libertinism pleads for restraint (1.2.125–30), he essentially confesses his sins and accepts his punishment, thereby ratifying the power and righteousness of the punishing agent.[24] The performative nature of Claudio's public confession (delivered, in my production, from the slip-stage) seems clear from the very different tone and attitude he adopts once permitted to converse privately with Lucio, to whom he proclaims his innocence and protests his punishment (1.2.144–71).

Nor can Angelo, strictly speaking, be called a sadist, primarily because, once incited by lust, he lacks the sadist's passionlessness: "[T]he true sadist is self-controlled to the point of apathy," says Deleuze, "Sade deplores the pornographer's 'enthusiasm.'"[25] By Sade's standard, Angelo is a deranged pornographer who insists on enacting his fantasy of mastering a helpless "feminine" figure.[26] That the "feminine" figure is initially a man only underlines his status as the pornographer's chastened double. The persecuted Claudio could be said to function as a kind of male intermediary between Angelo and the person who comes ultimately to occupy the position of degraded "feminine" double: Isabella. The cataclysmic lust that Angelo unleashes against her suggests that his severe, desexualized persona is a self-suppressing fiction. The sexual insurrection that he undertakes to defeat arises not simply in Vienna but within his own psyche. In mortifying Claudio, he not only punishes a criminal but pummels the principal adversary in his own *psychomachia,* forcing Claudio to play the villainous Flesh. He chastens Claudio's body in place of his own.

The sadopornographic spectacle of Claudio's degradation has ample historical sanction.[27] The exorbitant abuse of law-breakers was a popular form of public entertainment in Shakespeare's England. Chastised criminals were regularly submitted to a voyeuristic, sadistic public gaze. A Londoner on his daily rounds could amuse himself with a chained robber hanging in a gibbet, a petty thief in the pillory, a scold in the ducking stool, a murderer drawn to the gallows on a hurdle.[28] Executions, sometimes featuring grisly torture, were likewise turned into public spectacles. Such sadomasochistic events dramatized the reparation of a metaphorically shattered sovereignty. Because every criminal assaults the metaphorical body of the ruler, the ruler retributively assaults the criminal's physical body, publicly imprinting on his vulnerable flesh the irrefutable evidence of the sovereign's power.[29]

In the sense that Claudio represents Angelo's fleshly double, he must be punished for doing willingly what Angelo abhors and can only be hood-winked into doing: having sexual relations with the woman he has sworn to marry. On the one hand, Angelo's dismissal of Mariana for reasons of "levity" seems simply a moralistic cover for a cold financial maneuver— deserting a dowerless and hence undesirable woman. On the other, his vilification of Mariana manifests a psychological need to distance himself from female sexuality. According to Deleuze, sadism derives from a "nega-tion of the mother" and an "exaltation of the father who is beyond all laws."[30] With her maternal name and unabashed, unextinguishable desire for him, Mariana assumes the image of the devouring oedipal mother, an overtly sexual, emasculating figure. So Angelo rejects this mother-figure and becomes ruthless enforcer of the Law of the Father, affecting a severity that, as later events confirm, counters a contrary pull toward the feminine. Mariana essentially plays Helena to Angelo's Bertram. Like Bertram, Angelo runs from her, breaking his betrothal in order to avert emasculation. Claudio, however, who succumbs to Juliet's allure, is punished for not averting it.

Angelo also punishes Mariana's double, Juliet, the "fornicatress" (2.2.223) whose "groans" (2.2.15) evoke both labor pains and orgasm, whose visible pregnancy confirms her transgressive sexuality. The disguised Duke ratifies this reading of Juliet's pregnancy, characterizing her fetus as the "sin she carries" and contending that her crime—refusing to repel the passion she ignites—is greater than Claudio's (2.3.26–28). The Duke essentially reads the female body as both sign and source of sin. Claudio seems to concur, equating his desire for Juliet with poison, with a rat's "proper bane" (1.2.129–30).

If Juliet were to accompany Claudio on his penitential trek, the speechless dialect of her visible pregnancy (the sin she carries) would become the sign of his guilt, as he himself attests, "the stealth of our most mutual entertainment / With character too gross is writ on Juliet" (1.2.154–55). Claudio writes on Juliet's body the heedless lasciviousness of his own, which he must now make femininely "credulous" to Angelo's print. He, too, must be made to carry sin visibly. His public chastisement becomes the equivalent of Juliet's pregnancy, the physical, feminizing marks of his transgressive seduction by the corruptive female body. Juliet's participation in this scene foregrounds woman's status as the bearer of meaning that man makes, portraying the female body as a site for patriarchal inscription.[31] Because Angelo condemns Claudio to death for fornication, Juliet's visible pregnancy signifies not simply his sin but his death—or at least the incontrovertible evidence that sends him to death.

### SPEECHLESS DIALECT: Isabella's (Lacking) Sexuality

Juliet and Mariana both embody a potentially devouring female sexuality that Angelo safely contains. He dispatches the "fornicatress" to prison and drives the desirous woman to the moated grange. He cannot so easily disarm Isabella's sexual threat. She presents herself, involuntarily, as a more threatening version of Juliet, an alluring female body that recalls him to his own. By stridently rebuffing his lecherous overtures, however, she makes him alone bear the burden of the lust she arouses, impregnates him with "the strong and swelling evil of [his] conception" (2.4.7). In effect, she turns him into Juliet, a fallen "feminine" body, source of sin.

By afflicting Angelo with desire, Isabella forces him to retrieve the degraded sexual self personified by Claudio. When Angelo exclaims, "O let her brother live! / Thieves for their robbery have authority when / Judges steal themselves" (2.2.174–76), he makes the very concession Isabella labors so strenuously to secure: he and Claudio, the condemned fornicator, are kin. While such fellow-feeling has the effect of moving him momentarily to mercy, ultimately it breeds a vindictive desire to punish Isabella for having effected it. Beset by degrading lust, he stands in relation to Isabella as Claudio previously stood to him—a wretched lecher humbled by a hallowed figure of righteousness. When Isabella, lamenting her powerlessness before the unyielding Angelo, exclaims, "I would to heaven I had your potency and you were Isabel" (2.2.67–68) she evokes the very reversal of power—and of gender—that Angelo suffers. She has his phallic potency and he, castrated, becomes Isabel.

Angelo endeavors to reclaim masculine potency by returning Isabella to the body she seemingly wishes to transcend, by converting her to a fleshly receptor of his phallic power, fitting her body to the "destin'd livery" of sexual subservience. As in *All's Well,* masculinity in *Measure for Measure* substantiates itself through women's bodies. Isabella therefore takes Claudio's place as the object of Angelo's retributive violence, as the "feminine" self that Angelo must reject and punish, the horse who must feel the rider's "spur" (1.2.159–62). No sooner has he safely enchained and imprisoned Claudio than Isabella, figuratively speaking, enchains and imprisons Angelo. So he must, in turn, enchain and imprison her.

Isabella seems scarcely aware of the power she wields. "My power," she protests to Lucio when he bids her "assay" it on her brother's behalf, "alas, I doubt," (1.4.75–77). Claudio has already defined that power, telling Lucio

> in her youth
> There is a prone and speechless dialect,
> Such as move men; beside, she hath prosperous art
> When she will play with reason and discourse,
> And well she can persuade.
>
> (1.2.182–86)

The "speechless dialect" that "moves" (arouses) men is Isabella's sexual charisma—her body language, as it were. The word "prone," connoting both recumbence and receptivity, suggests that Isabella's body speaks the language of sexual availability.[32] Isabella, however, has gotten herself to a nunnery, silencing that language. The effect of Claudio's summons is to return her body—and her voice—to male control, to subsume her subjectivity to the oedipal plot. Only at play's end, when that plot becomes apparent to her, does Isabella seem to have a chance of reclaiming them.

Like Helena, Isabella is compelled to repress her sexuality and embrace a feminine lack. On one level, her choice of the cloister reflects a genuine religiosity, amply evidenced by her recurrent concern for the condemned Claudio's soul (2.2.84; 2.4.38–40; 3.1.106), her celebration of God's grace when urging Angelo to mercy (2.2.73–79), and her conviction that the aggrieved Mariana would be better off leaving this world (3.1.231–34). There is evidence to suggest, however, that Isabella's monastic withdrawal is an act as much of self-suppression as of self-fulfillment, that she begins the play having already enacted a more extreme version of the sexual renunciation that Helena undertakes through her pilgrimage. In a telling exchange with Angelo, Isabella agrees with Angelo that women are "frail":

> Ay, as the glasses where they view themselves,
> Which are as easy broke as they make forms.
> Women? Help heaven! men their creation mar
> In profiting by them. Nay, call us ten times frail,
> For we are as soft as our complexions are,
> And credulous to false prints.
>
> (2.4.124–30)

Isabella presents female sexual experience as a process of loss, of breaking chastity and making false forms—that is, begetting bastards.[33] She presents a woman's sexual experience as one of despoliation, impregnation, and abandonment (such as Juliet and Kate Keepdown actually suffer), implicitly defining female sexuality as submission to male dominance. Isabella's construct presupposes not only male rapacity—men "break the glass" and "mar their creation" by using women—but female compliance. Men corrupt women because women are corruptible, receptive as well as vulnerable to sexual use. Isabella refers to women as "they" and then as "we." By implication she portrays herself as sexually susceptible, suggesting that she would rather restrain her sexual impulses than pursue them into a ruinous encounter with a rapacious male. In short, she takes the path precisely opposite to that of her "cousin" Juliet, constraining the sexuality that Juliet so catastrophically liberates.[34]

Isabella's impulse toward self-regulation seems evident from her opening lines in the play. Critics have often noted that her first speech expresses a request for "more restraint," a wish that the notoriously strict order of St. Clare were even stricter. What has been less noted is the peculiarity of the question that precedes it: "and have you nuns no farther privileges?" (1.4.1). It seems strange that a young woman coveting "farther stricture" should begin by asking after farther privileges. Either she masochistically equates stricture with privilege or she chafes under stricture but is shamed by Francisca's testy reply—"are these not large enough?"—into shamming a desire for more.[35] In either case, she seems ill-suited to the cloister, either balking at sexual renunciation or embracing it with a vigor that invites suspicions of sexual guilt, as if the severity of the restraint she covets matches the fervor of the passion she wishes to restrain. Whether Isabella perceives the promised stricture as too much or too little, her retreat to a sanctuary of "lack," coupled with the sexual corruptiveness of the world she flees, tempts the conclusion that she must curb sexual drives that might otherwise propel her into the perilous territory of male sexuality.[36]

That territory is, however, precisely where Isabella finds herself. Whereas Helena voluntarily ends her renunciation and resumes her aggressive pursuit of Bertram, Isabella is propelled along a course charted exclusively by male desire. Her own desire remains inaccessible and indeterminate. Whereas Helena functions as desiring subject, would-be adaptor of the oedipal plot, *Measure for Measure* positions Isabella as object of desire, unwitting appendage to the oedipal plot. If Helena voluntarily enacts femininity to vindicate her perilously unfeminine ends, Isabella is manipulated into enacting it, giving up unfeminine autonomy.

Isabella's speechless dialect is a male-centered language, a signifier of the sexual availability that Claudio (and all the other men who come into contact with her) assign to her body. Although she demonstrates impressive rhetorical skills in her first meeting with Angelo (the "prosperous art" that Claudio praises), her impassioned speech is simply part of the dazzling sensual onslaught of her alluring (from Angelo's standpoint) body language. When Isabella urges Angelo to "go to [his] bosom, / Knock there, and ask your heart what it doth know / That's like my brother's fault," he remarks to himself, "She speaks, and 'tis / Such sense that my sense breeds with it" (2.2.141–42). That Angelo's sense "breeds" with the "sense" of these lines suggests that he responds not (only) to the "sense" of her argument but to the sensuality of its presentation, not to the abstract idea of male lust that links him with Claudio but to the physical sensation of lust that Isabella's impassioned imploring stirs in him.[37] On one level, Angelo's line means that Isabella—or, more precisely, her body—"speaks sex." He responds to her display of female passion, to the spectacle of her body pitched in impassioned supplication, to (as Bernice Kliman puts it) her "flashing eyes," "heaving bosom,"[38] and especially her open mouth—in Shakespeare's era a signifier of sexual availability, evidence of an "openness" at odds with the cultural paradigm of closed femininity.[39]

Francisca explains to Isabella the restrictions that ensure closedness for the St. Clares:

When you have vow'd, you must not speak with men
But in the presence of the prioress;
Then, if you speak, you must not show your face,
Or if you show your face, you must not speak.
(1.4.10–13)

To expose oneself to a male look *and* to speak, as Isabella does with Angelo, is to invite desire, to be transgressively open.

Angelo's attraction to Isabella stems from the fact that she is both closed and open, an alluring and passionate young woman clinging to an asexual persona. From Angelo's perspective, she is a walking provocation, a walking conundrum. Robin Phillips's 1975 Stratford, Ontario, production aimed to dramatize this conundrum by costuming actress Martha Henry in a nun's habit of "incredibly soft jersey" so that, "although she was buttoned from neck to ankle the movement of the material constantly showed the female form beneath."[40] Phillips replicated for his audience the effect of Isabella's sexuality on Angelo, aligning his spectators with a male look reading "proneness" in Isabella's body—and, at least potentially, implicated them as colluding in Isabella's objectification.

Angelo essentially demands that Isabella turn in her nun's habit for the "destin'd livery," a cultural costume of feminine subservience confirming the availability that her body inadvertently advertises. To eschew the destin'd livery, Angelo insists, is to be "more than a woman" and therefore "none" (or "nun"). When Isabella acknowledges female frailty, Angelo "arrest[s] [her] words"—a phrase with a provocatively double meaning. He "stops her words" because her verbal speech discourages the overtures that her speechless dialect incites. But he also "takes her at her word," choosing to construe her admission of female weakness as an invitation to debauchery, a confession of her own susceptibilities. In Isabella's response, "I have no tongue but one; gentle my lord, / Let me entreat you speak the former language" (2.4.139–40), one hears an echo of Hermione's protest to Leontes, "you speak a language I understand not." In Isabella's case, the complaint might more precisely be, "you make me speak a language I understand not." The scene confirms the difficulty of a woman's making her voice heard when asked to speak as Woman and ventriloquize the voice-of-the-Father. Her own dialect cannot be comprehended within a phallocentric register that hears resistance as coded encouragement. Isabella's observation that women are "credulous to false prints" and "make forms" (2.4.130, 126) refers not only to the biological process of conceiving and delivering but to the cultural process of bearing the meaning that man makes.

This female "lack" seems particularly evident in the trial of Pompey and Froth, which turns on the question of what happened to Elbow's wife when she strayed into Mistress Overdone's brothel. Mrs. Elbow herself never appears, and her husband fails in his attempt to portray her as the victim of an attempted rape. The elusiveness of Elbow's language allows Pompey to convert his tale of female victimization into one of female wantonness. Pompey essentially transforms Mrs. Elbow into a whore—a widely "respected" woman who craved "stewed prunes" and submitted to multiple sexual handling (2.1.89–171). Whether represented by Elbow or Pompey, her sexuality is an effect of male discourse, in the first instance non-referential and in the second referable only to the degrading category of whore. The scene makes farce of the acquittal of a probable rapist whose attorney blames the victim. It offers a comic version of the Duke's dismissal of Isabella's accusations against Angelo. The absent Mrs. Elbow functions as Isabella's unlikely alter ego, a victim of male sexual aggression whose "complaint" lacks credibility. In fact, because Mrs. Elbow never appears and because her husband's testimony is so hopelessly convoluted, the scene leaves her innocence open to question, making the character even more elusive. As in Helena's virginity speech, female sexuality seems unrepresentable within the oedipal plot.

By making unavailable a body that speaks availability, Isabella may be regarded as enacting a refusal of "feminine" sexuality. In effect, when Lucio, at Claudio's behest, retrieves Isabella from the convent for the purpose of "making friends" with Angelo (1.2.180), he asks her to perform femininity, to adapt herself to a prescribed code of corporeal deportments that signify femininity. "Go to Lord Angelo," Lucio exhorts Isabella,

> And let him learn to know, when maidens sue,
> Men give like gods; but when they weep and kneel,
> All their petitions are as freely theirs
> As they themselves would owe them.
>
> (1.4.79–83)

In one sense, in urging Isabella to sue, weep, and kneel, he merely urges her to perform a supplicant's role. Yet Lucio specifically genders supplication "feminine"—when *maidens* sue, *men* give like gods. In so doing, he affirms the attractiveness of female abjection to men, describing an essentially sadomasochistic dynamic. By submissively gratifying male fantasies of mastery, Lucio suggests, a woman achieves mastery. The sexual component of this admonition becomes clear when Lucio repeats it during Isabella's

ineffectual supplicating of Angelo. "Kneel down before him," he commands, "hang upon his gown; / You are too cold" (2.2.43–46). Isabella's
"coldness" springs from her initial attempt to dissociate herself from the
sexuality that impelled Claudio's crime, "a vice that most I do abhor, / And
most desire should meet the blow of justice" (2.2.29–30). Lucio urges
"proneness" (or at least submissive kneeling) as the remedy for this unfeminine frigidity. He directs her to perform a *passionate* subservience. When
Isabella warms to her task and begins to weaken Angelo's resolve, Lucio
celebrates her success in language suggestive of sexual arousal: "O, to him,
to him, wench! he will relent. He's coming; I perceive't" (2.2.124–25). Like
Lafew, Lucio eroticizes a young woman's entreaty to male authority. Like
Helena, Isabella overcomes scruples of "feminine" modesty and unleashes a
passion that subdues a dominant male. She shifts not simply from coldness
to passion but from supplication to contestation, from submission to
dominance. It is ultimately not her abjection but her power that excites
Angelo. Like Helena, Isabella displays an unfeminine forwardness. She
stands up to Angelo, challenging his masculine authority and, in so doing,
provokes an unmasculine urge for surrender.

Yet Isabella's power is greatly circumscribed by the male look that frames
her supplication. Lucio and the Provost function as spectators to this scene
and, particularly if they stand upstage of its action, lend it an explicitly
performative frame, situating Isabella's impassioned plea within spectacle,
subjecting her body to a dominating male look.[41] That look feminizes
Isabella's unfeminine forwardness, turning her plea into a seduction. Claudio, through the agency of Lucio, succeeds in exploiting Isabella's sexuality
for his own ends, effectively pimping his sister. Once seduced, Angelo takes
over the look, at first masochistically disavowing Isabella's "lack," then
sadistically discovering it. Isabella's power is revealed to be the familiar
"feminine" one of sexual attractiveness. Such power is perilously temporary, however: the unspoken corollary to a woman's getting her way by
arousing a man is that she will eventually have to let him have his way.

Forced to enter a spectacle authored, directed, and observed by men,
carrying out a seduction and defending a sexual license that she in principle
opposes, Isabella performs femininity throughout her dealings with Angelo.[42] Yet unlike Helena, who manages to convert her position from object-
of-the-look to personified gaze, Isabella remains in spectacle for most of the
play; when, in the final scene, she absolves Angelo of wrongdoing by
claiming her good looks corrupted him, she seems resigned to the status of
object.

## ANGELO'S SADOMASOCHISTIC FANTASY:
### Propositioning Isabella

Angelo's determination to project "lack" onto Isabella eventually takes on sadistic dimensions. He essentially becomes consumed by a pornographic fantasy. The most telling phrase of his first soliloquy is "What is't I dream on?" (2.2.178). Angelo struggles not so much against sexual feeling in general as against the specific image of sexual intercourse with the saintly Isabella, a struggle that lies at the heart of his second soliloquy. Here Angelo assumes a position similar to Claudio's: he finds his prayers to heaven empty and unavailing, unable to exorcise the guilt derived not from the actual commission of a sin (like Claudio's) but from the obsessive contemplation of one. Angelo's attempt to confess and repent his sexual fantasy only intensifies its imaginative rehearsal and tempts its enactment. In my production, the scene opened with the image of Angelo flagellating himself, conveying not simply the ferocity of his guilt but the power of the fantasy engendering it.

Angelo's fantasy transports him to a tortured fluctuation between sadism and masochism. Male masochism, according to Deleuze, reverses the dynamics of sadism, enacting the negation of the father and the exaltation of the mother, a submergence in the "feminine" and dismissal of the "masculine."[43] The masochist fetishizes his female tormentor—an image of the forbidden, desired mother—symbolically endowing her with the phallus and investing her with the power of law. He achieves sexual pleasure by purging through pain the guilt of desiring her, desexualizing his relation with her in order to achieve resexualization.[44]

On one hand, Angelo flirts with masochistic feminization. "This virtuous maid / Subdues me quite," he declares (2.2.184–85), implicitly admitting his subjugation and emasculation. Desire for her has made him "fond" (2.2.186), he admits—foolish and infatuated and thus potentially feminized like the "fond father" of a Duke whose "rod" is "more mock'd than fear'd" (1.3.23, 26–27). As a consequence of his degrading passion, Angelo would exchange his "gravity" for levity, for "an idle plume / Which the air beats for vain" (2.4.9–12), masochistically identifying with an unmasculine "vanity" that invites "beating." He covets lightness and insubstantiality, longing to lose what he later calls the "credent bulk" of his authority. His emasculating desire for Isabella betrays his inability to "fill the place" of phallic authority:

O place, O form,
How often dost thou with thy case, thy habit,
Wrench awe from fools, and tie the wiser souls
To thy false seeming!

(2.4.12–15)

Desire for Isabella shatters Angelo's cherished self-image as invincible saint. Like the liminal Duke, he becomes a ghostly father, unable to accept "lack" and desire unrestrainedly and yet unable to sustain his identification with the place he fills, the habit he wears.

Angelo comes close to embracing emasculation, investing Isabella with phallic authority by elevating her to the status of goddess—one who competes with God for his prayers:[45]

When I would pray and think, I think and pray
To several subjects. Heaven hath my empty words,
Whilst my invention, hearing not my tongue,
Anchors on Isabel; heaven in my mouth,
As if I did but chew his name,
And in my heart the strong and swelling evil
Of my conception.

(2.4.1–7)

In verbally flaying himself for his forbidden desire, Angelo implicitly assumes a masochistic posture, as though enslaved by a guilt-inducing sexual vexation that can only be purged through pain. In imagining himself pregnant with his "conception"—the sexual fantasy that Isabella has implanted—Angelo evokes a parody of the virgin birth in which his God, Isabella, descends from on high and impregnates him, leaving him with the unwanted child of lust, the sin he carries.[46] Angelo is, in Janet Adelman's resonant phrase, "pregnant with his own sexuality," and Isabella is the inseminating agent.[47] Angelo also evokes a parody of the Eucharist: he does not consume God's body but is consumed by a longing to consume the body of his goddess.

Angelo cannot, however, like the masochist, desexualize the object of his desire, so his masochistic self-excoriation becomes auto-erotic self-stimulation. His obsessive fixation on the sexual fantasy of ravishing his goddess clearly arouses him: in concrete physical terms, the "swelling" to which he refers can only be phallic. In positioning Isabella as God, he positions her as Other, the end to which his vexatious, insatiable desire drives him.[48] Angelo's pornographic fantasy manifests a longing for *jouissance*, linking his visionary erotic obsession with the more rarefied goals of monastical flagellants: mystical union with the unattainable beloved (Christ the bridegroom). In both cases, self-abuse leads to self-transcendence.

Angelo seems to be attempting such auto-erotic transcendence in the second soliloquy. He heightens his arousal by flagellating himself—verbally if not physically—and keeping his imagination fixed on union with Isabella. His fixation takes him "beyond reason": he asserts that sexual passion (the "blood" that "muster[s] to [his] heart") has disrupted the proper functioning of his psyche ("dispossess[ed] all my other parts / Of necessary fitness" [2.4.20–23]). Angelo describes a psychic upheaval conducive to the dominance of fantasy: passion shatters reason's judgment, breaks free of the will's restraint, and gives birth to the fantasy that sustains it. From this perspective, Angelo impregnates himself—just as Leontes seems to do in exclaiming, "Affection! Thy intention stabs the centre!" (1.2.138). Angelo too is stabbed in his center by his own sexual passion, an image that links his auto-erotic proclivities with the metaphorical condition of being pregnant with his own sexuality.

Yet Angelo elects not to confine himself to mystical auto-eroticism but to enact his pornographic fantasy, a version of the despoiling-the-virgin scenario discernible in Bertram's intended conquest of Diana.[49] Angelo seeks to demystify his own mystification of Isabella as exalted, unattainable goddess, to expose her as pure flesh, to affirm her essential sordidness. In Angelo's first soliloquy, his fantasy takes shape as an urge to degrade an exalted object: "having waste ground enough, / Shall we desire to raze the sanctuary / And pitch our evils there?" (2.2.169–71). Angelo compares satisfying desire to eliminating bodily impurities, associating sex with excrement. "To raze the sanctuary and pitch [my] evils there" is to put Isabella "prone" and empty his befouling fluids on her.[50] Angelo, pregnant with his own sexuality, essentially asks Isabella to duplicate and thereby terminate his pregnancy. He wishes to confirm her violation of him by violating her in return. He aims to transfer the sin he carries to Isabella, to make her pregnant—if only metaphorically—with a "staining" sexuality. By attempting to defile the goddess remade in the image of whore, Angelo seeks to regain his "masculine" identity, to mortify the fleshly, "feminine" self by mortifying Isabella.

In short, Angelo's fantasy shifts from masochistic to sadistic in the face of what he believes is Isabella's deliberate provoking of a lust she refuses to gratify. "Lay by all nicety and prolixious blushes / That banish what they sue for" (2.4.162–63), he demands, now believing her chastity to be a seductive affectation. Angelo comes to associate Isabella with the strumpet whose "double vigor" of "art and nature" (2.2.183) suggests a cunning enhancement of sexual allure. Previously he measured Isabella's attractiveness in terms of her difference from the whore (2.2.167–69, 182–85). Now he collapses the difference.

Angelo's derelict courtship culminates in a proposition that Isabella initially repels, threatening him with retributive speech:

> I will proclaim thee, Angelo, look for't!
> Sign me a present pardon for my brother,
> Or with an outstretch'd throat I'll tell the world aloud
> What man thou art.
>
> (2.4.151–54)

Angelo's response is to silence Isabella's voice by preying upon the vulnerability of her body—and of Claudio's as well:

> Redeem thy brother
> By yielding up thy body to my will,
> Or else he must not only die the death,
> But thy unkindness shall his death draw out
> To ling'ring sufferance.
>
> (163–67)

Here Isabella's status as mortified stand-in for Claudio becomes explicit. If the violently aroused Angelo cannot have his way with Isabella's body, he will have his way with Claudio's, subjecting him to protracted torture. Angelo makes clear that his passion for Isabella impels him to brutalize Claudio: "Answer me tomorrow," he tells her, "Or by the affection that now guides me most, / I'll prove a tyrant to him" (167–69).[51] Claudio, having suffered for his own entanglement with female sexuality, may now suffer on account of Angelo's. Angelo's lust, which he perversely calls love, transmutes into a sadistic urge to subjugate and inflict suffering. Isabella must "yield" to him, submit to his "sharp appetite." His violent language turns his vicious demand into the verbal equivalent of a rape. Angelo aims to transfer his "lack" forcibly to Isabella, to subject her body to the proof of his phallic fullness. For Angelo, pornographic fixation begets sadistic enactment, bringing to mind Robin Morgan's famous aphorism, "pornography is the theory, and rape the practice."[52]

The bed-trick simply extends his auto-eroticism. In the final scene, Mariana, upon unveiling herself, exclaims

> this is the body
> That took away the match from Isabel,
> And did supply thee at thy garden-house
> In her imagin'd person.
>
> (5.1.210–13)

Mariana embodies an erotic fiction conceived in Isabella's image. She becomes a creature of Angelo's pornographic imagination, a body upon which to exercise a masturbatory excitation.

Ironically, Angelo plans to reassert his masculinity in a setting that underscores his feminization: the garden, as Robert Watson points out, is the "iconographic home of the Virgin Mary."[53] In *All's Well,* Helena awaits Bertram's sexual entry in a female enclosure (Diana's house) that he must penetrate. In *Measure for Measure,* Angelo not only awaits Isabella's sexual entry but hands her the keys she requires to penetrate *his* enclosures. The site of the tryst subtly reinforces Angelo's identification with the figure of the corrupted virgin.

After his supposed tryst with Isabella, Angelo feels himself "unshaped" and "unpregnant"—not so much delivered of the "strong and swelling evil of [his] conception" as further divested of his gravity, of the "credent bulk" his authority "bears" (4.4.20, 26). Angelo suffers an abortion or miscarriage of his own sense of self, an unshaping of his "eminent body" (4.4.22) once deemed sufficient to fill the place of patriarch. To the extent that his "swelling evil" initially signified an erection, Angelo associates detumescence with impotence, a lack of phallic sufficiency.

### ISABELLA'S SADOMASOCHISM

Isabella too seems to fluctuate between sadistic and masochistic positions. In seeking to harness her own sexuality rather than wear the harness (or "livery") of sexual vassalage, Isabella resembles Angelo and the Duke: she wishes to achieve "masculine" self-mastery, to disown and mortify the fleshly feminine self. Yet, once catching the drift of Angelo's proposal, she expresses her fantasy of self-mastery in masochistic terms, positioning herself as recipient rather than dispenser of discipline:

> Were I under the terms of death,
> Th' impression of keen whips I'd wear as rubies,
> And strip myself to death as to a bed

That longing have been sick for, ere I'd yield
My body up to shame.

(2.4.100–104)

Through this image, Isabella imaginatively stages a kind of sadomasochistic drama, a bed-trick in which she strips herself naked and chooses Death rather than Angelo as her lover, spurning sexual intercourse in favor of punitive beating. She puts her mortified body on imaginative display, costumed only in the bleeding lashes inflicted by the whip. Isabella's masochistic fantasy implicitly posits a gaze that specularizes and shames her body for its transgressive urges, a monastic or heavenly authority for whose sake she must submit to penitential flagellation. At the same time, her sexual imagery, stirred by the subtextual erotics of her skirmish with Angelo, invites a desiring and—to the extent that it conjures a sexual act—voyeuristic look. In a sense, Isabella covers the keyhole where she herself has placed Angelo. From his standpoint, her exhibitionistic fantasy is a tease, a vividly sexual image that denies sexual availability.[54]

On one level, Isabella simply employs the imagery of martyrology, reiterating with martyrish intensity her oft-protested readiness to die on Claudio's behalf (2.4.55–56, 3.1.102–104), identifying herself with legendary female saints whose submission to "ling'ring sufferance" made them, through the pictorial arts, feminine icons of Christian masochism. This variety of masochism, according to Kaja Silverman, requires the exhibition of a mortified body in a manner evocative of "the master tableau": "Christ nailed to the cross, head wreathed in thorns and blood dripping from his impaled sides."[55] Angelo's mortification of Claudio, as I staged it, could be said to evoke this tableau.[56] So too could Isabella's picture of her bleeding, abject body.

The violently erotic scenography of her fantasy links the imagery of martyrology with that of pornography, coupling the "master tableau" with sadomasochistic ritual in a manner chillingly similar to the pornographic slide shows favored by theologian Paul Tillich, as described by his wife:

There was the familiar cross shooting up the wall. . . . A naked girl hung on it, hands tied in front of her private parts. Another naked figure lashed the crucified one with a whip that reached further to another cross, on which a girl was exposed from behind. More and more crosses appeared, all with women tied and exposed in various positions.[57]

This admixture of Christian and sadomasochistic imagery—the erotic dreamscape of a famous theologian—seems frightfully apposite to Isabella's fantasy.[58] In a sense, she puts herself on one of those crosses, savoring a version of *imitatio Christi* that exercises as well as disciplines a "sick" sexual longing. Her beating fantasy evokes the desexualized ecstasy sought by the most zealous monastical flagellants, who mortified the flesh to achieve unfleshly union with Christ the bridegroom.[59]

Like the self-abusing Angelo, Isabella exercises an auto-erotic masochistic fantasy. Yet, while *imitatio Christi* for Angelo entails a radical negation of normative masculinity, for Isabella it implies emphatic acceptance of normative femininity. The jewel-like bleeding wounds that Isabella wears so proudly conjure the bleeding wound foundational to female sexuality in a phallocentric economy. They become homologous with the "destin'd livery," a displayed lack that ensures her place in the oedipal plot, her surrender of active sexuality and embrace of masochistic eroticism. By commingling the sexual act with flagellation, Isabella both affirms a libidinal drive and acquiesces in the libidinal disinvestiture culturally required of female subjects. Through the imagined beating, Isabella's body achieves integration with lacking femininity.

To the extent that Isabella's beating fantasy manifests guilt for a sexual longing deemed "sick," it bespeaks a guilt-ridden compulsion to punish her own sinning flesh. Isabella may be sufficiently aware of her provocation of Angelo, sufficiently appreciative of the power she thereby commands, and sufficiently distressed by a sting of reciprocal attraction to feel that her own stimulated, errant flesh stands in need of corrective flaying. From this perspective, Isabella's beating fantasy enacts an atonement for oedipal guilt, for incestuous desire of the forbidden father-figure, Angelo, the ruthless enforcer of paternal law. Her erotic imagery suggests that the beating she envisions both chastens and gratifies a sexual vexation.[60]

Isabella's beating fantasy—and its implied oedipal guilt—sheds light on her condemnation of Claudio. Throughout their turbulent interview, she implicitly assigns Claudio the role of surrogate father—an asexual protector who will save her from the sexually menacing bad father, Angelo.[61] If Claudio were to acquiesce in her degradation, Isabella suggests, the resulting shame "would bark your honor from the trunk you bear, / And leave you naked" (3.1.71–72). Thus, when Claudio rejects the idea of ignominious ransom, vowing to "encounter darkness as a bride / And hug it in mine arms" (83–84), Isabella celebrates his likeness to her father: "There spake my brother; there my father's grave / Did utter forth a voice" (85–86). When, however, Claudio implores her to meet Angelo's demand, she emphatically negates the likeness, transforming him into his mother's son: "Heaven shield my mother play'd my father fair! / For such a warped slip of wilderness / Ne'er issu'd from his blood" (140–42). Her mother, like Juliet, becomes the carrier of sin, and Claudio, conceived in illicit sexuality, its embodiment. Isabella stigmatizes and implicitly disavows the female sexuality with which she had previously empathized. She resists identification with a sexualized mother and clings instead to a fantasized, asexual relationship with her father. In so doing, she rejects the incestuous image of sexually corrupting him or, to the extent that Angelo represents the Father, being corrupted by him. In explicitly charging Claudio with incest (3.1. 138), she conflates two sexually illicit acts. Claudio would "take life" from her "incestuous" union with the father-figure Angelo and, by colluding with Angelo in her corruption, would himself incestuously ravish her.

Claudio's refusal to facilitate Isabella's desexualization transforms her from masochist to sadist. She proceeds to brutalize him verbally, transforming him, as did Angelo, into a personified corrupt flesh that must be mercilessly lacerated. Claudio once more plays the part of Angelo's chastened surrogate. Made complicit in Angelo's assault on his sister, he suffers a vituperation that surely feeds on rage against Angelo even as Hamlet's chastisement of Ophelia channels disgust with his mother. At the same time, Claudio plays the part of Isabella's chastened surrogate, a whipping boy absorbing whatever guilt she feels for igniting—and perhaps reciprocating—Angelo's desire. She identifies Claudio with her own unruly flesh and punishes him as a feminized ego-substitute, assigning him the role she had assigned herself in the fantasy of flagellation. Claudio now stands in relation to Isabella as Isabella does to Angelo.

In a sense, the desexualized, protective father-figure of Isabella's imagining corresponds to God the father, illuminating another aspect of Isabella's attraction to the nunnery. When the Duke steps forward from the prison's shadows and offers miraculously to resolve her seemingly irresolvable crisis, saving both her brother's life and her chastity, he essentially takes over the role of protective, desexualized father-figure that Claudio declined to play. He also assumes the figure of the God to whom she initially wished to devote herself.

In rescuing Isabella, the Duke sees to it that her erotic energies remain directed to fantasy, devising a bed-trick in which a woman avowedly desirous of Angelo takes Isabella's place. "The *image* of it gives me content already," Isabella announces (3.1.259, emphasis mine), as though vicariously savoring her surrogate's satisfaction of a desire she must repress.[62] If Helena's alliance with Diana depends upon exploiting a desirability she cannot claim, Isabella's confederacy with Mariana depends upon exploiting a desire she cannot admit.

## GESTIC STAGING

The creation of a feminist gestus for *Measure for Measure* depends, first of all, upon redeeming Isabella's choice of chastity over her brother's life.[63] Juliet Stevenson, who played Isabella for Adrian Noble in 1983, puts the matter quite well:

> Outside of Catholicism, notions of "perjuring the soul" and "eternal damnation" have become quaint, and they make Isabella an eccentric. If her decision is not one the audience can identify with positively, they will judge her. This means that the production has got to place the play so that the line "More than our brother is our chastity" can be spoken with integrity. The production—if its objective is that the audience will recognise Isabella's dilemma as opposed to merely observing her in critical detachment—has to support Isabella. Otherwise the audience will not really be challenged by the play, they'll be let off the hook.[64]

In short, a feminist gestus, far from simplifying the play, actually assists in capturing its complexity, sharpening the critique of gender it enables. One way to elicit greater sympathy for Isabella's choice is to redefine chastity in secular terms as a value constitutive of personal integrity and dignity, the loss of which breaks not simply the mirror of virginity but the "glassy essence" of selfhood.[65] My production aimed to achieve this revaluation through two particular gestic stagings: turning Angelo's brutal threats into an attempted rape and turning Claudio's plea for Isabella's compliance into an inadvertent reenactment of it. In the first instance, an attempted rape simply physicalizes the violence of Angelo's words. "[Angelo's] filth within being cast," Isabella exclaims to Claudio, "he would appear / A pond as deep as hell" (3.1.92–93). Isabella imagines Angelo's degrading speech as a demonic ejaculation, a vomiting forth of a bottomless pit of filth. Isabella thus suggests that Angelo "speaks sex" too, seemingly linking semen with vomit even as Angelo linked it with excrement.

Previous productions have indeed characterized Angelo's brutal proposition as a kind of rape. In Barton's production, Angelo, once rejected, butted Isabella across the room with his groin onto a table, where he "roughly caressed her body."[66] In Bogdanov's, Angelo thrust himself against her after professing his "love," wedging her against the desk until he mimed an orgasm.[67] In Hytner's (RSC, 1987), Angelo ripped off Isabella's veil, struck her down, and "straddle[ed] her as she sobbed passionately."[68] In Nunn's, Angelo threw a screaming and kicking Isabella onto a couch and forced himself on her, an action "as horribly near a rape as this scene can ever have come."[69] Isabella's choice of chastity over her brother's life becomes much more sympathetic when viewed as a defense against sexual violence. Such chastity expresses not an exaltation of virginity but an abhorrence of rape, of a "pollution" not imagined but threateningly real. Audiences could therefore be expected to grasp that Isabella stands to lose something far more than virginity if she gives in to Angelo. While "chastity" would not normally seem the correct word for this precious, irreplaceable "something," it can, in the context of an attempted rape, take on that meaning. Stevenson, addressing members of the Shakespeare Association of America (Vancouver, 1991), explained that she played the line, "more than our brother is our chastity" as a discovery, registering surprise at her own choice. I instructed my actress to follow Stevenson's advice and also to pause slightly before the word "chastity," as though saying or at least understanding the word for the first time, newly coining and claiming it.

The second gestic moment aims to mitigate the harshness of Isabella's tirade against Claudio by underlining her status as the victim of an intended rape. On the line, "be ready, Claudio, for your death tomorrow"(3.1.106), Isabella urged him to kneel beside her in prayer. He initially complied but then broke away, returning to her side for his meditation on the terrors of death. On his concluding line, "Sweet sister, let me live," he desperately, forcefully embraced her and, as she recoiled, ended up on top of her, in a position distressingly similar to the one Angelo had assumed in his attempted rape. Although Claudio's only intention was to plead for his life, the parallel to Angelo's assault impeached the integrity of his request to live and made Isabella's ferocious response—in particular her charge of "incest"—much more understandable and presumably less objectionable.

Another attempt to articulate a feminist gestus took the form of "staging the look." In the preshow, an audience of inebriated, lecherous men looked at and made bids on a group of prostitutes "auctioned off" by Mistress Overdone. The theatrical audience observed a process of objectification rather than, as in film, colluding in objectification by looking directly at fetishizing close-ups of the women themselves. This exhibition of female objects contested the male look it elicited by planting a mediating image of disreputable surrogates. The image deflected the male look away from the women-as-objects to the men who are objectifying them and then back to the women-as-subjects. In the play's final scene, the male look was disrupted by, and ultimately yielded to, a female look, constituted in the course of the Duke's spectacle by the sequential arrival of female spectators: townswomen, whores, nuns, and Mariana's friends. When the Duke proposed to Isabella, the remaining witnesses were all women.

Also crucial to the gestus was a piece of sadomasochistic ritual that opened the show: a young man knelt before a dominatrix, flagellated himself, and then extended his arms to her in a gesture at once supplicating and exalting. This image anticipated other key moments in the production: Angelo's kneeling and flagellating himself at the beginning of 2.4, Angelo's kneeling and extending his arms to Mariana (dressed like Isabella) at the outset of the bed-trick, and the Duke's kneeling and extending his arms to Isabella in the play's final moment. This parallel underscored the extent to which these characters are themselves enmeshed in sadomasochistic transactions, enacting sadistic scenarios that belie the masochistic poses. The intent was to portray sadistic enmity as the flip side of masochistic awe. Both dispositions have the effect of submitting women to symbolic erasure, the first by stigmatizing, the second by mystifying a feared difference.

The dominatrix glimpsed in the opening image became Kate Keepdown, who personified this male fear, stalking Lucio throughout the play, forever emerging from dark corners in an effort to claim him. She functioned as a female bogey, a spectre of castration, a figure of the dreaded yet desired (m)other. Her silence became a signifier of her utterly constructed identity, her status as the projection of a male fantasy. At the end, when finally allowed to claim Lucio, she extended his public humiliation, slapping a collar and leash on him and leading him off on all fours.[70]

The feminist gestus can also rest on more fundamental matters of relationship and characterization. Because the women in this play are mostly estranged from each other, my production sought to underscore the kinship of Isabella and Mariana.[71] After securing Mariana's participation in the Duke's plot, Isabella helped her dress in a white novitiate's outfit identical to her own, which she wore for the remainder of the play. Mariana functioned not simply as Isabella's surrogate during the bed-trick but as a "sister" during the final scene, both the secret sharer of her covert sexuality and the public sharer of her sexual shame. For a significant portion of the scene, Mariana and Isabella stood together on the slip stage, two scorned, exhibited "giglets" (5.1.347) trying to sustain each other. Isabella greeted the Duke's first astonishing proposal by crossing away from him to Mariana, as though seeking her comfort and counsel.

It is also highly important to defamiliarize the image of Isabella as frigid or repressed.[72] Her aversion to Angelo's proposed violation need not express an aversion to sexuality itself, nor does her compulsion to contain her sexual drives imply a fear of them. With Stevenson's refreshing and engaging performance in mind, I worked with my actress toward creating an Isabella who was warm and sensual as well as formidably intelligent and self-possessed. She did indeed harbor an unconscious attraction to Angelo that increased the combustiveness of their scenes together. This choice makes sense dramatically as well as psychologically. If Isabella is a passionate young woman whose only outlet for passion in this patriarchal society is the impassioned championing of monastical chastity, then the task of "moving" Angelo provides a new outlet, one which, far from submerging her in institutionalized masochism, provides for the temporary release of power: Isabella dominates and sexually arouses the most dominant, seemingly most desexualized man in the land. It seems plausible that she has some awareness of her effect on Angelo, that she discerns his faltering resolve and enjoys the experience of subduing him. "I am come to know your pleasure" (2.4.31), she announces upon arriving for their second interview, a perhaps guileless greeting that nonetheless registers a double, sexual meaning, as though Isabella were acknowledging—consciously or not—the sexual undercurrents of their encounters. In this instance, actorly imperative and psychoanalytic insight work together: deciding that Isabella harbors a covert desire for Angelo is the strongest, most emotionally generative choice, the one that maximizes internal conflict.

## THE DUKE'S SADOMASOCHISTIC SPECTACLE

In the play's final scene, the Duke orchestrates a kind of sadomasochistic spectacle in which he rescues people from the shame and humiliation to which he himself subjects them, effectively hurting them in order to please them. With Isabella in particular, the Duke concocts a deception that conduces to—and possibly aims at—her reception of him as savior and husband. Certainly the Duke seems determined to make her feel as helpless as possible. He resolves to keep her ignorant of Claudio's survival in order, he says, "to make her heavenly comforts of despair / When it is least expected" (4.3.110–11). The Duke's goal, if not his strategy, resembles Petruchio's: transforming a strong-willed woman into a submissive wife. Like a shrew, Isabella demonstrates a transgressive unruliness, a daunting capacity for fearless raillery, and a provocative "openness" that invites patriarchal enclosure.[73]

When Isabella, stung by the news of Claudio's death, vows to "pluck out [Angelo's] eyes," the Duke overrules her urge toward "masculine" revenge and recommends a retreat into iconic femininity, urging "wisdom," "patience," and "forbearance" (118, 124). "Give your cause to heaven," he instructs her. That he really means "give your cause to me" seems clear from his ensuing admonition that she seek "grace of the Duke" (4.3.119–36). The Duke effectively manipulates her into assuming the same supplicatory proneness before him that Lucio coached her to assume before Angelo, "suing and weeping," possibly even "hanging upon his gown," femininely enabling the male fantasy of "giving like a god."

In the final scene, then, Isabella finds herself trapped within the Duke's spectacle, despite balking at the dissimulations required of her: "[T]o speak so indirectly I am loath; / I would say the truth." She would, at last, speak with her own voice. "Be rul'd by him," Mariana urges, (4.6.1–2, 4). Isabella proceeds "to tell the world with outstretch'd throat" of Angelo's reprobation, just as she had threatened, but her accusations are fictional, her speech performative, even if venting a genuine sense of violation. Once more Isabella submits an impassioned supplication to a male look, provocatively opening her mouth and displaying her speechless dialect. Indeed, Isabella is at her most "open" in this scene, daring to disrupt the Duke's ceremonial lauding of Angelo, implicitly presenting herself as a sexual (because sexually violated) woman.

Just as Helena did to Bertram, the Duke orchestrates the public besmirching of Isabella's honor. He manipulates her into "unchaste" public utterances that he scornfully censures, accusing her of madness and wantonness, thus converting her defamations of Angelo's reprobation into admissions of her own. He places her under arrest. If, in performance, he also places her in chains, the stage picture recalls the mortified Claudio, the original image of the body shamed. The image may also recall the humiliations of Pompey and Mistress Overdone, whose arrests were also turned into mortifying public spectacles in my production. Isabella thus becomes linked with a fornicator, a bawd, and a brothel-keeper. In fact, in my production the key moments of spectacle in the final scene—the Duke's tribute to Angelo, Isabella's accusation, and Mariana's unveiling, for instance—all took place on the slip-stage that had first been employed in the production's preshow, principally for the fantasy auction that underlined the exploitation of female bodies. The Duke's display of the shamed Isabella therefore becomes homologous to Pompey's and Overdone's display of prostitutes; in both instances women enter spectacle to fulfill male fantasies of mastery. In addition, the chains that bind Isabella serve not only to link her with other shamed transgressors but to forecast the Duke's attempt to bind her in the chains of a possibly unwanted wedlock.

The Duke also makes a spectacle of Angelo, punishing him as Angelo punished Claudio, converting him to the personification of a wayward flesh that must be disciplined, emasculating him for falling prey to the female sexuality whose clutches the Duke manages to escape. Having publicly exposed and shamed Angelo's treacherous lechery, the Duke forces him to marry a formidably desirous woman whom he has already rejected. This forced marriage is sadistic in effect if not in intention, a punishment that fits the crime: Angelo, who had sought to dominate one woman, must now submit to another. The Duke implicitly consigns Angelo to the permanent status of "lack," enforcing an emasculating subjugation to a markedly sexual woman whose desires he must now service. Angelo ends the play where Bertram finds himself at mid-point, coerced into marrying a woman whose sexuality he fears, without the opportunity afforded Bertram to overcome his aversion.

In my production, the Duke went even further in making a spectacle of Angelo by actually summoning an executioner who led him to the "block." As two of the Duke's officers began to undress him and a priest (Father Peter) administered the last rites, Mariana desperately implored Isabella to appeal for Angelo's pardon. This staging not only imparted additional suspense to the outcome of Mariana's appeal but also linked the mock execution of Angelo to a mock execution in the preshow that was explicitly marked as a piece of sadomasochistic ritual. When Mariana finished her supplication, Isabella turned and slowly walked stage left in order to face the exhibited Angelo, who stood on the slip-stage upstage of her. The executioner and priest backed away, and Angelo, in chains and naked from the waist up, turned slowly to face her. As she stared at him, he began to weep. This act of looking conveys a drastic reversal of power, as though Isabella's earlier wish were granted: she now has Angelo's "potency" and he is Isabel. Indeed, by entering the space of shame, of feminine degradation, Angelo trades places not only with Claudio but with Isabella as well. Because Isabella's look operates free of desire, it approximates the gaze, shaming and controlling the vulnerable Angelo. Although this look precedes her decision to sue for his forgiveness, it is intrinsically sadistic, fixing the exhibited Angelo in a "lacking," feminized position. Because Isabella's back is to the audience, the emphasis falls not on the drama of decision-making but on her visual capture of Angelo. The audience looks at Isabella looking at—and dominating—Angelo.

Even Isabella's act of forgiveness extends Angelo's punishment. Because her appeal for his pardon directly contradicts his explicit wish to die (5.1.370–74, 474–77), she assists, consciously or not, in punishing him with an unwanted wife, sharpening his shame by once more making him (as he was in the bed-trick) an object of exchange between two women. In addition, because Isabella's appeal favorably answers Mariana's, it may derive as much from sisterly compassion (toward Mariana) as from Christian charity (toward Angelo). Remembering her own powerlessness before Angelo, Isabella possibly sees an image of herself in the desperately pleading Mariana.

In my production, Angelo was an utterly broken man by the time the Duke dismissed him to his marriage with Mariana. She collected his clothes and led him down from the slip-stage and began dressing him. On one hand, these intimate ministrations affirmed Mariana's love for Angelo and, inasmuch as he permitted them, signaled the possibility of a reconciliation. At the same time, his submissiveness signaled his capitulation to the dreaded (m)other he previously spurned, underscoring his emasculation. In returning Angelo to maternal domination, the Duke publicly exhibited his insufficiency to the paternal function. Angelo, as he has been hitherto constituted within the field of vision, goes out of focus even as the liminal Duke comes into it. His urgent wish to die may be read as a desire to escape the punitive gaze altogether, to crawl into a hole in the ground—literally.

The Duke also orchestrates the public humiliation of Mariana, shaming the unchaste discourse he himself elicits, calling her "pernicious woman" (5.1.241), and allowing Angelo to scorn her as a kind of whore—or at least a woman whose "reputation was disvalued / In levity" (5.1.221–22). He puts her through the emotional wringer, first threatening her with punishment (5.1.240), then wedding her to Angelo, then condemning him to death, then returning him to her—but as a virtual zombie, unresistant yet unresponsive to her loving, maternal gestures.

Angelo's liminality reinforces Mariana's, leaving her cloaked in a figurative veil long after she removes the physical one. Mariana, like Helena, enters as the "shadow of a wife." Unlike Helena, however, Mariana is neither the name nor the thing. She declines to be identified as wife—having not yet been officially married to Angelo—nor will she answer to the names of "maid" or "widow." The only other identity available to her as a woman—

as Lucio gleefully points out—is whore. The Duke pronounces her "noth-ing" and, indeed, Mariana presents herself as a marginal being, a body awaiting inscription into the Symbolic Order, a statue that can only be animated by Angelo's acceptance of her as wife:

> He knew me as a wife. As this is true,
> Let me in safety raise me from my knees,
> Or else for ever be confixed here,
> A marble monument!
>
> (5.1.230–33)

The pose in which she proposes to freeze herself is that of the prone supplicant, submissively on her knees, enabling Angelo to "give like a god," to become her lord and master. Like Helena, she dominates, through her patriarch's authority, a man to whom she wishes to submit. Her subjectivity is even more invested in marriage than Helena's, and her husband even more enigmatically taciturn. As Angelo never acknowledges her as wife, she effectively remains veiled and liminal, no maiden but a monument.

The Duke also subjects Lucio to public mortification. Initially sentencing him to death, the Duke relents and merely orders him to marry Kate Keepdown, a remission that Lucio decries as worse than the original punishment: "Marrying a punk, my lord, is pressing to death, whipping, and hanging" (5.1.522–23). Indeed, in an earlier scene, Lucio admits having once perjured himself before the Duke in order to avoid marrying Kate (4.3.169–74). The Duke's response—"slandering a prince deserves it" (5.1.524)—marks the marriage as unmistakably punitive. Like Angelo, Lucio suffers consignment to an unwanted marriage that shames and emasculates him. His punishment parallels Angelo's because he shares Angelo's status as scapegoat, representative of the Duke's abjected sexual self.

Lucio functions as the Duke's discredited double in a second sense: his subjectivity also seems primarily an effect of theatricality, of improvisa-tional adaptation to circumstances. He too is a trickster and exhibitionist—a "fantastic" who shares with the "fantastical" Duke a fondness for dark corners. Like Parolles, he is an utterly constructed fashion-monger, man-about-town, and self-proclaimed soldier.[74] When Lucio tries to excuse his slander of the Duke on the grounds that, "I spoke it but according to the trick" (5.1.504–505), the double meaning of "trick" ("custom" and "hoax") confirms his status as both man of mode and antic dissembler. Whether following fashion or improvising a jape to disconcert the uptight Duke,

Lucio lives histrionically in the moment. Just as the Duke intervenes to save Isabella's honor and ultimately publicly dishonors her, so Lucio earnestly praises her as a "thing enskied and sainted" at the nunnery yet cracks lewd jokes at her expense in the final scene, exploiting her public shaming in order to aggrandize himself, to clear a space for himself in the Duke's spectacle (5.1.273–77, 79–80). Lucio essentially tries to upstage the Duke in the final scene, ceaselessly interjecting self-promoting commentary despite the Duke's repeated reprimands. He comes to occupy center stage, figuratively and perhaps literally, when accusing and then unveiling the disguised Duke. Lucio receives the Duke's harshest punishment not simply for yoking him to a corrupt sexuality but for exhibitionistically disrupting his attempt to exhibit himself as gaze.[75]

FINAL MOMENTS: "What Do You Think This Is?"

When the Duke reveals himself, he promises Isabella,

> as I was then
> Advertising and holy to your business,
> Not changing heart with habit, I am still
> Attorneyed at your service.
>
> (5.1.382–85)

The Duke essentially assures her that he will continue to play the role of the salvific, desexualized father-figure, an image of the God she initially wished to marry. He undertakes to fulfill his original promise to save both her brother's life and her chastity. To the extent that he "resurrects" her brother and hopes to convert her gratitude into devotion, he continues to play God. To the extent that he rescues her from sexual shame, not simply by proving her innocence but by offering to marry her, he seems still to play the protective father-figure who safeguards her chastity.[76]

His offer to marry her, however, also radically alters his fatherly role, introducing the provocative possibility of a sexual relationship. Having protected her from the sexually rapacious Angelo, he presents himself, at least potentially, as another "bad father." While Mariana took Isabella's place in the bed-trick, the Duke carried out another trick, setting up a second opportunity for Isabella to realize an oedipal fantasy, assimilating for her sake the seemingly irreconcilable roles of "father" and lover. In a sense, he does for her what Helena did for Bertram, enabling her to fulfill a forbidden desire involuntarily. In another sense, the Duke tricks Isabella in much the same way that he tricks Angelo. Isabella thinks that she has been safely intimate with one man (the desexualized holy friar) and discovers that, in fact, she has been far more provocatively intimate with another (the newly sexualized Duke). The Duke has known Isabella while she knew not that she ever knew him. She still does not know him, except perhaps as a man capable of deceiving and humiliating her—which must complicate whatever admiration she could reasonably be expected to have for him.

Like Bertram at the end of *All's Well*, she requires clarifying knowledge of the mystifying figure presenting himself as spouse. The extent to which she may reciprocate his desire (or at least his interest in marrying her) remains provocatively mysterious—even more so than Bertram's feelings toward Helena. Even those productions (such as my own) that hint at a possible attraction between the two do not always end with Isabella's unequivocal acceptance of the Duke. What she learns about him seems likelier to undercut than enhance her attraction.

If Isabella balks at fulfilling her fantasy, the Duke seems ready to realize his, one that strongly resembles that of his more predatory double, Angelo. In seeking to marry and enjoy conjugal relations with this "fair and gracious daughter" (4.3.112), this "sister" (3.1.151), this chaste would-be nun, the Duke similarly seeks to convert an exalted, forbidden female figure into a sexually accessible woman. Certainly he positions her as the figure of conquest/closure for his oedipal quest, the symbolic (m)other out of whom he wishes to create himself, the redemptive "feminine" force who enables his paternity, restores his potency, and affirms his sovereignty—in short, makes a man of him. The Duke attempts to coerce and manipulate Isabella into playing the same role that Helena so desperately wished to play for Bertram. There is no overt evidence, however, that Isabella complies. Helena, desiring subject and would-be object of desire, and Isabella, object of desire and arguably desiring subject, each distinctively enacts the central contradiction of female subjectivity within a phallocentric order: forging a self that is always already implicated in symbol.

The Duke appears to achieve a victory of sorts when Isabella, attempting to excuse Angelo's misconduct, accepts the status of desired object she has heretofore strenuously resisted: "I partly think / A due sincerity govern'd his deeds / Till he did look on me" (5.1.445–47). Isabella seems ready not only to surrender her body to patriarchal spectacle but to make her voice a mouthpiece for patriarchal values. In implicitly arraigning herself for inciting Angelo's assault, Isabella ventriloquizes the Duke's voice, evoking the same double standard by which he judged Juliet's crime greater than Claudio's, implicitly blaming women for the desire they provoke. Isabella seems close to donning the destin'd livery.

By kneeling before the Duke for the second time in the scene—this time as Angelo's advocate rather than his accuser—by once more assuming a submissive, supplicatory posture, Isabella physicalizes her status as object of a fetishizing male look. She once more plays the role assigned her in the Duke's spectacle, gratifying his fantasy of mastery. Indeed, by consenting to "take [Mariana's] part," Isabella implicitly assumes Mariana's statuesque pose of eternal proneness, inadvertently enacting the wifely subservience the Duke may intend for her in marriage. In urging Isabella to "say nothing," in assuring her "I'll speak all," Mariana essentially asks Isabella to facilitate a double ventriloquism: Isabella speaks for Mariana, who speaks for the patriarchal voice—traceable to the Duke—ordaining marriage as a means of achieving normative femininity.

When the Duke extends his hand to Isabella at the play's end, he implicitly encourages her to assume a prone position one final time. Isabella, of course, says nothing in response to his proposal. Her silence has generated voluminous debate and multifarious performance choices, ranging from joyful, unhesitating acceptance to outright revulsion.[77] Yet the complexity of the play seems to require a less simplistic resolution. Certainly Isabella's silence could signify resignation, as though the Duke had hounded her into mute submission. Yet it might also manifest resistance, evoking if not reenacting her original rejection of the destin'd livery, signified by the vow of silence she was poised to take at the convent. Her muteness may not signify the helplessness of an actress who has run out of lines, as Marcia Riefer suggests,[78] but the recalcitrance of a woman who no longer wishes to speak someone else's. Indeed, given her previous willingness to subordinate speech to the Duke's design, her silence may signify her refusal to speak according to the trick, to end her collusion in ventriloquism, to cease being the Duke's dummy.

My own staging, seeking a feminist gestus in accord with the play's complexity, aimed to shift the question attending the play's final moment from "will she or won't she?" to "what do you think this is?" After the Duke had dismissed all his subjects, Isabella stood downstage right. The Duke stepped down from the stage on which he had concluded his spectacle, took off his ceremonial robe, and crossed to Isabella, now prepared to court her as a man. After delivering his final lines (in this production, "what's mine is yours and what is yours is mine") he dropped to one knee. She stepped toward him and, in response, he brought the other knee down as well. This particular pose, which was held for only a brief instant, was meant to have erotic undercurrents, as the two were momentarily in an intimate space, in a suggestive position. Isabella then quickly turned and walked upstage, as though intending to exit and to reject the proposal. The Duke remained on his knees but shifted and turned upstage to watch her. Suddenly, she stopped. Then came a sound cue—a reprise of the same ethereal music that had accompanied the entrance of the nuns in 1.4 (in my production an aborted wedding presenting Isabella as would-be bride of Christ). Isabella turned to face the Duke and took a step toward him. In response, he stretched out his arms to her. At the same time four figures returned to the second-level balcony: two nuns and two whores, who consequently became spectators to this final moment. Isabella took another step toward the Duke, who extended his arms even further. As the lights began to fade, the ethereal "nun music" shifted into the dark, grinding, industrial music that had underscored the frenzied decadence of the sex club and had also concluded Angelo's first soliloquy and introduced his second. This sequence of movements and images aimed at asking the question "what do you think this is?" by inducing spectators to question the meaning of the Duke's proposal. What exactly does he offer—or fail to offer—Isabella? To what extent does that offer intersect with her inclinations? To what extent is she a pawn, to what extent a desired object? If mostly the former, how can a purely ceremonial marriage accommodate her complex subjectivity? If mostly the latter, to what extent does she reciprocate or even accept the Duke's desire? Does the marriage rescue her from a self-suppressing sexual renunciation or oppress her by robbing her of sexual autonomy?

When Isabella first stepped into an intimate space with the Duke, sex was unavoidably in the air. He assumed a "prone" position, ostensibly transferring power to her, on his knees as though willing to service her. In turning sharply and beginning to exit, she appeared not simply to reject his proposal but to reject sexuality, as though understanding that the power the Duke extends to her derives from her excitation of male desire. The music cue, which coincided with her arrested exit and seemed to motivate her turning back to the Duke, suggested, by reprising the music associated with the purity of the convent, that marriage to the Duke might be compatible with the maintenance of her chastity, that the urge for purity could be translated into holy matrimony. The audience could presumably entertain this possibility. In my production, the Duke was a sensitive, well-intentioned man who was utterly unaware of the dubiousness of his tactics and who had enjoyed a warm relationship with Isabella. At the same time, the music, together with the Duke's outstretched arms, signified his *summoning* of Isabella. If the beautiful music and worshipful pose worked to situate her as madonna, the grasping arms suggested a sexual covetousness capable of converting her into a whore. Given the parallel between the Duke's pose, that of Angelo in the bed-trick, and that of the flagellating "slave" at the outset of the show, Isabella occupied a position similar to that of two creatures of male fantasy: the madonna/whore and the dominatrix.

The coarsening of the music and dimming of the lights as Isabella took another step toward the Duke further contested the compatibility of chastity and marriage, underlining the uncertainty of Isabella's position. So too did the presence of the nuns and whores who witnessed these final moments. Like Lavatch at the end of *All's Well*, they personified an unanswered, perhaps unanswerable question: does there exist for Isabella a possible subject position other than madonna or whore? Are her only alternatives the institutionalized repression of the nunnery and the institutionalized (sexual) subservience of marriage? Or does the Duke offer her "something more" than consignment to lack?

By failing to answer the Duke's proposal, Isabella leaves herself undefined. Her silence registers an ambivalence and irresolution that return her to the position she assumed when first forced to reenter the world of men: "at war twixt will and will not" (2.2.33). She no longer attempts to articulate her betwixtness, however, but instead mimes the absence of a subjective voice capable of expressing it. Her silence signifies neither "yes" nor "no" nor even "maybe" but enigmatically manifests the impossibility of reply, of expressing an experience irreducible to oedipal logic.

In effect, Isabella's silence lends her a doubleness comparable to that of Helena. On the one hand, she is still in spectacle, still implicated in the oedipal plot, still a part of the Duke's story. On the other, her silence creates a space for her own story, evoking an "elsewhere" unassimilable to the patriarchal narrative that has previously constrained her. She remains in spectacle but not coherently, resisting capture by the male look, eluding consignment to lack.

In the play's final moment, Isabella's dialect becomes truly speechless, exclusively bodily, yet *other* than the language of seduction it was previously made to speak. Like Helena in the staged bed-trick, Isabella offers a nonmimetic body, unreadable but incontestably "there," speechless but unsilenceable. Isabella, through the actress who represents her, remains a body that cannot be easily fitted to the destin'd livery, despite the Duke's intention: "[W]hat's mine is yours, and what is yours is mine," he proclaims (5.1.537). As she would seem to have no dowry, what else can she give him—what else is "hers"—besides her body?[79]

By greeting the Duke's proposal with silence, Isabella implicitly claims her body as hers, if only for a moment. Yet, because that moment coincides with the final moment of the play, it becomes indefinitely extended in the audience's imagination, a kind of permanent "now." In real time Isabella would eventually have to resolve her ambiguous silence and give the Duke a definite answer. The play allows her, as it were, the last word. Her control of the final moment enables Isabella, like Helena in the staged bed-trick, to arrest the narrative momentum of the oedipal plot, evoking a "different narrative temporality." Her silence strands both herself and the Duke in Elsewhere, a no-man's land of unsubstantiated gender. If such suspension imperils the Duke's achievement of mythical masculinity, it also rescues Isabella from lacking femininity, allowing her to be the source of her own meaning, even if that meaning cannot be coherently articulated within the world of the play. To be in no-man's land is to escape phallocentric capture, to assert a difference alien to man's land.

In sum, *Measure for Measure* greatly extends the tensions that strain the resolution of *All's Well That Ends Well*. The Duke is a more troubled and troubling manipulator of events than Helena, Angelo a more daunting reprobate than Bertram, Isabella a more aggressed-against virgin than Diana. At the end of *Measure for Measure,* one has cause to question not one but three marriages, as only Claudio and Juliet seem clearly in love. The play's anti-comic dissonances are sharper and its comic ending even more dubious than that of *All's Well.* The Duke becomes an embattled, surrogate comic dramatist, straining to effect a happy ending by enforcing marriage, the conventional medium of comic amelioration. Indeed, he tries to do through overzealous imposition of marriage what Angelo fails to do through merciless imposition of law: restrain sexual passion.[80] Because three of the four marriages lack credibility, however—or, more to the point, lack the overt consent of both parties—they seem insufficient to arrest and redeem desire, to ratify the law of the father.

Inasmuch as the comic plot coincides significantly with the oedipal, especially in positioning women as figures of closure, the play's ending, by resisting comic resolution, also resists oedipal imperative. *Measure for Measure* exposes the duplicities of the oedipal plot by exposing the duplicities of the oedipal plotter, dramatizing resistance to his coercive maneuvers. Not only does Isabella greet the Duke's marriage proposal with enigmatic silence but Juliet deflects his indictment of her as a fallen woman, Claudio defeats his efforts to reconcile him to death, Angelo reneges on his agreement to pardon Claudio, Barnardine refuses to die and supply the head the Duke requires, Lucio vehemently protests his marriage, and Angelo fails to validate his.

If the Duke's efforts to impose comic oedipal order fall short, so too does his effort to affirm paternal sufficiency. Isabella's nonreply to his proposal effectively suspends his oedipal narrative. As in *All's Well*, the play's major characters fail to fit themselves to culturally imposed myths of gender, fail to lay hold of a stable identity or a secure destiny. Isabella and Mariana essentially end the play as bodies awaiting signification. Will Mariana become other than nothing? Will Isabella's otherness escape a similar negation? Similarly, the Duke and Angelo fail to fill out the masculine shape to which they aspire: neither proves equal to the status of Symbolic Father. The four seem not so much subjects-in-process as subjects either coveting or resisting erasure. If *All's Well That Ends Well* ends as well as it can, then *Measure for Measure* ends as unwell as it ought.

# 3

# Troilus and Cressida

*Troilus and Cressida* is the most problematic of the problem comedies, the most removed from the ameliorative comic structures that lend *All's Well That Ends Well* and *Measure for Measure* a provisional integrity. It deploys the largest screen for its projected crisis in gender, turning the epic Trojan War into a vast spectacle of emasculation, and leaves its drama of sexual difference even more unresolved. It more provocatively deconstructs its sources, deflating heroic legends instead of fracturing folk tales. For these reasons, I am discussing *Troilus and Cressida* last, even though, chronologically speaking, it is the first of the problem comedies.

Shakespeare depicts the Trojan War as an arrested collective oedipal plot in which the quest for masculinity is frustrated by the unavailability and inadequacy of its object/obstacle/ objective. Victory in war—achievement of manhood—depends upon possessing Helen, and Helen is unpossessable. To the extent that she underwrites the warriors' heroic endeavors, she exists as a purely mythical construct—the awesome beauty of legend—and, therefore, cannot be possessed. To the extent that she is a mere woman, she also proves unattainable, an emasculating seductress unamenable to male governance. Helen the woman is utterly unequal to her legendary image, unworthy of the carnage she causes. Like the Duke, she is a signifier of lack who is herself lacking, a figure of the veiled phallus.[1]

In the Trojan Council scene, Hector attempts to expose Helen's lack, protesting the "mad idolatry" that "attribute[s]" to her a value she does not intrinsically possess (2.2.56–60). In effect, Hector decorously translates Thersites' aspersion of Helen as a "placket," a slur collapsing Helen with the female sexual organ, which, in a phallocentric frame of meaning, signifies nothing. For Hector, Helen is nothing but a transgressive wife—subject to the laws of men—who ought to be returned to her husband (2.2.173–88). Troilus, by contrast, equates her with the male sexual organ, or at least with the organ of the king's power, which he locates in a vast protrusion from the waist. "Fie, fie, my brother!," he exclaims,

> Will you with counters sum
> The past proportion of his infinite,
> And buckle in a waist most fathomless
> With spans and inches so diminutive
> As fears and reasons?
>
> (2.2.25–32)

To retain Helen is to sustain the Father's erection—or at least to allow his fathomless waist to protrude unchecked. Troilus invents a mythically powerful father-figure—one vastly different from the ineffectual Priam—in order to borrow from him a phallus for Helen. In so doing, Troilus publicly indulges in the profligate fetishizing of Helen that he had privately denounced: "Helen must needs be fair," he had protested earlier, "when with your blood you daily paint her thus" (1.1.90–91). To "paint" Helen is either to beautify her with cosmetics or to paint her picture. In either case, she becomes more an effect than a cause of the war, a mythical being spawned from male bloodshed.

The empty Helen functions as a signifier for the emptiness of the whole enterprise of the Trojan War. Not only is what the armies strive for not worth having, it is scarcely "there" at all. In Euripides' *Helen*, the title character never goes to Troy at all, but is (mis)represented by a phantom. In Shakespeare's play, she goes to Troy—but she is still misrepresented by a phantom: a projection of the warriors' need to substantiate their quest for masculinity, a masculinity preemptively denied them from the outset.

Ulysses confirms this essential male "lack" in decrying the futility of redressing the collective emasculation inflicted on the Greek generals by Helen's cuckolding of Menelaus: "O deadly gall, and theme of all our scorns," he exclaims, "for which we lose our heads to gild his horns (4.5.30–31)! The Greek warriors "lose their heads" (submit to emasculation) while aggrandizing the emasculated Menelaus.

The Trojan soldiers are as essentially "lacking" as the Greeks: "you have the honey," Priam scolds Paris, "but these [his fellow warriors] the gall" (2.2.144). The Trojans also lose their heads for a woman they cannot possess. Nor does Paris truly possess her. Helen, it is clear, possesses *him*: "I would fain have arm'd today," Paris tells Pandarus, "but my Nell would not have it so" (3.1.135–36). Paris puts down his own arms in order to lie in Helen's, surrendering male potency to lose himself in a female bower of bliss. At the scene's end, Helen promises to disarm Hector upon his return from battle—an "unmetaphoring" of her seductive capacities.

Helen's seductiveness derives from her willingness to inhabit the warriors' misrecognition, to be forever unassimilable to her seductive image and thus forever uncapturable, defeating their efforts to constitute themselves in her capture.[2] To paraphrase Viola, they'd be better off capturing a dream. If Helena of *All's Well* displays a subjectivity exceeding the lack assigned her, Helen of *Troilus and Cressida* displays a lack contradicting the distinction awarded her. Her one scripted scene amply dramatizes her defectiveness. Idly lounging with the besotted Paris, persistently interrupting Pandarus in order to request a randy song, she cuts a frivolous, vacuous figure ill-befitting her status as "theme of honor and renown" (2.2.199).

At the same time, performance could confirm her formidable seductiveness. The director could stage the scene as a virtual fulfillment of the male fantasy embedded in Troilus' longing to "wallow" in Elysian "lily-beds" (3.2.12, 22): presenting Paris and Helen in luxuriant repose, listening to music while nibbling on fruits and nibbling at each other—enacting the specifically oral gratifications that Troilus evokes in his speech, offering an image of the recovered lost plenitude for which he longs.

Helen dispels the fantasy of blissful fusion at the scene's end, however, asserting her difference from the image of compliant sex-object by reaffirming her unpossessability. "[B]y my troth, sweet lord, thou hast a fine forehead," Helen says (3.1.107–108). Editors have been inclined to assume she addresses this line to Pandarus, but she could just as easily say it to Paris. In fact, in the quarto version, the line reads, "by my troth, sweet *lad*"—an appellation better suited to Paris than Pandarus. In that case, Pandarus' response, "you may, you may," could be addressed not to Helen (as in "you may have your joke") but to Paris (as in "you *may* have a fine forehead one day—when Helen cuckolds *you*"). By raising the specter of emasculation, Helen asserts her unmasterable otherness.

In performance, Helen's status as seductive image could also be conveyed through a series of fetishizing tableaux that parallel in visual terms the play's recurrent verbal references to her. These tableaux would establish her status as gaze, the phallus transferred to the visual field. She could be omnipresent throughout the play's action, framed in contemporary images of adulation: trailed by adoring fans and autograph hounds, swarmed upon by paparazzi, lovingly and lavishly attended by a sycophantic entourage. Helen is the gaze as center of attention, focus as well as founder of the spectacle, deriving power not from looking but from being looked at. Her essential persona could be that of the world's preeminent supermodel, the apotheosis of "feminine" glamor and celebrity, serving not simply as specular treat for men but as mirror of misrecognition for women, modeling a fabricated femininity.

Images of Helen's vanity and vapidity could provide ironic counterpoint to the weighty debates, heated passions, and frenzied fighting that she implicitly incites, underscoring her inadequacy as the war's "theme."[3] One moment, in particular, could assist in this gestus: during the Trojan Council scene, when Troilus and Paris praise Helen's peerlessness, she could be seen savoring the lavishments of her worshipful entourage, as they dress and coif her and apply her makeup, confirming her status as constructed icon.

Helen's status as gaze could be established from the outset. The play could open with a startlingly contemporary yet gestically potent image: a video featuring Helen simulating a supermodel's photo shoot, assuming the obligatory sultry and pouty poses to the accompaniment of soft-rock music.[4] As the video ends, the play could move to another gestic moment: Helen, now glamorously clad in a shimmering gold gown, takes the stage accompanied by a smartly dressed older gentleman, basking in the attention of frantically jostling photographers. When her dandified consort, Pandarus, raises his hand, Helen and the photographers freeze into a tableau. Pandarus then speaks the lines of the prologue, literally cuing the arrival of the enemy armies, the "princes orgillous" from Greece (2) on one side of the stage, and the "sons of Troy" (13–19) on the other, each freezing into fiercely combative poses.[5] Having conducted Helen, the subject of the quarrel (8–10), to a position between the two armies, Pandarus then waves his arms, cuing the eruption of war; the two armies rush ferociously to meet each other, all the while yelling and heaving and thrusting. Helen, a poised, glittering jewel, drifts among these hacking behemoths, unobserved and undisturbed, dominating the spectator's field of vision, ratifying her status as gaze. As the fighting progresses, she sits on a golden chair attached to wires and is lifted slowly above the savage combat, serenely observing the slaughter until she ascends out of sight.

## THE WAR AS EMPTY SPECTACLE

Helen's status as phallus/gaze, as signifier of the warrior's disarmament, figures crucially in the play's apocalyptic imagery. Ulysses' speech on violated degree records a fear of female dominance suggestive of Helen's emasculating power: "the bounded waters / Should lift their bosoms higher than the shores, / And make a sop of all this solid globe" (1.3.111–13). Ulysses' striking image expresses dread not of castration but of engulfment, portraying a catastrophic flood as a profusion of breast milk—or at least of a liquid emitted from perilously unbounded "bosoms." The lines manifest fear of losing masculine solidness and becoming infantilized sops for female bodily emissions, of regressing to a state of subjugation by a powerful female force.

Thersites also records the cataclysmic consequences of elevating Helen to the status of phallus, but in terms of a plague of venereal disease rather than a flood of female liquid. Remorselessly trumpeting the theme of "war and lechery," he wishes on both armies the "Neopolitan bone-ache" and the "dry suppeago"—the fitting curse, he suggests, for "those that war for a placket" (2.3.18–19, 74, 19–20). Because the goal of both armies is to possess a whore, their proper fate is to contract venereal disease. The war is contaminated at its source. So too are its warriors, infected by their contact with the corrupt woman who delivers them to ravaging combat. Like Lavatch and Lucio, Thersites circulates the dread of female sexuality that underlies male efforts to claim power and autonomy.

These images of emasculation, engulfment, and infection mark male subjectivity in the play as always already lacking. *Troilus and Cressida* offers a representation of the Trojan War—and of male heroism—that foregrounds its absence.[6] Today's spectator may not know the story of Troilus and Cressida but will almost certainly remember the Trojan War as a great heroic legend. In place of that heroic legend, the play offers a jolting parody, an empty spectacle in which the war not only falls startlingly short of its fabulous model but scarcely qualifies as a war at all. Until its concluding scenes, the play substitutes posturing, vaunting, plotting, and speech-making for dramatized combat. Acting substitutes for action, exhibitionism for productivity.

In short, the play radically destabilizes a masculinity defined by military prowess. It turns a traditional field of "masculine" self-substantiation into a degraded theater of "feminine" self-display. The effort of the play's "lacking" heroes to match their heroic legacies—to actualize imposed myths of themselves—suggests the perils of a purely textual subjectivity. As in Lacan's Symbolic Order, "lacking" would-be subjects become objects of spectacle and attempt to fit themselves to culturally prescribed identities.

One moment that amply illustrates this male specularity comes when Pandarus trains Cressida's look on the returning Trojan warriors: "Hark, they are coming from the field," he tells Cressida, "shall we stand up here and see them as they pass toward Ilium?" (1.2.177–79). Pandarus presents this public processional as an exhibition of male glamor, reading the implements of war—the bloody swords and hacked helmets on display—as signifiers of masculine allure, costumes worn by contestants in a male beauty pageant, with Troilus the clear winner ("Look you how his sword is bloodied, and his helm more hack'd than Hector's" [1.2.232–33]).

The director, of course, must determine the extent to which the processional matches Pandarus' glitzy mediations—the extent to which the warriors consciously make spectacles of themselves.[7] Given the play's persistent deflation of military posturing, however, and its deferral of battle scenes to its denouement, one can certainly make a case for staging the Trojans' entrance as a full-fledged spectacle, with a boisterous throng lauding and ogling a bevy of preening, muscle-bound warriors. John Barton's 1969 RSC production achieved something of this effect, with narcissistically self-aware, glamorously burnished warriors disporting themselves in "minute, coquettish, pleated kilts," costumes that converted rugged "masculine" materials into implements of feminized exhibitionism.[8] The warriors in Barton's production coveted one another's admiring looks, embracing specularity with a "feminine" sensuality and self-consciousness.[9]

Such flagrant exhibitionism confirms the warriors' consignment to a spectacle in which they are preemptively effeminized, displaced to a world of appearances in which they must do what women have been encouraged to do within a phallocentric order: cover their "lack" with seductive display. Their masculinity amounts to a strenuous resistance to emasculation, a culturally mandated charade of power.[10]

Even Achilles, the play's most illustrious figure, is revealed to be kin to Parolles, an avatar of the disreputable braggart soldier, whose valor is derived from display and attribution. Certainly, Achilles does nothing within the world of the play to merit his reputation. Indeed, it is precisely by doing nothing that he hopes to enhance his greatness—a greatness simply posited as fact, a legacy of the lost original. We rarely see him on the battlefield—and, when we do, he disgraces himself with his cowardly ambush of Hector. Like Helen, Achilles is essentially a celebrity, famous for being famous. He proves himself as bogus an exemplar of masculinity as Helen is of femininity, as much the recipient of a mass delusion, as much a figure gilded and exalted by an adoring public gaze. He is, as Thersites puts it, an "idol of idiot-worshippers" (5.1.7).

Nestor affirms Achilles' status as constructed idol when, contemplating Hector's proposed "sportful combat," he asserts that the Greek champion (meaning Achilles)

shall give a scantling
Of good or bad unto the general,
And in such indexes (although small pricks
To their subsequent volumes) there is seen
The baby figure of the giant mass
Of things to come at large. It is suppos'd
He that meets Hector issues from our choice.
And choice (being mutual act of all our souls)
Makes merit her election, and doth boil
(As 'twere from forth us all) a man distill'd
Out of our virtues, who miscarrying,
What heart receives from hence a conquering part
To steel a strong opinion to themselves?
Which entertain'd, limbs are his instruments,
In no less working than are swords and bows
Directive by the limbs.

(1.3.341–56)

The reference to "pricks" underlines Achilles' function as phallic signifier: his small *pricks* (individual feats) are the index of their collective masculinity ("the giant mass of things to come at large").[11] His valor reflects and elicits theirs. The opinion owed him in victory will animate their stricken limbs and enable them to wield their weapons once more—an unmistakable image of restored masculine potency.

Yet the Achilles celebrated here is a mythical figure, a construct from which they wish to construct themselves, the "issue" of their "choice" (born in an act of collective male parthenogenesis) who is also pregnant with their reputation (thus in danger of "miscarrying"). Achilles becomes the repository of their fantasies of ideal masculinity, the mirror in which they misrecognize themselves.[12]

Achilles essentially aims to meld with this seductive image of himself by withdrawing from the war. He achieves the Helen-like status of gaze, drawing the attention of all the warriors and inspiring some, like Ajax, to emulate him (1.3.185–96). He reconstitutes the spectacle by placing himself at its focal point, achieving through his absence the preeminence denied him when he was present. Achilles' withdrawal is an act of exhibitionism, a histrionic disarmament that converts effeminate retreat into masculine self-assertion. He gives up masculine production for feminine seduction, achieving mastery over those who would deny him a power commensurate with his productive prowess. By shying away from his fellow generals and enshrining himself in a seductive image, Achilles engages them in a game of courtship, drawing power from his status as desired object. Like Helen, he subdues them through imagery. He ceases to be a warrior and becomes the sign of one, invincible and indisposable as he could never be in actual battle. The disarmed Achilles represents a veiled phallus, the unpossessable object of the army's desiring look, the absent signifier who fixes them as "lacking."

Achilles' act of disarmament is also a contemptuously mimetic gesture, a way of representing what he perceives to be the Greek generals' fundamental "lack." He carries this scornful mimesis one step further by eliciting Patroclus' mocking caricatures of Nestor and Agamemnon, which function as derogations not simply of the generals themselves but of their "plots, orders, preventions"—their "policy," which, says Ulysses, Achilles calls "cowardice" (1.3.197). Inasmuch as Achilles "esteem[s] no act / But that of hand," he reads the generals' stratagems as signs of effeminacy, as a *lack* of manly action (199–200). Their "wisdom" is "*no member* of the war" (emphasis mine) but mere "bed-work, mappr'y, closet-war" (198, 205), images that connote unmanly consignment to domestic spheres, with a suggestion (particularly in the phrase "bed-work") of degrading prostitution or even of auto-erotic self-stimulation.[13] It is as if the Greek generals, having lost the ennobling text of the heroic Trojan War, try to substitute a text of administrative expertise and find themselves transformed, through Patroclus' contemptuous impersonations, into punctilious cowards and exhibitionists, who offer the show of warriorship rather than the substance. Achilles' tent theater—his conversion of the war into a private spectacle for his entertainment—mockingly mirrors their closet war. Patroclus' caricatures debase the Greek generals by underlining their counterfeit status, their unlikeness to the legendary models they implicitly strive to actualize. Already second-rate replicas, they become, through Patroclus' derisive "pageant," imitations of imitations. In fact, Patroclus' caricatures—which the contemporary director would be well-advised to stage—could be closer to Shakespeare's characters than those characters are to their Homeric originals. Agamemnon, after all, is so unlike his image as "god in high office" that Aeneas, bearing Hector's challenge, fails to recognize him, even when directly addressing him (1.3.215–56).

In Barton's production, Achilles, too, engaged in histrionic mimicry, dressing in drag for much of the play. This decision, which discommoded many reviewers, simply confirms the mimetic dimension of Achilles' disarmament, his interest in mocking the generals by mirroring their effeminacy.[14] Wearing a dress asperses their manhood, not his. As Barton explains, "what we did was show him *playing* at effeminacy and homosexuality in order to mock and outrage the Greek generals."[15] In the production I'm imagining, the director could go even further, costuming Achilles in a gold dress identical to the one Helen wears. Besides underlining Achilles' status as a parallel Helen, the image registers his ironic embrace of "feminine" seductiveness as well as his contempt for the war the generals wage— conveyed through mimicry of its contemptible origin.

Achilles' partner, Patroclus, might seem a better candidate for cross-dressing since he could be considered—and could be played—as a figure of the boy actor. His "pageant" of the generals marks him as an actor, and Achilles and Thersites, despite wildly divergent opinions of him, establish him as a "boy" (5.5.45, 5.1.14). While it seems unlikely that Patroclus could be as young as the boy actors of the Tudor-Stuart stage, he could be conspicuously younger than the other Greek warriors; as he professes "little stomach to the war" (3.3.220), one may infer that Patroclus withdraws not simply out of loyalty to Achilles but out of his own aversion to combat, an unwillingness to embrace war-making as a means of proving his manhood. Patroclus thus enacts the emasculating disarmament that Achilles only affects.

His resistance of the phallic masculinity of soldiership matches his dephallicized status as Achilles' catamite. Thersites reviles him not for homosexuality but for effeminacy, not for loving a man but for being like a woman. Patroclus, according to Thersites, is a "male varlot," a "masculine whore," and therefore a "preposterous discover(y)"—preposterous in a literal sense, it seems, for putting his behind in front and hiding the organ that defines him as male (5.1.15–24).[16] If Achilles' effeminacy fortifies his manhood, Patroclus' effeminacy represents a renegade self-emasculation.

The contemporary director could amplify Patroclus' resemblance to the boy actor and enhance his renegade status by having him cross-dress in two distinct ways. First, Patroclus—rather than Achilles—could don Helen's dress, expanding his repertoire of mocking impersonations. This drag act could represent both a subversive teasing of his own dephallicized status and an ironic theatricalization of *his* role as a parallel Helen—the disarming, desired object whose seductive charms keep Achilles from the war. Patroclus-as-Helen could even engage Achilles in an erotic pantomime virtually identical to the one I've imagined for Helena and Paris (at the beginning of 3.1). In this manner, Achilles and Patroclus theatricalize their own erotic relationship, turning it into a stinging parody of the war's disreputable origin.

Second, Patroclus might engage in an unhistrionic, unparodic trans-vestism aimed not at female impersonation or masochistic self-shaming but at subversive indistinction. Patroclus—or, rather, the actor playing him—could disdain the stereotypical effeminate mannerisms that would render him too easily legible (and dismissable) as a "queen" and thereby resist absorption into a phallocentric economy of meaning.[17] If Patroclus—although boyish, pacifistic, and disposed to cross-dress—conforms in all other respects to expectations of normative masculinity, the resulting incongruity renders him unreadable in phallic terms. His cross-dressing serves not as a straightforward affirmation of effeminacy but as an ironic confounding of it—and therefore as a confounding of the masculinity that effeminacy reifies by inverting. Patroclus could be seen as refusing the gender that his body, mannerisms, and vocalizations evoke, embodying a difference that cannot be readily assimilated to the phallocentric gender system. He becomes an outlaw in gender not because he is effeminate but because he is undefinable. By demonstrating gender's constructedness, Patroclus implicitly discredits his own lover's attempt to concretize an heroic masculinity.

Prying Achilles from his seductive image is precisely the strategy that Ulysses employs. Ulysses counters the Patroclus-Achilles spectacle with a charade of his own, contriving—in collusion with the other Greek generals—to transform Ajax into an imitation Achilles, promoting him as the new Greek champion. In fashioning the doltish Ajax in Achilles' image, Ulysses gives Achilles a taste of the degrading impersonation he so gleefully inflicted on the Greek generals. Like Nestor and Agamemnon, Achilles finds himself replaced by a caricature of himself. Having transformed himself into a seductive image, Achilles finds that the image can be replicated. Cut loose from his myth, Achilles becomes disposable, lacking.

Ulysses deprives Achilles of his status as gaze, the observed of all observers, by urging his comrades to transfer their worshipful looks to Ajax (3.3.38–49). He aims to wrest from Achilles his control of signification, to resituate the spectacle within the arena of war, and thus to place Achilles outside it, where he cannot signify or can signify only as a degraded noncombatant. Instead of mirroring the generals' effeminacy, Achilles' disarmament becomes a signifier of *his* effeminacy—as evidenced by the shifting presentation of his motives for withdrawal. Initially, Ulysses blames inflated pride for Achilles' abstention (1.3.142–45). But, once resolved to decenter Achilles, Ulysses charges him instead with effeminizing desire (3.3.195–215). Patroclus himself confirms the shift by urging Achilles to reclaim his manhood in battle: "a woman impudent and mannish grown / Is not more loath'd than an effeminate man / In time of action" (3.3.217–19).

Having chosen spectacle as his means of self-substantiation, Achilles faces a degradation of self when Ulysses takes over his play.

Ulysses impresses upon Achilles the perils of specularity, the menace of inhabiting a "self" constituted in the look of the other, of inhabiting a world in which the degree whose "vizarding" Ulysses so expansively laments is simply a vizard for purely relational distinctions. Achilles himself affirms:

> The beauty that is borne here in the face
> The bearer knows not, but commends itself
> To others' eyes; nor doth the eye itself,
> That most pure spirit of sense, behold itself,
> Not going from itself; but eye to eye oppos'd,
> Salutes each other with each other's form;
> For speculation turns not to itself
> Till it hath travell'd and is mirror'd there
> Where it may see itself.
>
>                       (3.3.103–11)

The passage yields a peculiarly Lacanian sense of subjectivity. The subject is visible to himself only through the mirror of the other, in whose reflection he substantiates himself. Ulysses goes even further, however, in contending that the other does not merely reflect but "forms" the subject: a man cannot know his "parts," cannot know of what he "consists," until "he behold them formed in th' applause / Where th' are extended" (3.3.115–20). Achilles is what others make of him; he *consists* in their regard. Ulysses impresses on Achilles the necessity of recreating himself in the "rich beholding" of his comrades (3.3.91), rescuing himself from the invisibility to which he has consigned himself by eliciting visible reflections of his worth.

Ulysses' speech confirms what his strategic promotion of Ajax implies: that Achilles is a disposable creature of attribution. Of course, Ulysses' ultimate goal—inducing Achilles to return to battle—presupposes precisely the opposite: his indisposability, his intrinsic worth as a warrior, his manifest *difference* from the oafish Ajax. Certainly there is much comic mettle to be mined in Ajax's ungainly attempts to assume Achilles' image. Still, the play also registers his essential likeness to Achilles. Like Achilles, Ajax reads his heroic image in the idolizing looks of his comrades, assuming the "screen" receptive to their exalted image of him, even if imperfectly. Like Achilles, Ajax is propped up by opinion as the imitation of a lost original. Like Achilles, Ajax draws criticism for his insolence and unsociability (in the very act of taxing Achilles for these faults [2.3.208–11]). Ajax's incompetent mimicry becomes an inadvertent form of mockery. His swaggering, self-absorbed brutishness serves as the distorted mirror of Achilles' masculine vanity. Ajax also carries to parodic, farcical extreme Achilles' attempt to meld with his own image, becoming so transported by his new identity as awesome champion that he loses the self he formerly inhabited and becomes "a very landfish, languageless, a monster," a macho warrior turned womanish, "ruminat[ing] like an hostess that hath no arithmetic but her brain to set down her reckoning" (3.3.263, 252).

When Achilles finally reenters the spectacle of the war, he succeeds only in proving himself shockingly unequal to the misrecognized image of exalted warrior he means to authenticate. Finally engaging Hector in one-on-one combat, he finds himself overmatched, blames his prolonged idleness (5.6.13–20), then returns with his Myrmidons. Catching Hector unarmed and vastly outnumbered, he orders his ambush (5.8). He proceeds to exalt the killing he did not actually carry out: "On Myrmidons, and cry you all amain, / 'Achilles hath the mighty Hector slain!'" (5.8.13–14). His promise to drag Hector's corpse about the battlefield (5.8.21–22) in conformity to Homeric precedent only reinforces his essential unlikeness to the Homeric figure. Achilles' ignoble behavior belies Agamemnon's earlier distinction between "the bold and the coward" (1.3.23) or Nestor's confident claim that "valor's show and valor's worth divide / In storms of fortune" (1.3.46–47). Achilles' cowardly dispatching of Hector not only aligns him with "valor's show" but undermines the ideal of valor itself, discrediting military prowess as a measure of masculinity. Achilles, the male ideal, turns out to be a fraud. Shakespeare's play exposes the lack disavowed by the collective look in which Achilles and Helen "consist." As Thersites suggests, Achilles is the "picture of what [he] seemest" (5.1.6), the semblance of a semblance, unable to transubstantiate the idealized masculine self he represents.

## TROILUS AND CRESSIDA: The Limits of Sexuality

Troilus offers another image of male subjectivity at the margins, beginning the play disarmed, enmeshed in an emasculating passion for Cressida, pronouncing himself unfit for manly combat. In a startling image, Troilus positions himself female in a grotesque act of intercourse, in which Pandarus "pours" into Troilus' bleeding hole ("the open ulcer of my heart") Cressida's imagined body parts ("her eyes, her hair, her cheek, her gait, her voice" [1.1.53–54]). Displacing his mouth to a lower bodily opening, Troilus consumes Cressida's body piecemeal, an eerie instance of both the oral fixation that pervades his expressions of desire and his penchant for fragmenting Cressida. By protesting that Pandarus, with his ecstatic tributes to Cressida, "lay'st in every gash that love hath given me / The knife that made it" (1.1.62–63), Troilus implicitly blames Cressida for the bleeding gashes inflicted on his femininely penetrable body.

If Troilus strikes a masochistic pose, wearing (imagined) bloody wounds as badges of his abject longing, he eschews the masochist's acceptance of emasculation as punishment for desiring a woman placed beyond desire's reach. Nor does he emulate Angelo's retributive scheme of sadistically violating the exalted female for lashing his body with shameful desire. Troilus wishes neither to descend into dephallicized servility nor to resort to vindictive phallic aggression but to step outside the phallic register altogether—to purify sex by reconfiguring it as presexual delectation, an unmediated consuming of maternal sustenance. Deprived of Cressida's nurturance, he regresses into infantile helplessness:[18]

> I am weaker than a woman's tear,
> Tamer than sleep, fonder than ignorance,
> Less valiant than the virgin in the night,
> And skilless as unpractic'd infancy.
>                         (1.1.9–12)

Several scenes later, anticipating Cressida's arrival, Troilus imagines himself on "Stygian banks" awaiting Charon's "waftage" to the watery realms of Elysian lily beds, where he proposes to "wallow" (3.2.8–13). Through this image of static, blissful, watery oblivion, Troilus portrays his desire for Cressida as a wish to return to the womb, to the primordial mother-child dyad. He goes on to express his sexual excitement as a longing for preoedipal bliss:

> I am giddy; expectation whirls me round;
> Th' imaginary relish is so sweet
> That it enchants my sense; what will it be,
> When that the wat'ry palate tastes indeed
> Love's thrice-repured nectar? Death, I fear me,
> Sounding destruction, or some joy too fine,
> Too subtile, potent, tun'd too sharp in sweetness
> For the capacity of my ruder powers.
> I fear it much, and I do fear besides
> That I shall lose distinction in my joys,

As doth a battle, when they charge on heaps
The enemy flying.

(3.2.18–29)

Troilus not only dephallicizes the imagined act of love, presenting it as exclusively oral, but transforms Cressida into an image of the preoedipal maternal body, a transcendent dispenser of heavenly nectar. The desire Troilus exercises in this speech goes through a Lacanian circuit, moving past its ostensible object to an originary, mystified (m)other.[19]

At the same time, Troilus marks the perfect fusion for which he longs as a kind of death, the loss of the "distinct" masculine self that depends upon resisting regression to female domination. Such a regression invites the very chaos of violated degree that Ulysses imagined: losing phallic hardness in a flood of female liquid. Troilus' dread evokes the necessity of hardening the masculine self within the triadic structure of the Symbolic Order, in which female otherness is not exalted but converted, by virtue of phallic law, into a masterable opposition.

Yet Troilus' speech also hints at the confounding limits of phallic sexuality. His fear of finding the exquisite sensations of sexual union unendurable evokes a less abstract dread of losing hardness—specifically, a fear of premature ejaculation. In a later speech, Troilus affirms overtly that the phallic register condemns desire to perpetual frustration, substituting limited acts of discharge for acts of unlimited consumption: "This is the monstruosity in love, lady, that the will is / infinite, and the execution confin'd, that the desire is / boundless, and the act a slave to limit" (3.2.81–83). From Troilus' perspective, every ejaculation is premature. To achieve orgasm is to die, to spend desire rather than to fulfill it, in a confined execution unequal to it, returning from a temporary transcendence to a terrible finitude.[20] Troilus' lament calls to mind Lacan's description of desire as both inexpressible and insatiable, a drive surpassing its object or any act that would express it, a volatile nomadic signifier futilely seeking an anchoring signified. Such narcissistic desire is forced to arrest itself with attempts to possess what is ultimately unpossessable: an other capable of articulating the self.[21]

Implicit in Troilus' lament is an indictment of the female lack so feverishly disavowed in his "giddy" speech. By depicting "the act" as essentially auto-erotic (omitting any reference to its object), he confirms the desired female's negligibility; and by depicting it as unfulfilling, he confirms her inadequacy. He no longer portrays the female body as a transcendent source of unlimited nectar but as a disposable receptacle of his limited discharge.

By enabling the spending of male desire, the desired female destroys the source of her own value, rendering her unworthy of the passion she arrests, confirming her status as flawed substitute for an unrecoverable original.

Troilus' behavior following the tryst seems to confirm Cressida's inadequacy. Affecting a concern for her health, he enforces their separation, sending her back to bed, making clear his determination to leave, despite her pleas for him to stay (4.2.1–20). His eagerness to depart suggests an instinctive recoil from a limited act far removed from imbibing exquisite nectar. Ironically, Troilus seems to enact the very scenario of "distast[ing] what [he] elects" that he decries when protesting the proposed return of Helen: he "turns back" the "silks" he has "soiled," tossing the "remainder viands" into an "unrespective sieve" (2.2.61–71).[22]

This experience of despoliation is precisely the fate that Cressida fears. Her initial strategy of "holding off" derives from the dread of losing the power and value she achieves by denying satisfaction of the desire she elicits. She fears the shift from adored goddess to disposable receptacle:

> Women are angels, wooing:
> Things won are done; joy's soul lies in the doing.
> That she belov'd knows nought that knows not this:
> Men prize the thing ungain'd more that it is.
> That she was never yet that ever knew
> Love got so sweet as when desire did sue.
> Therefore this maxim out of love I teach:
> Achievement is command; ungain'd, beseech.
> (1.2.286–93)

If one must be an object, better to be an unattainable one; better to conceal a reciprocal desire than, by confessing it, leave oneself vulnerable to a disclosure of lack.

Like both Helena and Isabella, Cressida confronts the difficulties of representing herself as a desiring subject within a phallocentric register in which she can function only as an object, a prize to be won or a body to be used, either fetishized (when ungain'd) or found lacking (once achieved). The inescapability of this register within the world of the play forces her to try on a series of culturally available "feminine" guises that fail to capture her complex interiority and condemn her to incoherence and fragmentation, to a succession of self-befuddling performances that summon Kristeva's famous phrase, "that's not it" and "that's still not it."[23]

In her first scene, for instance, Cressida essentially constructs herself as the emasculator of Troilus' imaginings, transferring lack to him as though confirming his bleeding wound. When Pandarus praises Troilus' attributes as "the spice and salt that season a man," Cressida replies, "Ay, a minc'd man, and then to be bak'd with no date in the pie, for then the man's date is out," metaphorically castrating him (1.2.256–57). In an earlier exchange, Cressida also casts doubt on Troilus' phallic sufficiency. Told by Pandarus that Helen loves Troilus, Cressida brazenly returns, "Troilus will stand to the proof, if you'll prove it so" (1.2.129–30).

Cressida's bawdy deflections of Pandarus' lewd solicitings recall Helena's ribald evasions of Parolles. She, too, initially refuses the role of compliant sexual object appointed her, duplicating Helena's portrayal of sexual intercourse as an act of male aggression: "If I cannot ward what I would not have hit, I can watch you for telling how I took the blow—unless it swell past hiding, and then it's past watching" (1.2.267–70). Anticipating Helena's image of "blown-up" women, Cressida portrays pregnancy as the swelling wound that results from the "blow" that a woman sustains during intercourse.

As with Helena, Cressida's wisecracking bawdry covertly vents a sexual avidity that she must otherwise evade and suppress. Once Pandarus departs, she executes a *volte-face* even more startling than Helena's, shifting from jaded anti-romantic to distressed lover. She not only confesses her desire for Troilus but betrays a likeness to him by wistfully longing for a sexual satisfaction outside the phallic register: "that she was never yet that ever knew / Love got so sweet as when desire did sue." In suggesting that a woman cannot "get" the "love" promised her by a desiring male, Cressida expresses a longing for *jouissance*—or at least for satisfaction on her own terms, beyond mere fulfillment of male desire.[24]

Confined to the phallocentric economy of lack and fetish, however, Cressida's sexuality must become defensive, negative, and secretive. The bodily space of desire's fulfillment she calls "what I would *not* have hit" and the "thing *ungain'd*" (emphasis mine). Her remark that she depends upon "secrecy, to defend mine honesty," though partly jocular, nevertheless evokes a private realm of forbidden desire whose disclosure would prove her unchaste (1.2.261–62). Similarly, when she taxes Troilus, after their tryst, "you men will never tarry," she sounds like a veteran of clandestine affairs (4.2.16), or at least the owner of a sexuality more developed than she explicitly divulges.

As the scene ends, Cressida seems determined to disavow her sexuality. She moves in the direction opposite of Helena—toward "feminine" helplessness instead of away from it—resolving to suppress desire instead of fulfill it. When Cressida does opt for fulfillment, her decision is not dramatized. If Helena expresses her sexual intentions cryptically and evasively, Cressida does not express hers at all. Pandarus expresses them for her, in his characteristically puerile voice. While on a mission to persuade Paris to invent an excuse for Troilus' absence from supper—from which one may *infer* Cressida's assent to an assignation—Pandarus tells Helen, "My niece is horribly in love with a thing that you have" (3.1.97–98), crudely reducing Cressida's sexual desire to a craving for Troilus' sexual organ, effectively imprisoning her in the phallic realm.

## SEDUCTION

In agreeing to meet Troilus for a tryst, Cressida implicitly overcomes her dread of despoliation and reaches for a meaningful intimate relation. Troilus, however, proves himself less interested in relation than in seduction. Beset by consciousness of what Baudrillard calls the "quick, banal end" of sex, Troilus turns to the unending drama of seduction, in which the seducer continually challenges his victim to go to ever greater lengths to prove her limitless love, to prove herself completely seduced.[25] Troilus seeks the sustenance of unequivocal conquest rather than the nurturance of a preoedipal merger unrecoverable in genital sex. His erotic goal is to seduce Cressida into assuming the role of seductress in order to play out the scenario of *his* seduction—thus substantiating his preferred self-image as doomed transcendent lover, betrayed by Cressida's characteristically female incapacity to reciprocate his undying devotion. Reifying his myth as ontologically true requires subduing Cressida to her inherited role as congenitally false.[26]

Troilus is not a self-conscious seducer. He does not so much artfully manipulate a world of appearances as permanently reside there, unable to distinguish himself from his own seductive myth. He therefore dodges the specter of lack that disrupts Achilles' attempt to substantiate his image, the consciousness of inhabiting a spectacle whose integrity is impeached from the outset by the absent female who founds it. Troilus resists such emasculation by gaining access—in a private realm of desire—to a surrogate Helen and contriving to discover her lack in order to fortify his fragile masculinity. Achilles, confined to a world of men, cannot be the gaze. Troilus, engaged in a game of seduction with a single woman, can be.

Troilus thus declares himself "truth's authentic author," not simply the standard but the origin of truth (3.2.181). To be the origin of truth in a world of appearances is to be the origin of fiction, to take on the status of the veiled phallus, regulating the culturally encoded signs that construct "truth" in the symbolic srder. The "truth" that Troilus authors is the fiction of his own truth, the fiction of the substantiality of the spectacle he means to regulate, of the story of which he is a part. Troilus becomes not simply a character in an inherited tale but the custodian of its legacy, the guarantor of its fixity. The traditional story of Troilus and Cressida becomes *his* play, with Cressida assigned the reductive role of seductress. His impenetrable superficiality defeats her depth; his unawareness of the constructedness of the reality he inhabits condemns her to it. His insistence on the fiction of his essence converts her potentially adaptive, decentered core self into an utterly textualized cipher.

Cressida's subjectivity is thus constricted by a gender ordinance disguised as a textual legacy. To seduce Troilus, to love him and leave him, is to fulfill the destiny appointed her by literary tradition. Yet this literary tradition is complicit with a patriarchal script that portrays female seduction as the original sin and makes all women potential seductresses. The notorious identity mapped onto Cressida's body is merely a patriarchal "destin'd livery," a "lacking" representational overlay recording the absence of a coherent self. Cressida is ultimately unidentical to her infamous model.[27] Troilus endeavors to erase the distinction.

Pandarus assists in this erasure, enabling Troilus to seduce Cressida into assuming a seductive image so that she may be misrecognized as a vessel of transcendent sex. Until Pandarus brings them together, the play offers no evidence of direct contact between them. At first their attraction is based entirely on his mediation of their desiring looks. Pandarus carries out what Baudrillard identifies as the covert operation of all seduction: "the transubstantiation of sex into signs."[28] He channels a reciprocal attraction of bodies into a symbolic register, personifying the signifying media that define desire and regulate its circulation, that ultimately seek to arrest its erratic trajectories by anchoring it to a misrecognized object of satisfaction. Pandarus projects the culturally available imagery through which Troilus and Cressida read each other's bodies. They "consist" in each other's culturally mediated looks.

"I cannot come to Cressid but by Pandar," Troilus declares (1.1.95). Troilus at first comes to Cressida through the seductive image that Pandarus projects to her, using the peerless Hector as screen; in asserting at length that Troilus surpasses Hector in masculine allure (as evidenced by his more lavishly hacked helmet [1.2.60–91]), Pandarus positions Troilus as epitome of Trojan manhood.[29] Yet the constructedness of this image becomes clear when Cressida, parrying Pandarus' extravagant tributes, mischievously inquires, upon Troilus' entrance, "what sneaking fellow comes yonder?" And Pandarus, not immediately recognizing him, replies, "Where? Yonder? That's Deiphobus—'Tis Troilus!" (1.2.226–29).

Pandarus also offers *himself* as an image of Troilus, serving as surrogate wooer as well as saucy emissary. Declares Cressida, "words, vows, gifts, tears, and love's full sacrifice, / He offers in another's enterprise" (1.2.282–83). Yet Pandarus does not simply mirror Troilus to Cressida; he also mirrors Cressida—or an image of her as desirous and seducible—to herself, modeling the transports of feminine infatuation, demonstrating the swooning adoration to which his projected image of Troilus ought to move her:

> Brave Troilus, the prince of chivalry! . . . O brave
> Troilus! Look well upon him, niece. Look you how his
> sword is bloodied, and his helm more hack'd than
> Hector's, and how he looks, and how he goes. O
> admirable youth!
>
> (1.2.228–35)

Pandarus also enacts for her emulation the ecstasy of eliciting Troilus' desire, of "consisting" in his look: "I could live and die in the eyes of Troilus!" he exclaims (1.2.246–47), hoping to move her to a comparable bondage.

Pandarus must not only help seduce Cressida but fashion her as seductive in order to gratify Troilus' wish to be seduced. By comparing Cressida favorably to Helen (1.1.41–43, 73–75), he posits the ultimate figure of seductive femininity as the screen upon which to project Cressida's alluring image. Accordingly, in performance, when Pandarus begins to praise Cressida's beauty, a huge banner bearing her likeness could be unfurled. Or her picture could be *projected* as a backdrop for this scene and all others focusing on the two lovers, corroborating Pandarus' role as projector of seductive imagery.[30] This picture could present a Cressida constructed in Helen's image, assuming one of the alluring poses that Helen struck in the preshow video, positioning herself as a culturally mediated male fantasy.

Whenever Cressida appears, she must compete with this looming, counterfeit, dream-girl image, which inevitably overwhelms and diminishes her, making evident her inability to "measure up." It provides a potent gestus for Cressida's "doubleness." From the outset, the spectator receives a visual cue that she is unidentical to her image, that "this is and is not Cressida." The weight of Troilus' expectations bear down on her—as does the weight of her notorious identity. For contemporary audiences unfamiliar with the Troilus-and-Cressida tale, this larger-than-life picture of Cressida as seductress conveys her burdensome, inherited image as not only desirable but (due to her resemblance to Helen) deceitful. Like Helena in *All's Well*, Cressida is continually accompanied by an imposed image of herself but, unlike Helena, she cannot assimilate it. To become the image is to collude in her own erasure, to accept the role of seductress that Troilus—and her notorious identity—appoint her.

When Cressida first meets Troilus for the tryst, she seems prepared to become a seductress, to embrace a new "feminine" guise as impersonal, compliant sexual object. She enters wearing a veil, and says nothing until inviting Troilus to enter her bedchamber. Her position is strangely analogous to that of Helena and Mariana during their bed-tricks: she veils herself in "shadow and silence" and enables the fulfillment of a male sexual fantasy, taking care not to contradict Troilus' image of her, not to let him know that she is *other.* In that sense, her position also is analogous to that of Diana and Isabella: she is both the woman whose misrecognized image drives the fantasy and the woman who lends her body to its enactment.

Her veil reflects her liminal status as a spectre summoned from the limbo of Troilus' fantasies, a living "picture" (as Pandarus calls her [3.2.47]) which, once unveiled, must be confirmed as real. The kiss Troilus gives her confirms Cressida's tangibility, the availability of her heretofore unavailable body. The kiss becomes the equivalent of Leontes' exclamation, "O, she's warm" when confirming the reality of the liminal Hermione in *The Winter's Tale.* When her veil is removed, Cressida returns Troilus' look; she ceases to be an unapproachable picture and becomes a possessable mirror, reflecting to Troilus his preferred self-image as potent lover.

However, having led Troilus to the threshold of fulfilled fantasy ("O, Cressid, how often have I wish'd me thus!" he exclaims when she invites him in [3.2.61]), Cressida suddenly balks, unable to maintain her pose as serviceable object. "That's not it," she seems to say. She attempts to represent herself as *other* than his image of mystified (m)other, a subject in her own right, torturously desirous of Troilus but unable to meld with his misrecognition. "I have a kind of self resides with you," she tells Troilus, "But an unkind self, that itself will leave / To be another's fool" (3.2.148–50). The "kind of self" is a self that is kind to Troilus (like him, formed in his image), but unkind to itself (not like itself, not itself).[31]

Cressida fears the loss of distinction that will attend wholesale surrender to the role of seductress. "To seduce," says Baudrillard, "is to die as reality and reconstitute oneself as illusion. It is to be taken in by one's own illusion and move in an enchanted world."[32] Cressida seems to have one foot in this enchanted world and one foot out, essentially remaining liminal. She cannot completely die to herself, cannot transform herself into the "Cressida" of Troilus' fantasy. So she remains perpetually divided, forever watching herself, aware that she competes with Troilus' image of her, which, in the performance I imagine, watches *her.*

Cressida's difficulty in representing herself becomes clear when she proceeds to destabilize the core self she has just struggled to establish—the self to which the self she fashions for Troilus is unkind. First she discredits her own testimonial to its existence: "where is my wit? I know not what I speak" (3.2.151). Cressida disjoins the speaking self and the core self, portraying the former as an inadequate substitute for the latter, a would-be kind self that is also unkind. By implication, she portrays the core self as unrepresentable and the speaking self as incoherent, as her strangulated, contradictory outbursts seem to confirm. Next, as though saying "that's still not it," she suggests that the speaking self may not be ineptly mimetic but cunningly performative: "Perchance, my lord, I show more craft than love, / And fell so roundly to a large confession, / To angle for your thoughts" (3.2.153–55). Cressida's statement does not so much deny her undeniable passion as dispute the coherence of her self-presentation by underlining its presentationality. Cressida asserts her illegibility as a subject, her essential alienness—to herself as well as to Troilus.

Cressida also reiterates her need for a distinct satisfaction, countering Troilus' implicit indictment of female lack with a protest against male inadequacy—the true source of "monstruosity" in love.

> They say all lovers swear more performance than they are
> able, and yet reserve an ability that they never
> perform; vowing more than the perfection of ten, and
> discharging less than the tenth part of one. They that
> have the voice of lions and the act of hares, are they
> not monsters?
>
> (3.2.84–89)

Cressida portrays herself as the victim of frustrated desire, the unlucky recipient of limited male "discharge," implicitly casting doubt on Troilus' capacity to satisfy *her.* She once more evokes the impossibility of *jouissance* within a phallocentric economy of desire.

Pandarus corroborates Cressida's status as a sexual subject with daunting testimonials to her insatiable desire. When Troilus concludes his kiss with Cressida by exclaiming, "you have bereft me of all words, lady," Pandarus replies, "Words pay no debts, give her deeds; but she'll bereave you o' th' deeds too, if she call your activity into question" (3.2.55–57). Pandarus not only exhorts Troilus to make love to Cressida ("give her deeds") but also warns that she may wear him out ("bereave you o' th' deeds") and still remain unsatisfied ("call your activity into question").

Yet Cressida's attempt to assert herself as desiring subject only increases her disposability as an object. In confessing desire for Troilus, she reveals herself to be even more "open" to him and thus more vulnerable to the disclosure of lack, renewing her fear of disempowerment and devaluation. "If I confess much," she protests to Troilus, "you will play the tyrant" (3.2.119). Having "achiev'd," he will "command." Consenting to have sex with Troilus is one thing, but in confessing desire for him she reveals herself to be seduced.

Moreover, Pandarus, once bringing the lovers together, becomes more distinctly the medium of a "male gaze," defeating Cressida's efforts to be anything other than a sex-object. He frames the entire tryst as a kind of pornographic peepshow, the object of which is removing the veil of mystery from Cressida's fetishized body. He begins by literally unveiling her to Troilus' desiring look and proceeds (through his eager preparation of the trysting place, his voyeuristic savoring of their kisses and endearments, and his ribald, incontinent punning) to undress both lovers metaphorically and turn their soaring, fretful rhetoric into so much foreplay. When visiting them afterward, he verbally "screens" a flashback of the tryst that focuses specifically on Cressida's deflowering. First he positions Cressida as a sexual performer, naughtily inquiring, "how go maidenheads?" as though addressing a prostitute (4.2.22). Next, he conjures the act itself: when Cressida protests, "you bring me to do—and then you flout me too," he obscenely ripostes, "to do what, to do what, let her say what!" (26–27) Finally, he executes the equivalent of pornography's anatomical zoom, zeroing in on Cressida's genital zone: "has't not slept tonight? Would he not, a naughty man, let *it* sleep?" (32–33, emphasis mine).

Pandarus' "close-up" corroborates the demystifying consequences of Troilus' conquest of Cressida—the conversion of her once exalted body into a site of unimpeded access (Troilus "would not let it sleep"). Troilus himself seems to confirm this devaluation when, emitting a Pandarus-like snicker, he willfully misconstrues Cressida's summons to her chamber—provoked by her fear of detection—as a sexual come-on, as though joining in Pandarus' depreciation of her as a common gamester (4.2.35–40). Troilus drops the delirious rapture of the ardent lover for the coarse familiarity of the jaded customer.

## THE LIMITS OF SUBJECTIVITY

Cressida's quest for subjectivity is derailed by her seduction into disclosing lack—and not simply in the sexual realm. Even before the tryst, Troilus anticipates a far more cataclysmic discovery of her inadequacy, asking for a satisfaction more rarefied and permanent than sex could ever provide. The satisfaction he requires is evidence of her indisputable satisfaction by him— an absolute fidelity confirming his masculine adequacy, retracting her doubts about his sexual performance. Having extracted from Cressida a confession of desire, Troilus reaches for a vow of unequivocal devotion capable of seducing him into the expectation of constancy:

> O, that I thought it could be in a woman—
> As, if it can, I will presume in you—
> To feed for aye her lamp and flames of love,
> To keep her constancy in plight and youth,
> Outliving beauties outward, with a mind
> That doth renew swifter than the blood decays!
> Or that persuasion could but thus convince me
> That my integrity and truth to you
> Might be affronted with the match and weight
> Of such a winnowed purity in love!
> How were I then uplifted! but alas,
> I am as true as truth's simplicity,
> And simpler than the infancy of truth.
>                    (3.2.158–70)

Troilus here posits female *jouissance* as the measure of male sufficiency ("how were I then uplifted!"). As Stanley Cavell puts it, the gift of female *jouissance*—"something more," as Lacan calls it[33]—represents the gift of the world to a male subject beset by the withdrawal from the world of a transcendental signifier: "[I]s she satisfied, and is her satisfaction directed to me? There is no satisfaction . . . apart from a favorable conclusion here."[34] The desired woman becomes a possessable gaze, whose reciprocal look substantiates the male subject's cherished self-image. Troilus needs Cressida to be constant not only to him but to his preferred image of her as an image of himself. He wishes her to be constantly possessable, enabling a symbolic colonizing of difference that founds his own subjectivity.

Cressida seems prepared to satisfy Troilus' expectations, as though seduced into embracing the new "feminine" guise of faithful beloved. Told of her exile to the Greek camp, she affirms her satisfaction by Troilus in the most extravagant terms. She dispels the qualms that shadowed her previous professions of love. "My love admits no qualifying dross," she tells Pandarus, "no more my grief, in such a precious loss" (4.2.9–10). Twice she asserts her determination to defy her banishment (4.2.94, 109). Like Helena, she insists that she has "forgot" her father. "I know no touch of consanguinity; / No kin, no love, no blood, no soul so near me / As the sweet Troilus" (4.2.96–99). In making Troilus her only kin—her only *kind*—she implies that the self that is kind to Troilus is kind to its kind and therefore cannot be, as she had previously asserted, unkind to itself. Like Helena, she locates her own subjectivity in her beloved's desire. She reconceives herself in his image, offering Troilus precisely the sort of prodigious fidelity he had solicited, locating love in a realm beyond the bodily:

> Time, force, and death,
> Do to this body what extremes you can;
> But the strong base and building of my love
> Is as the very centre of the earth.
> (4.2.101–104)

Cressida not only pledges a love "outliving beauties outward" but proposes to mar those outward beauties, to "tear my bright hair and scratch my praised cheeks" (4.2.107)—a gesture not only of grief but of fanatical devotion.

Cressida's hyperbolic pledges of constancy affirm her likeness not only to Troilus' preferred image of her but to Troilus himself. She appears to solve the problem of representing herself by imitating him. However, because Troilus is unassimilable to his notorious identity—too readily reconciled to estrangement to qualify as unwaveringly devoted—Cressida could be said to imitate an imitation. She tries to transcend the world of appearances by mirroring the appearance of Troilus' inordinate adoration, involuntarily discrediting her own vows of fidelity by speaking them in his voice. Even at her most strenuously sincere, Cressida cannot escape displacement into lacking representation.

Having seduced Cressida into directly mirroring his chosen self-image, Troilus raises the stakes yet again, challenging her to accept her banishment and still remain constant, to represent her satisfaction not only nonsexually but nonrelationally—to transfer it from their covert, dyadic netherworld to the light of the Symbolic Order. Her satisfaction must be *represented* by becoming demonstrable as a choice of him over others—specifically, over the handsome Greek warriors whose seductive wiles he explicitly fears (4.4.76–91). The question, "is she satisfied, and is her satisfaction directed to me?" implies that it could be directed to someone else. Cressida must convince Troilus that he alone suffices.

Troilus surrenders her to the world of men governed by the Law of the Father, in which women function as exchangeable commodities in the marketplace of masculine self-affirmation. If Cressida stays true to Troilus, if she disdains the inevitable advances of the comely Greek warriors to whom he unfavorably compares himself, then she projects her satisfaction by him into the very sphere of male endeavor in which he must substantiate himself. Cressida's preference for Troilus lends him the mirror of the rejected Greeks in which to read his own validated manhood.[35]

In addition, Cressida's banishment saves Troilus from a sustained intimate relationship with her, from a sustained confrontation with sexual difference. Having subdued difference by seducing her into emulating him, he aims to subdue sexuality by fashioning her as his own celibate votary, conferring upon her a retroactive purity that lends her a second try at dispensing maternal nurturance—this time to his psyche rather than his body.

Yet Troilus, wedded to his inherited tale of female treachery, betrays his expectation that she will fail him—that she *must* fail him. His pleas for constancy inevitably disclose a foreboding of her failure. Requesting her reciprocal purity, he exclaims, "O that I thought it could be in a woman— / As, *if* it can, I will *presume* in you . . . but alas" (emphasis mine). Troilus strongly implies that women are incapable of the constancy he requires and, when bidding Cressida farewell, proceeds to make clear his distrust of her, assaulting her with incessant admonitions to fidelity as though expecting her to betray him—as though expecting her to prove herself just like a woman.

"O heavens, you love me not!" she concludes (4.4.82). Cressida must betray him because that's what a seductress (that's what a woman) does. As Cressida, as Woman, she must fail to satisfy and fail to be satisfied, dispelling the image of transcendent nurturer narcissistically projected onto her. Cressida's displacement to the Greek camp enables the betrayal Troilus requires in order to confirm the insufficiency of the female object of desire, to fulfill the scenario of his own seduction, a scenario subsumed by the myth of Troilus and Cressida, itself subsumed by the myth of female inconstancy.

Cressida's imprisonment in the myth is especially evident in the scene in which she and Troilus exchange vows by citing their notorious identities. Put on the defensive by Troilus' coercive mistrust, Cressida pledges her devotion in terms that evoke the very role of seductress she wishes to disclaim: "If I be false . . . let memory upbraid my falsehood. . . . When th' have said 'as false / As' . . . let them say . . . 'As false as Cressid'" (3.2.184, 191–92, 196). Cressida tries to protest her faithfulness; what one hears instead are invocations of unfaithfulness. At least Pandarus seems only to hear them, negating Cressida's oath by translating her "if" into a "when": "[L]et all constant men be Troiluses, all false women Cressids," he declares (3.2.202–203). Yet Cressida had stipulated that false women could be called Cressids only if she herself proved false. Pandarus simply assumes that she will, or so his "conclusion" implies. He turns her protestation of fidelity into a portent of infidelity. Cressida is here overburdened by textuality: the received text of Troilus and Cressida, the patriarchal text of female wantonness, the oedipal text that dramatizes the subduing of female difference. Having to cite her own legendary inconstancy while pledging her constancy illustrates the inescapability of subjugating gender myths—imaged in performance by the looming picture of Cressida-as-Helen, Cressida-as-seductress.

## FEMINIST GESTUS

The feminist gestus I have in mind would underline, rather than mitigate, the play's fragmenting of Cressida, presenting her subjectivity as a masquerade, a sequence of adaptations to imposed images of femininity. As Cressida strikes a different attitude in virtually every scene in which she appears, she could also sport a different look in virtually every scene—which would, in turn, always be referable to the omnipresent, projected fantasy image, at times startlingly convergent, at others wildly divergent. In the opening scene, for instance, Cressida ought to look distinctly different from the projected image—just recognizable enough to accentuate the discrepancy.

When she first meets Troilus, by contrast, she could look virtually identical to it, underlining her self-presentation in the scene as a desperate glamorous make-over, an effort to refashion herself in Helen's image. If she enters the scene not only veiled and silent but clad in a dress identical to Helen's, she could even, at first, be mistaken for her. Her attempt to animate the picture only measures her distance and her difference from it. Her erratic behavior in the scene with Troilus—which could be rendered visually as movements toward and away from him—conveys her moments of conformity to and deviation from this reductive fantasy image.

In her farewell scene with Troilus (4.4), Cressida could once more look distinctly different, dropping her sex-kitten guise while not entirely disdaining seductive display, in keeping with her curious position: feverishly professing her love in a manner sufficiently close to Troilus' histrionics as to seem emulative and performative—another version of an essentially reactive femininity.

Cressida's kissing game with the Greek generals (4.5)—which has seemed to some critics a violation of the character's integrity, the point at which her psychological coherence is sacrificed to her notorious identity[36]—may instead be read as yet another performance, the adopting of a new "feminine" persona suitable to the circumstances. Having sampled the roles of caustic anti-romantic, forlorn inamorata, conflicted dream girl, and would-be transcendent lover, she now takes the part of calculating sex object.[37] The feminist gestus turns Cressida's fragmentation into an advantage, into the very basis for her characterization.

In this scene, then, Cressida dons an overtly provocative costume and proceeds, through her strategic exhibitionism, to control this potentially threatening situation. She implicitly reenacts her dictum that "achievement is command, ungain'd beseech," deriving power from her exploitation of male desire—the only power available to her. She gives Ulysses a taste of that power, demanding that he beseech her for a kiss: "why, beg then." Although he declines, asserting that he will claim a kiss from her "when Helen is a maid" again (i.e., "never"), Cressida still effectively humiliates him, linking him with the emasculated Menelaus as the only unkissed Greek generals (4.5.48–52).

Upon her exit, Ulysses denounces her "speechless dialect":

> Fie, fie upon her!
> There's language in her eye, her cheek, her lip,
> Nay, her foot speaks; her wanton spirits look out
> At every joint and motive of her body.
> O, these encounterers, so glib of tongue,
> That give accosting welcome ere it comes,[38]
> And wide unclasp the tables of their thoughts
> To every ticklish reader! set them down
> For sluttish spoils of opportunity,
> And daughters of the game.
>                               (4.5.54–63)

This is and is not Cressida. In the scene I envision, Cressida does indeed seductively display her physical charms, does indeed "give accosting welcome ere it comes," does indeed make a spectacle of herself. Her exhibitionism so provokes Ulysses because it fixes him as lacking; she is the object of his desiring look (consumable, as she was for Troilus, in parts) who becomes a representative of the gaze. At the same time, the audience is positioned to view Cressida's "wantonness" as performative, an adaptation to the Greek generals' image of seductive femininity. She once more consents to inhabit a misrecognition, to collude in male self-deception, to seduce. Ulysses' speech testifies to the success of Cressida's seduction, her mastery of the world of appearances that constitute "reality" within this heavily textualized playworld.

Some recent productions, sympathetic to Cressida, have taken a different tack with this scene, essentially demonstrating that the lascivious "encounterer" of Ulysses' censure is emphatically *not* Cressida—or, to the extent that she is, she is forced to be. Two productions, in particular, have treated the scene as a kind of gang-rape in order to acquit Cressida of any lascivious intentions. In Libby Appel's 1984 production for the Utah Shakespeare Festival, Cressida became a "hapless victim" who was "literally thrown from one Greek hero to another."[39] In Howard Davies's 1985 RSC production, Cressida was subjected to "brutally violent kisses" that shocked and appalled her; she then proceeded to turn the tables on the Greek generals, however, "tartly" demanding that Ulysses beg for his kiss and "snapping her fingers to indicate that he should kneel."[40]

I am sympathetic to this treatment of the scene, which, like Angelo's near-rape of Isabella, aims to make explicable and sympathetic an action that might otherwise be alienating and incomprehensible. Both approaches affirm continuity between the Cressida who consorts with the Greek generals and the one who pledges her devotion to Troilus. They also depict a vulnerability to male brutality that casts Cressida's later behavior with Diomedes in a less incriminating light.[41]

Still, presenting a fragmented Cressida offers an even more promising means of dramatizing her plight, accenting the discontinuity between the exhibitionist of this scene and the plaintive exile of the previous one. Seen in isolation, a flirtatious, body-flaunting Cressida may appear to be a "daughter of the game"; seen in the context of successive adaptations to male-enforced images, she becomes an embodiment of a female subjectivity vexed and constricted by the oedipal plot. Cressida is unidentical to any self she assumes or constructs, including that of her notorious identity. The "kind" self that performs the version of femininity circumstantially required must forever be unkind to itself. Cressida not only cannot be "true" to Troilus, she cannot be true to herself. She cannot be constant when her essential difference from him—and from the other men who "encounter" her—must be converted to varieties of mastered opposition. Her fate exposes the limits of Baudrillard's celebration of the female's seductive power. To control the world of appearances is to be forever confined to it, without the possibility of achieving depth, coherence, or meaningful relation.

Cressida's "infinite variety"—in particular, her manipulation of costuming—offers an instance of Irigarayan mimicry, demonstrating the theatricality of "femininity." This mimicry takes part in a feminist gestus by destabilizing the play's mimetic structure, forcing the audience to ask, "Who is Cressida?" She functions as a site of proliferating signifiers, expressive of yet excessive to any discernible signified, thus dislocating the phallocentric economy of meaning that constructs her. If Helena's subjectivity seems excessive to the feminine role she chooses to play, Cressida's feminine mimicry seems excessive to the subjectivity she wishes to forge.

The danger, of course, is that a Cressida who constitutes herself in wildly divergent, discontinuous looks may so recede as a character as to seem, in performance, an impenetrable, unengaging cipher, unable to interest the audience in the *drama* of her fragmentation, her failed attempt to forge a coherent subjectivity.[42] She must have an accessible core of provisional selfhood in order for her discontinuities to signify dramatically—a core perhaps not easily recognized if Cressida looks and even acts differently in every scene in which she appears.

One tactic that could help, while adding to the gestus of masquerade, would be for Cressida to be greeted after each of her exits by Helen, standing next to an imposing clothes rack. Helen would then pull Cressida's next outfit off the rack, display it briefly, and hand it over to her. (She might once or twice actually hold it up to Cressida and nod approvingly.) This business could help establish Cressida's core self by dissociating her from whatever specific masquerade she concocts, whatever accoutrement of "femininity" she employs. (It might be effective if Cressida were to put on each outfit in view of the audience, provided such business does not steal undue focus or stir undue prurient interest.) Helen's dispensing of costumes has rich gestic potential, transforming the familiar act of shopping for clothes into an image of shopping for an identity, as the utterly constructed Helen tries to find Cressida the correct image with which to meld.

Ultimately, the actress must provide the "strong base and building" of the character, not simply through her irrefutable embodiedness but through an imaginatively sympathetic creation of interiority. The actress must internally unify an externally fragmented character; she must achieve psychological coherence in order to be gestically legible. The audience may not be able to define the self that Cressida conjures, but if they discern its embattled, fitful manifestations, they may be drawn into the drama even as her discontinuities distance them. By giving Cressida a "spine," the actress exacerbates rather than mitigates her puzzling variability, making it an attribute of a beleaguered subject-in-process rather than that of a confounding blank.[43]

Yet another Cressida emerges in her scene with Diomedes, one unidentical to the figure of traitress that Troilus constructs. Once more she struggles to reconcile her complex interiority to an image of a male-constructed seductive female. Once more she destabilizes the role she is destined to play, vacillating between complying with Diomedes' demands—thereby confirming her notorious identity—and honoring her vows to Troilus.

The performative basis of her new persona is made evident by the presence of spectators: her flirtation with Diomedes is framed as spectacle by the spectatorship of Troilus, Ulysses, and Thersites—a collective male look predisposed to read the flirtation as unambiguous betrayal. The scene's presenter, Ulysses, essentially repeats his earlier characterization of Cressida as "daughter of the game" by seconding Troilus' imputation of "familiarity" to her: "She will sing any man at first sight" (5.2.9).

Troilus' true fellow voyeur and secret sharer is not Ulysses, however, but Thersites. Like Lavatch and Lucio, he functions (in this scene at least) as an unlikely alter ego to the play's central male figure, articulating the unpresentable sexual subtext of the hero's crisis. His own overt voyeurism—the titillation he derives from the spectacle of Cressida's ungainly coquetry—literalizes the metaphoric language of sexual arousal encoded in Ulysses' remonstrances to Troilus' bodily convulsions ("you are mov'd . . . you shake . . . come, come" [5.2.36, 49, 51]). This parallelism could be underlined in performance by positioning the two as mirror-images, partners in voyeurism, even if unseen to each other. Thersites' leering mediations turn Troilus' spasms of passion into harrowing parodies of the dizzying rapture that he displayed in his meeting with Cressida.

Thersites articulates Troilus' darkest thoughts, contemptuously identifying Cressida as a cunning whore from the outset: "[A]ny man may sing her if he can take her cliff" (5.2.10–11). He construes her retrieval of the love-token and dismissal of Diomedes ("visit me no more") as mere tactics for heightening his desire: "[N]ow she sharpens. Well said, whetstone" (5.2.74–75). If Thersites reads Cressida's acts of resistance as seductive gamesmanship, Troilus simply ignores them, seizing instead on her expressions of encouragement to Diomedes (5.2.35, 45–46, 52, 67). As such, they both misrecognize Cressida and misrepresent the scene, substituting a simplified, degraded version of what takes place—as performance could make clear.[44]

The first part of the scene consists of Cressida's trying to wriggle free from her agreement to have sex with Diomedes. "Tempt me no more to folly," she exclaims, later adding, "do not hold me to mine oath" (5.2.18, 26). When her (whispered) attempt to placate him fails, she promises compliance and fetches a token in order to allay his doubts. The second part consists of Cressida's vigorously renewing her resistances, shamed by the token into remembering her promised fidelity to Troilus. She engages in a virtual tug-of-war with Diomedes over the sleeve and, having lost, negates his victory: "I will not keep my word," she asserts (5.2. 98). When Diomedes threatens never to see her again, she again affirms her willingness to have a tryst, but without much enthusiasm: "Ay, come—O Jove!—do come.—I shall be plagu'd" (5.2.105). Much of what Cressida does is equivocal, even contradictory, and much of what she says is inaccessible. On two occasions, she whispers something into Diomedes' ear (5.2.7–11, 34–43); on another, her exchanges with Diomedes are inaudible—or so they would have to be, as they are not specified in the script (5.2.49–58).

This is, and is not, the scene of Cressida's betrayal. Certainly, she does not make love to Diomedes here in any sense of the phrase. She strokes his cheek at one point (so, at least, Troilus says [5.2.52]), offers him a few endearments (or at least calls him "sweet" on three occasions [5.2.7, 18]), and eventually promises to honor her original promise to sleep with him. But the play does not dramatize or even substantiate the fulfillment of that promise, and therefore does not dramatize or substantiate her betrayal. When Diomedes asks, "What, shall I come? the hour?" Cressida replies that he should come, but she conspicuously declines to specify the hour (5.2.103–104). The betrayal is deferred to an altogether uncertain future. Perhaps when they next meet she will once again stall and equivocate; perhaps she will put Diomedes off indefinitely, forever vacillating between her attraction to him and her sworn fidelity to Troilus. Perhaps she will persevere in constancy while awaiting one of the visitations that Troilus promised her (4.4.66–67, 72–74) or, failing that, simply await the end of the war.

Of course, none of these scenarios squares with Cressida's notorious identity. But, one may well ask, how much authority should that identity be granted, particularly when Shakespeare declines to ratify it unequivocally and contemporary spectators cannot be expected to know it? As a demonstration of Cressida's proverbial inconstancy, the scene is inadequate, lacking, unequal to its literary predecessors—a misrecognition of the scene for which it insufficiently substitutes. Particularly in performance, the discrepancy between Cressida's ambivalent lapse and Troilus' thundering denunciations could underline the extent to which he willfully misreads the scene as proof of the inconstancy he requires.

Cressida does, of course, end the scene by denouncing herself for an anticipated infidelity:

> Troilus, farewell! one eye yet looks on thee,
> But with my heart the other eye doth see.
> Ah, our poor sex! this fault in us I find,
> The error of our sex directs our mind.
> What error leads must err; O, then conclude,
> Minds sway'd by eyes are full of turpitude.
> (5.2.107–12)

Cressida laments the depravity to which a woman's desiring look—the "eye" that leads the "heart"—drives her. She refers her own errant desire to a mythology of female turpitude ("ah, our poor sex! this fault in us I find"), finally buckling under the burden of textuality, not so much the received text of "Troilus and Cressida" as the fundamental myth of female corruption it reiterates. She prepares to surrender to her notorious identity by reaching past it to its originary myth. The word "fault" conflates error with female genitals ("this fault in us I find"), as does the phrase "the error of *our sex*" (emphasis mine). If Isabella blames herself for being a desired object, Cressida blames herself for being a desiring subject and converts her sense of guilt into a pretext for transgression, as though compelled to submit her inherited sense of depravity to corroborative display. She essentially says, "I feel like a whore—I might as well act like one." With this speech, Cressida begins to recede as a subject. She simplifies her conflicted, desiring subjectivity by misrecognizing herself in the image of a depraved sex maniac. She proves herself hopelessly self-divided, acceding to an unkind self that consents to be another's fool: Diomedes' concubine, Troilus' seductress, patriarchy's female wanton.[45]

Yet Cressida is not finished vacillating. As one may infer from Troilus' description of its contents (5.3.108–12), the letter that Pandarus delivers to Troilus essentially recants her farewell speech, or at least repledges her fidelity to Troilus. She tries to negate the text of inherited depravity with her own text. Because the letter represents her final statement in the play, she recedes even further as a subject, essentially becoming the text of her letter, which Troilus, disbelieving, tears into pieces and scatters to the wind, once more fragmenting and now silencing her, underlining her failure to cohere as a subject within the oedipal plot. Yet Troilus certainly errs in asserting "my love with words and errors still she feeds, / But edifies another with her deeds" (5.3.111–12). Within the world of this play, Cressida has "done the deed" only with him; it is Diomedes to whom she offers only words.

Of course, from Troilus' perspective, Cressida does not actually have to do the deed with Diomedes. Her promise to do it, her farewell, her brazen "familiarity" with Diomedes are sufficient to establish his insufficiency, his incapacity to satisfy her.[46] She claims to have one eye yet that looks on Troilus, but she has trained her gaze away from him, deprived him of the reciprocal look he requires to fill a place in the social spectacle. To withdraw her satisfaction is to withdraw the world:

> Instance, O instance, strong as Pluto's gates,
> Cressid is mine, tied with the bonds of heaven;
> Instance, O instance, strong as heaven itself:
> The bonds of heaven are slipp'd, dissolv'd, and loos'd;
> And with another knot, five-finger-tied,
> The fractions of her faith, orts of her love,
> The fragments, scraps, the bits, and greasy relics
> Of her o'ereaten faith, are given to Diomed.
> (5.2.153–59)

Cressida, who once seemed capable of dispensing "thrice-repured nectar" to Troilus, now offers repellant scraps of greasy left-overs to Diomedes. The image recalls that of the fragmented body parts ("her eyes, her hair, her cheek, her gait, her voice") that he consumed through the "open ulcer of [his] heart" as well as the scraps of her letter that he scatters to the wind.

Her conversion into gross, fragmented material reflects his consignment of her to a fallen female body. Cressida demonstrates a sexuality unassimilable to his image of female purity, derived from a nurturing, maternal body. If the dissolution of their sexual relationship had restored Cressida's potential value as an exemplar of "winnow'd purity," her assertion of a sexual desire outside the circuitry of his own needs and drives disqualifies her as provider of lost plenitude:

> Think, we had mothers; do not give advantage
> To stubborn critics, apt, without a theme
> For depravation, to square the general sex
> By Cressid's rule. Rather, think this is not Cressid.
> (5.2.130–33)

In distancing her from a maternal ideal, Troilus confirms Cressida's fulfillment of her destiny as flawed substitute for an unrecoverable original.

Troilus manages, however, both to preserve the mystified ideal and to excuse Cressida from it by proclaiming, "this is and is not Cressida" (5.2.146). The transgressively sexual woman becomes "Diomed's Cressida" (5.2.137), the vessel of purity "Troilus' Cressida." Troilus preserves the "rule in unity" Cressida supposedly violates by splitting her in two, as madonna and whore. He thus upholds the unity of the phallocentric economy founded on a female lack that can be either sadistically confirmed ("whore") or fetishistically disavowed ("madonna").

The former proves a more useful strategy to Troilus, allowing him to reify the feminine "false" that defines his masculine "true." Indeed, "Diomed's Cressida" deserves the name "Troilus' Cressida" more than the idealized construct to whom he gives it. The infidelity that incites Troilus' apparent disintegration actually enables his integration as betrayed eternal lover ("never did young man fancy / With so eternal and so fixed a soul" [5.2.165–66]). Troilus thus concludes his lamentation by unifying the divided Cressida in the image of corruptress, essentially declaring, "this is Cressida": "O Cressid! O false Cressid! false, false, false! / Let all untruths stand by thy stained name, / And they'll seem glorious" (5.2.178).

By assuming the role of "stained" seductress, however provisionally, Cressida confirms the success of Troilus' seduction, yielding to the reductive mythology of female treachery that Troilus, as "truth's authentic author," means to substantiate. The ultimate end of seduction, Baudrillard suggests, is the death of the seduced, self-annihilation as a gesture of absolute surrender.[47] Troilus' seduction of Cressida culminates in a kind of death for her, an incapacity to denote herself truly, a descent into terminal indefinition. Cressida's core self, the self to which her kind self is unkind, simply does not receive coherent articulation within the world of the play. It is missing, hidden, radically unstable. Cressida is not simply a mimic but an hysteric, excessive or inaccessible to the representational frame that seeks to contain her. Like Helena and Isabella, she ends the play as a body aspiring to yet escaping signification.

The play provides an image of the hysterical woman in the "mad" Cassandra, whose prophetic speeches are dismissed as nonsense.[48] If the fixed icon Helen sells her soul to phallocentric representation, the non-signifying Cassandra stands forever outside of it. Cressida, burdened throughout by the picture of herself in Helen's image, ends the play in a position much closer to Cassandra's—unassimilable to phallocentric con structs. In performance, one could attempt to establish Cassandra as Cressida's doppelgänger by having her shadow Cressida throughout the scenes at Troy, perhaps literally emerging from the shadows after each of Cressida's major scenes. When Cressida finally turns away from Troilus in order to leave with Diomedes in 4.4, she could find Cassandra standing directly in her path, as though confronting an image of her true exile—not to the Greek camp but to the hystera theater of nonsignification to which she is ultimately headed.

Following the Cressida-Diomedes scene, two additional pieces of staging could extend the feminist gestus. In the first, Troilus could conclude his jeremiad on Cressida's inconstancy by ripping her huge picture in half. If the image is a projection rather than a poster, Troilus could actually hurl himself at it and (depending on the material onto which the image is projected) wrestle with it, swim in it, bump and grind against it. A new image could then be projected: the same picture torn in half. Troilus' final speech could be accompanied by the mending of this fragmented image, either manually (in the case of a poster) or electronically (in the case of a projection). The image he assaults and consequently repairs is precisely the one he requires to authenticate his own myth: Cressida as seductress. Even as he disowns Cressida as irretrievably false, he retrieves the image conjuring her falseness, underlining his dependence on the very thing he vilifies.

More importantly, in the later scene when Pandarus delivers Cressida's letter to Troilus, Cressida herself could be brought on stage on a mobile platform (a "wagon") surrounded by mannequins outfitted in her various costumes, representing the various "feminine" personae she has assumed throughout the play. She herself would be dressed in simple, casual, contemporary clothes, the sort of outfit the actress playing her might have worn to early rehearsals. This tableau would serve, first of all, as an image of Cressida's fragmentation into lifeless images of femininity, into an array of different fashionable "looks" that define and constrict her subjectivity. The tableau conveys Cressida's doubleness, simultaneously registering her difference from and her similarity to the mannequins, signifiers of a constructed femininity. She is a single, sensate, unadorned woman amidst multiple, lifeless, glamorous, "feminine" caricatures but, at the same time, these lifeless figures relay the images through which she becomes representable within the world of the play. They constitute her signifying "screens." She is and is not a mannequin. Cressida becomes a kind of spectral actress, unrepresentable without her costumes, speechless without her lines, a would-be subject under erasure.

As Troilus surveys the missive, Cressida could turn to face him. When, having finished reading the letter, he tears it up and discredits its contents, she could turn back to the audience, the light on her fading as the platform is pulled offstage, as though she were condemned to this limbo of lifeless fragmentation. If Cressida's masquerade defamiliarizes normative femininity, it leaves her own subjectivity elsewhere.[49]

Yet this Elsewhere, this fragmented limbo, becomes as much a measure of Cressida's nonmimetic subversiveness as does the staged bed-trick for Helena and the protracted nonreply for Isabella. In this final tableau, Cressida's dialect also becomes speechless, exclusively bodily, opposing itself to the displayed markers of her feminine masquerade, establishing her as other-than-Other. If Cressida's elsewhere seems closer to nowhere than do the nonreferential registers of Helena and Isabella, it is because she comes closer to symbolic erasure than they do. Like them, she is confoundedly double, coexisting with her own negation. But the negation with which she coexists has the imposing force of literary tradition behind it. Thus, Cressida all but embraces her notorious identity in her farewell speech, donning the "destin'd livery" of treacherous seductiveness.

Yet because the play adumbrates a subjectivity for Cressida at odds with this identity, because it fails to provide an unequivocal image of her betrayal, and because it allows her the (albeit hidden and disregarded) last word, Cressida ultimately resists seduction, negating the negation that Troilus insists on projecting to her. The feminist gestus underlines this negated negation (this "not not, but"), accentuating Cressida's unassimilable otherness, lending her a subjective meaning inaccessible to the oedipal plot.

BETWEEN MEN: The Homoerotics of War

In the play's final scenes, Troilus undertakes a course similar to Bertram's. He flees female engulfment and goes to war, prepared to rescue his imperiled masculinity. Because of Troilus' protracted disarmament, the war functions for him, as for Bertram, as a male rite of passage, even though he has previously participated. Hector reinforces this image, treating Troilus as untested, excusing him from battle on the same grounds that the King evoked against Bertram: youth. "Let grow thy sinews till their knots be strong," Hector tells him, "and tempt not yet the brushes of war" (5.3.33–34). In response, Troilus chides Hector for his "vice of mercy" and makes clear his determination to "get the woman out": "[L]et's leave the hermit pity with our mother" (5.3.37–45).[50]

Troilus undertakes to realize his reputation as a second Hector—as "manly" as his brother "but more dangerous," in the words of Agamemnon (4.5.104). The war becomes his stage for proving himself the new Trojan champion, taking over for his slain brother. His replication of Hector, however, is less than perfect. The Greek generals describe both warriors as veritable juggernauts, exhibiting an invincibility driven by ferocious desire. But whereas Hector's "appetite" is disciplined by skill (5.5.19–29), Troilus' is recklessly promiscuous; he fights with "such a careless force, and forceless care / As if that lust, in very spite of cunning, / Bade him win all" (5.5.40–42). "That lust" channels Troilus' "boundless desire" into a jealous martial rage aimed specifically at Diomedes. The infinite will that sought transcendent satisfaction with Cressida now seeks frenzied revenge against her paramour. If Hector functions as the model of Troilus' awesome military feats, the image that drives them, the mirror into which Troilus looks, is that of Diomedes.

Diomedes assumes the figure of the seductive Greek youth against whom Troilus had warned Cressida, and against whom he had unfavorably measured himself. Diomedes uses Cressida as a tool for conquering Troilus, as his vaunting and taunting of Troilus during Cressida's exchange make clear. Cressida has value, he tells Troilus, as he desires her, not as Troilus praises her (4.4.116–20). "Use her well," Troilus warns Diomedes, or "I'll cut thy throat" (4.4.126, 129). To "use her well" means not to "use" her sexually. If Diomedes regards her as a penetrable body, Troilus will similarly regard his body on the battlefield. Diomedes dismisses the threat. "When I am hence," he returns, "I will answer for my lust"; he will vindicate his conquest of Cressida by conquering Troilus in battle, proving himself the better man (4.4.131–32). Diomedes' desire for Troilus' desired object manifests a desire for Troilus—a desire to render him "lacking" by depriving him of the signifier of his masculine potency, to read in the mirror of Troilus' humiliation the image of his own power.

Cressida accordingly is reduced to a pawn in a male power struggle. Rather like Helena, she stands silently by as two headstrong men debate her worth. Diomedes essentially replaces her as the source of Troilus' "lust." She becomes the catalyst for aggressive male bonding. "Hold thy whore, Grecian!" Thersites brays as Diomedes and Troilus ferociously clash, "now for thy whore, Trojan!" (5.4.24–25). After losing track of the combatants, Thersites exclaims, "what's become of the wenching rogues? I think they have swallow'd one another. I would laugh at that miracle—yet in a sort lechery eats itself" (5.4.32–35). Thersites' imagery is highly suggestive, given the play's association of desiring and feeding. The "wenching rogues" channel the desire to taste Cressida into a desire to swallow each other—a "lecherous" consumption carrying homoerotic overtones. Thersites' assertion that "lechery eats itself" corroborates Ulysses' image of "appetite" as a "universal wolf" that, "seconded with will and power," must "make perforce an universal prey, / And last eat up himself" (1.3.120–24). Thersites' repellant raillery is littered with images of eaten-up, disease-ravaged bodies—the wages, he clearly implies, of unchecked appetite. Thersites, like Pandarus, focuses on the body, but on its corruption and perishability rather than its eroticism. Thersites is Yorick's skull made animate, a talking death's head, serving the same function as the skull in Holbein's painting *The Ambassadors*. Yet, unlike the skull, Thersites is visible from every angle. He is everywhere.[51]

The Troilus-Diomedes conflict becomes an image of the Trojan War in miniature—a private war provoked by competitive desire for a "placket." The rivalry it exercises essentially erases the shared object of desire; the male bonding Cressida facilitates supersedes any male bond to her. Similarly, the entire war assumes the shape of triangulated homoeroticism. The rival armies' relation to each other is far more tangible and important than their relation to Helen; as the Trojan Council scene makes clear, she serves her purpose by enabling the pursuit of masculine distinction, the launching of a vast homosocial enterprise.

Both Cressida and Helen (each of whom is compared to a pearl) function as objects of exchange in a male economy of power and desire, tokens of purely attributive value used to purchase honor. Even Hector's proposed "sportful combat" posits woman as signifier of male distinction, throwing down the gauntlet of his "lady's" peerlessness: "[H]e hath a lady wiser, fairer, truer, / Than ever Greek did couple in his arms" (1.3.275–76). He challenges "Grecian[s] true in love" to avow their mistresses' "beauty" and "worth" in "other arms than hers" (1.3.279, 271–72). This image suggests a near continuum between homosocial bonding and homosexual coupling: the warrior forsakes the arms of his beloved for the arms of his cherished enemy.[52] Embracing Diomedes, Aeneas ecstatically declares, "no man alive can love in such a sort / The thing he means to kill, more excellently," conflating male-to-male love with murderous violence (4.1.24–25). Told by Aeneas that Paris has been wounded by Menelaus, Troilus responds, "Let Paris bleed, 'tis but a scar to scorn; / Paris is gor'd with Menelaus' horn" (1.1.111–12). Here the murderous violence is specifically imaged as penetration: Paris' bleeding wound reflects the penetrability of the male body.[53] And once more the female intermediary of the coupling males, Helen, recedes from view.

Barton's production was particularly attentive to the homoerotic dynamics of the war, inspiring one reviewer to observe, "the great love affair of this play is not Troilus and Cressida, but the Greeks and the Trojans."[54] Another critic put it even more forcefully:

> This war, [Barton] suggests, is a sort of lechery itself. War is sex and sex is war. Cressida destroys Troilus, and the Trojans meet the Greeks like lovers, almost naked, agog for the dark orgasmic flutter of killing or being killed.[55]

Within a war that fetishizes male bonding, the relationship between Achilles and Patroclus becomes transgressive not because it is homosexual but because it is anti-(homo)social, ensnaring both lovers in unmanly desire, as Patroclus himself affirms:

> A woman impudent and mannish grown
> Is not more loath'd than an effeminate man
> In time of action. I stand condemn'd for this;
> They think my little stomach to the war,
> And your great love to me restrains you thus.
> Sweet, rouse yourself, and the weak wanton Cupid
> Shall from your neck unloose his amorous fold,
> And like a dew-drop from the lion's mane,
> Be shook to air.
>                                    (3.3.217–24)

Achilles' effeminacy stems not from a specifically homosexual desire but from the emasculating effects of desire itself, its capacity to deflect a man from his narrative of competitive self-actualization. Patroclus once more takes a position usually reserved for a woman: the seductive siren who submerges the questing hero in sensual languor. Patroclus blames himself for effeminizing Achilles just after Ulysses blames Polyxena, a woman who, because she has previously not merited a single mention, seems almost a female alter ego for the effeminate Patroclus—or a convenient figure through whom Ulysses can indirectly indict Patroclus. When Ulysses counsels Achilles, "better would it fit Achilles much / To throw down Hector than Polyxena" (3.3.207–208), he implies that it would also better fit Achilles to throw down Hector than Patroclus. "Make war, not love," Ulysses seems to say, and it matters little whether Achilles makes love to Polyxena or to Patroclus: in either case unmanly desire deters him from combat. He must spurn a homosexual relationship with a seductive "varlot" and embrace homoerotic grappling with macho rivals. Within the world of this play, a man makes love to a man not through sex but through war.

The moment that marks Achilles' reanimation as ruthless warrior comes when he and Hector gaze into each other's eyes. Just after Patroclus exhorts him to shake off his effeminacy, Achilles asserts, "I have a woman's longing, / An appetite that I am sick withal, / To see great Hector in his weeds of peace" (3.3.237–39). Achilles' desire is womanish because it implicitly positions Hector not as a rival warrior armed for battle but as a potential lover outfitted in "weeds of peace." Hector confirms Achilles' lack by looking at him with insulting brevity, as though colluding with the Greek generals:

> Hector.   Stand fair, I pray thee, let me look on thee.
> Achilles.  Behold thy fill.
> Hector.   Nay, I have done already.
> Achilles.  Thou art too brief. I will the second time,
>            As I would buy thee, view thee limb by limb.
>                                          (4.5.235–38)

Achilles quickly shifts from a womanish, desiring gaze to a warrior's rapacious look, surveying Hector's body as a composition of penetrable, dismemberable parts—parts that he will soon "lack." "Why dost thou so oppress me with thine eye?" Hector, seemingly unnerved, inquires (4.5.241). "In which part of [Hector's] body, / Shall I destroy him?" (4.5.242–43) Achilles wonders, perhaps not simply surveying Hector's body parts but actually touching or thrusting at the parts to which he refers—"there, there, or there" (perhaps the last "there" indicates Hector's crotch—an arguably over-bold choice that would nevertheless effectively accentuate the violent homoerotics of war). Achilles, who, Patroclus suggests, had "gor'd" himself (3.3.228–29), must now restore his manhood by "goring" Hector—penetrating his body in a martial rather than sexual act. Hector returns Achilles' vaunt and projects his own dismembering gaze: "[S]tand again," he instructs Achilles, promising to kill him not "there, or there, nor there" but "everywhere, yea, o'er and o'er" (4.5.256). The conflating of looking, desiring, and dismembering in the scene underlines the essential sadism of war, in which "gor'd" men violently attempt to transfer lack to feminized surrogates.

Achilles' inventory of Hector's dismemberable parts becomes chillingly fulfilled as the Myrmidons ambush him, carrying out Achilles' orders, "empale him with your weapons round about" (5.7.5). Indeed, the scene could be staged not simply as an ambush but as a kind of grotesque gang-rape, as the Myrmidons—who have themselves suffered dismemberments at Hector's hands ("that noseless, handless, hack'd and chipp'd come to him" [5.5.34])—take turns thrusting their swords into his prone, penetrable body. Hector then becomes the very picture of what his sister Cassandra had prophesied: an assemblage of "bleeding vents" (5.3.82).

Hector's transformation into feminized victim coincides with his embrace of specularity. Despite his penchant for sparing the enemies he disables, Hector does not hesitate to kill a warrior whose sumptuous armor he covets. "Wilt thou not, beast, abide?" he vaunts, "why then, fly on, I'll hunt thee for thy hide" (5.6.30–31). Hector wishes to possess the sumptuous armor presumably because its visual splendor more emphatically advertises his greatness. By donning the glittering armor, he will be better able to make a spectacle of himself, constituting himself in the idolizing looks thereby elicited. Having won this prize, Hector disarms, effectively dephallicizing himself—leaving himself open to the thrusting swords of the Myrmidons.

In performance, this disarming could precede an actual attempt on Hector's part to don the glittering armor, clearly his eventual goal. Such a staging underlines the act of disarming as a register of "lack," as Hector exchanges his functional armor for a glorious costume, shifts from "masculine" productivity to "feminine" self-display. Hector is seduced by the armor, misrecognizing himself in its dazzling image and preparing to use it as a tool for seducing his fellow warriors' admiring looks. If the armor has the same golden hue as Helen's gown, then Hector's attempt to don it becomes a kind of cross-dressing, parallel to Achilles' donning of Helen's dress but without the representational frame that transforms it into an image of the generals' "lack." Hector's mirroring of Helen forecasts his death, his ultimate "lack." To be like the gilded, ghostly Helen is to court oblivion. As with Euripides' Pentheus, an act of cross-dressing not only portends but embodies disaster, setting Hector up for ignominious death and the brutal violation of his corpse recorded in *The Iliad*—the fate fixed by his notorious identity. In Richard E. T. White's 1984 production at the Oregon Shakespeare Festival, Hector attempted to defend himself with his new ornamental weaponry, which immediately broke.[56] If Hector is killed while wearing the armor (or part of it), the glittering costume becomes his tomb; he trades places with "the most putrefying core, so fair without" (5.8.1), imaging the corruptible flesh beneath the masculine glamor, a corrupting flesh associated in Thersites' mind with the corrupt woman who has caused the war. Given the visual parallel between Hector's golden armor and Helen's glittering dress, and the connection between male specularity and lack, one might say that Helen, signifier for the glossy emptiness of the war, has indeed disarmed Hector, just as she said she would.

## FINAL SCENES

Shakespeare gives the final word in the play to Pandarus, who, since the break-up of the lovers, has appeared only once, delivering Cressida's letter to Troilus and lamenting his own physical decline, complaining of a "tisick," of "rheum" in his eyes and aches in his bones, and prophesying his own death ("I shall leave you one o' th's days" [5.3.101–106]). In performance, Pandarus could look hideously transformed in his final appearances, a wheezing, disheveled old bawd bearing only the slightest resemblance to the natty *bon vivant* of the play's earlier scenes.[57] Pandarus functions as a repository of the very diseases that Thersites invokes in his bitter invectives against both armies. His diseases signify the wages of flesh-trading—in both sex and war. He becomes a kind of walking putrefying core, symptomizing the essential corruption of an image-mongering medium that stokes appetite by fetishizing the flesh.

Pandarus continues to play the role of mediator, bequeathing to the audience, in the play's final line, the diseases he seems to have inherited from Thersites (5.10.56). He turns Thersites' curse—"the burning devil take them all" (5.2.195–96)—into a chillingly jocular gift, essentially saying "the burning devil take *you* all." To the extent that Pandarus is going blind, he also bequeaths his voyeuristic look to the audience—or at least implicates them as fellow voyeurs, carrying on the flesh-trading (the mediation of erotic spectacle) that he must abandon. It might be highly effective if Pandarus were actually blind in the final scene, complete with cane and dark glasses, signifying the erasure of his glamorizing pseudo-gaze by corrosive "appetite."

The end of the play could be staged as an eerie reprise of the beginning. Instead of the cacophonous beginnings of a mammoth battle, the final stage image could present the eerily silent tableau of a battlefield littered with corpses, perhaps even including dismembered limbs and "bleeding vents." In the middle of Troilus' speech proclaiming Hector's death (5.10.4–31), some Trojan soldiers could enter with a litter bearing Hector's covered remains along with the sumptuous armor. This entrance could motivate Troilus' line, "stay yet" (5.10.23). He could then lift the covers and become palpably revolted and enraged at the sight of Hector's ravaged corpse (still hidden from the audience's view), which could, in turn, motivate his final furious vaunts ("you vile abominable tents, . . . I'll through and through you! and thou great-siz'd coward, . . . I'll haunt thee like a wicked conscience still" [5.10.23, 26, 28]). He could accompany these lines by preparing to put on the sumptuous gold armor, dismissing his army at the end of the speech. Pandarus, walking through the corpse-strewn field, tapping his cane against the bodies so as to avoid stepping on any of them, could reach Troilus around the same time, only to be rebuffed, thus proceeding downstage to deliver his final speech.

At the conclusion of his speech, the resplendent Helen could be lowered onto the battlefield, a glittering goddess descending from the heavens, gliding her way around the corpses as though unaffected and uncorrupted by them. In a reprise of the production's opening images, she could rejoin Pandarus. Completing the final tableau would be the reemergence from the shadows of Cressida's wagon, possibly pulled by Cassandra.

Helen's function as veiled phallus becomes particularly evident in these final images. Like Cressida, but on a vaster scale, she has colluded in a seduction, enabling a massive—and massively destructive—self-deception, spurring sadistically rapacious acts aimed at reifying an imperiled masculinity. She appears at the play's end as a kind of angel of death. She cued the play's opening battle, and now she returns as though having completed a mission of destruction, rejoining her once robust partner who has metamorphosed into a living corpse, as if he too were her victim. She looks unvaryingly, indefatigably glamorous and seductive, even while the world around her disintegrates.

The image of Troilus' donning Hector's armor offers another image of death, not simply by ensuring that the cycle of destruction will continue but by confirming his absorption into the same exhibitionistic, degraded masculinity that assured Hector's doom. As the play ends, Troilus struggles to fit himself to a masculine glory as fictitious as his legendary truthfulness. At the same time, the image of Cressida surrounded by her mannequins confirms her imprisonment in incoherence. Hector slaps on the armor of a mythical masculinity, while Cressida swims forlornly in the fragmented images of glamorous femininity.

If *All's Well That Ends Well* ends as well as it can, and *Measure for Measure* ends as unwell as it ought, *Troilus and Cressida* does not really end at all and renders standards of "wellness" or "unwellness" virtually irrelevant. Chronologically the earliest of the problem comedies, *Troilus and Cressida* offers the most extreme version of an unresolved crisis in gender. Cressida manifests a sexuality even more subversive than Helena's (because even more unamenable to a normative femininity) and a subjectivity even more elusive than Isabella's (because even more performative). Troilus ends the play where Bertram arrives at mid-point—in a hypermasculine warrior mode hostile to reconciliation with female difference. He has passed through an Angelo-like experience of frenzied misogyny and sexual disillusionment but lacks a Helena or a Duke to force him to confront otherness. The war enacts the crisis in gender on a grand scale, an empty, inglorious spectacle in which "lacking" warriors, maimed by a female phallus, sadistically hack at one another in hopes of affirming their manhood.

The problem comedies have enjoyed critical attention and a theatrical life in the last few decades that would have been unthinkable to earlier generations of critics and directors. To a significant extent, this startling renaissance may be ascribed to their provocative interrogation of erotic politics, their powerful exploration of the distresses and strains of the phallocentric gender system, and the volatile interplay of power and desire within it. In the problem comedies, gender becomes a highly unstable—and highly dramatic—process of negotiation, as male and female subjects struggle unsuccessfully to perform and reify myths of masculinity and femininity that cannot adequately regulate the vagaries of desire or tame the terrors of difference. The plays expose the representational limits of a phallocentric economy of meaning founded on the mastery of difference and persistently frustrate the oedipal plot, leading to their notorious open-endedness.

The problem comedies' critique of representational orthodoxy makes them particularly apt vehicles for gestic renovation on the contemporary stage—for exciting, provocative performances that would vitalize, within the plays' narrative and mimetic framework, the drama of difference uncovered by a criticism sensitive to issues of gender and subjectivity. My study has been propelled by the conviction that the process may also work productively in reverse, that an appreciation of gestic stagings both actual and hypothetical can lend crucial insight into the plays' critique of the sex-gender system and can expand their range of meanings. A theoretically engaged performance criticism seems essential. So much stands to be gained from making inquiry dramatic and drama inquisitive.

# NOTES

## Introduction

1. "*A Midsummer Night's Dream* and the Shaping Fantasies of Elizabethan Culture: Gender, Power, Form," in *Rewriting the Renaissance: The Discourses of Sexual Difference in Early Modern Europe*, ed. Margaret W. Ferguson, Maureen Quilligan, and Nancy J. Vickers (U of Chicago P, 1986), 80.

2. James I of England, letter to George Villiers [December 1623]. Letter 218, ed. G. P. V. Akrigg, *Letters of King James VI & I* (Berkeley: U of California P, 1984). I am grateful to Professor Nora Johnson of Swarthmore College for this citation.

3. See Linda Woodbridge's discussion of these transgressive women in *Women and the English Renaissance: Literature and the Nature of Womenkind, 1540–1620* (Urbana: U of Illinois P, 1984), 180–82. Jean E. Howard also insightfully discusses the phenomenon of female cross-dressing in Shakespeare's England in her essay, "Crossdressing, the Theatre, and Gender Struggle in Early Modern England," *Shakespeare Quarterly* 39 (Winter 1988), 420–22.

4. Peter Erickson argues persuasively for linking Bertram's military exploits with those of the Essex-Southampton group: "[I]n both cases an emphatically military definition of masculinity is placed under intense pressure and is ultimately frustrated. . . . Can all end well if female power undercuts male heroism?" (*Rewriting the Renaissance, Rewriting Ourselves* [Berkeley: U of California P, 1991], 57, 60). Eric Mallin links the deflation of the chivalric ideal in *Troilus and Cressida* to its decline in the Tudor court ("Emulous Factions and the Collapse of Chivalry: *Troilus and Cressida*," *Representations* 29 [Winter 1990], 145–79).

5. Josephine Waters Bennett gives the most extensive account of the play as a tribute to James (*Measure for Measure as Royal Entertainment* [New York: Columbia UP, 1966]). J. W. Lever assays most of the relevant parallels and sensibly concludes, "to see the Duke in *Measure for Measure* as an exact replica of James I would be to misunderstand both Shakespeare's dramatic methods and the practice of the contemporary stage. But to suppose that no parallel was to be drawn between the two characters . . . would seem to be just as untenable" ("Introduction" to the Arden *Measure for Measure* [London: Methuen, 1965], l). Jonathan Goldberg believes the parallel underlines James's attempts to constitute his power through strategic displays of presence-in-absence (*James I and the Politics of Literature* [Baltimore: Johns Hopkins UP, 1983], 231–39). Leonard Tennenhouse sees in the story of the patriarch's withdrawal and return a powerful metaphor for the monarchical transition and reads the play as an exploration of the

cultural anxiety that it generated ("Representing Power: *Measure for Measure* in Its Time," *Genre* 15 [1982], 139–58). According to Steven Mullaney, *Measure for Measure* enacts "an imaginary projection of a transition from one genre of government to another—from one structured along the lines of pastoral romance to one structured along the lines of pastoral inquiry and its theatricalization" (*The Place of the Stage: License, Play, and Power in Renaissance England* [Chicago: U of Chicago P, 1988], 107). For a critique of these "New Historicist" readings of the play, see Anthony B. Dawson, "*Measure for Measure,* New Historicism, and Theatrical Power," *Shakespeare Quarterly* 39 (Autumn 1988), 328–41; and James Hillman, *William Shakespeare: The Problem Plays* (New York: Twayne Publishers, 1993), 145–46.

6. See *A Natural Perspective: The Development of Shakespearean Comedy and Romance* (New York: Columbia UP, 1955).

7. Seminal feminist essays examining the conservatism of Shakespearean comic closure include Clara Claiborne Park, "As We Like It: How a Girl Can Be Smart and Still Popular," in *The Woman's Part: Feminist Criticism of Shakespeare* (Urbana: U of Illinois P, 1980), 100–16; and Shirley Nelson Garner, "*A Midsummer Night's Dream:* 'Jack shall have Jill; / Nought shall go ill,'" *Women's Studies* 9 (1981), 46–63.

8. *Alice Doesn't: Feminism, Semiotics, Cinema* (Bloomington: Indiana UP, 1984), 121.

9. *Bodies That Matter: On the Discursive Limits of "Sex"* (New York: Routledge, 1993), 126–27.

10. For particularly astute criticism of traditional Shakespearean performance criticism, see W. B. Worthen, "Deeper Meaning and Theatrical Technique: The Rhetoric of Performance Criticism," *Shakespeare Quarterly* 40 (Winter 1989), 441–55; see also his review in *Shakespeare Studies* 21 (1993), 300–12, of *Shakespeare and the Sense of Performance: Essays in the Tradition of Performance Criticism of Bernard Beckerman* (Newark: U of Delaware P, 1989). Although eloquently appreciative of the invaluable advances made by traditional Shakespearean performance critics, Worthen points out their tendency to subjugate performance to preset textual meanings and to elide "the intervening practice of acting or directing as a mediating discourse" ("The Rhetoric of Performance Criticism," 445). In a complementary critical move, Harry Berger, Jr., protests the efforts of "new histrionicists" to circumscribe textual meanings in accordance with the circumstances and constraints of playgoing (*Imaginary Audition: Shakespeare on Stage and Page* [Berkeley: U of California P, 1989]).

11. "Performance Criticism: From Granville-Barker to Bernard Beckerman and Beyond," in *Shakespeare and the Sense of Performance,* 15. I should like to make clear that I do not, in the least, wish to negate the tremendous value of traditional Shakespearean performance criticism. I simply want to clear a space within it for a critical discourse receptive to post-structuralist theory and to a wider variety of directorial and actorial mediations.

12. "The Authentic Shakespeare," *Representations* 21 (Winter 1988), 6–7.

13. Andrew Gurr similarly contends that recovering the original conditions and conventions of Shakespearean performance, while an indispensable scholarly endeavor, cannot be extended to contemporary performance: "[T]he original performance texts, all that intricate interaction between poet's mind and collective audience mind, mediated in the familiar structures of the Globe and its players, can never be reconstructed" ("The 'State' of Shakespeare's Audiences," in *Shakespeare and the Sense of Performance,* 174).

14. See, for instance, Hugh M. Richmond, "Peter Quince Directs *Romeo and Juliet*," in *Shakespeare and the Sense of Performance*, 219–27. I find Richmond's interpretation of *Romeo and Juliet* highly compelling, offering key insights and challenges to directors of the play. But I find problematic his claim to produce "an authentic Shakespearean interpretation" (219), his proposal to "remedy" the "misdirections" of other productions (221) by "recovering the consciously artificial modes of the Elizabethan stage and the audience detachment it implies" (226), an ambition that seems to presuppose the transhistorical transmissability of the semiotics of Shakespeare's theater.

15. "Parallel Practices, or the Un-Necessary Difference," *Kenyon Review*, n.s. 7 (Summer 1985), 57–65.

16. Thomas Clayton, "'Balancing at Work': (R)evoking the Script in Performance and Criticism," in *Shakespeare and the Sense of Performance*, 237. I want to emphasize that, although I disagree with the premises and conclusions of Clayton's essay, it is nevertheless one of the most thoughtful and provocative meditations I have ever read on the relationship between text and performance.

17. "The Interpreter's Wand," in *Prospero's Staff* (Bloomington: Indiana UP, 1986), 40.

18. Ralph Berry makes a similar argument in his insightful introduction to *On Directing Shakespeare* (London: Croom Helm, 1977), 15–18. See also Marowitz, "The Interpreter's Wand," 33; and H.R. Coursen, *Shakespearean Performance as Interpretation* (Newark: U of Delaware P, 1992), 57.

19. *The Empty Space* (New York: Avon, 1968), 12.

20. "Balancing at Work," 228–49.

21. "Balancing at Work," 235–36.

22. "Disciplines of the Text/Sites of Performance," *TDR* 19 (Spring 1995), 13–28, esp. 17.

23. See, for instance, Janet Adelman, *Suffocating Mothers: Fantasies of Maternal Origin in Shakespeare's Plays*, Hamlet to The Tempest (New York: Routledge, 1992), 134.

24. See "Transitional Objects and Transitional Phenomena," esp. 11–14, and "The Use of an Object and Relating Through Identifications," 86–94, in *Playing and Reality* (New York: Tavistock, 1971; rpt. Routledge, 1989). Winnicott specifically connects the transitional space to the realm of art and criticism: "This intermediate area of experience, unchallenged in respect of its belonging to inner or external (shared) reality, constitutes the greater part of the infant's experience, and throughout life is retained in the intense experiencing that belongs to the arts and to religion and to imaginative living, and to creative scientific work" ("Transitional Objects and Transitional Phenomena," in *Playing and Reality*, 14).

25. *The Empty Space*, 10.

26. *The Empty Space*, 11.

27. "Success [in performing Shakespeare] is then rated, not by the degree to which the performance approximates to an entirely unknowable state of Shakespeare's mind but by the extent to which the text now speaks with more or less coherent vitality," from Miller's letter to *The Times* of London (October 13, 1971), quoted in Berry, *On Directing Shakespeare*, 10. In his book *Subsequent Performances* (London: Faber and Faber, 1986), Miller develops this notion further, arguing for a limited kind of historical relativism, allowing for meanings unforeseen by the "original author" that nevertheless do not "imply that [the text's] meaning has altered" (71).

Miller contends that "common sense, tact, and literary sensitivity *should* prevent the director or actor from introducing interpretations or versions of the play that are profoundly inconsistent with the range of meanings understood as constitutive of the play's genre" (35). The constraints to which Miller appeals seem unrigorously subjective and generalized. How can "genre" be expected to prohibit contemporary misconstruings when "genre" is itself susceptible to historical reassessment? For some time, *Cymbeline* and *The Winter's Tale* have been thought to belong to a genre called "Romance," yet the folio does not list such a category and instead groups *Cymbeline* among the tragedies and *The Winter's Tale* among the comedies. To take an example closer to home, the folio lists *Measure for Measure* as a comedy, yet Miller himself, in his 1973 production, declined to stage it as such, choosing instead to have "a frigid Isabella . . . recoil in horror" from the Duke's proposal of marriage, "repulsed" by the very idea of wedding him" (see Michael Scott, *Renaissance Drama and a Modern Audience* [London: Macmillan, 1982], 70).

28. As Phyllis Rackin puts it, "stage illusion radically subverted the gender divisions of the Elizabethan world" ("Androgyny, Mimesis, and the Marriage of the Boy Heroine on the English Renaissance Stage," *PMLA* 102 [January 1987], 29–41).

29. For insightful discussions of the subversive effects of transvestite disguise in the comedies, see Catherine Belsey, "Disrupting Sexual Difference: Meaning and Gender in the Comedies," in *Alternative Shakespeares,* ed. John Drakakis (London: Methuen, 1985), 166–90; and Howard, "Crossdressing, the Theatre, and Gender Struggle."

30. For considerations of the homoerotic dynamics enabled by the boy actress, see Lisa Jardine, "'As boys and women are for the most part cattle of this colour': Female Roles and Elizabethan Eroticism," in *Still Harping on Daughters: Women and Drama in the Age of Shakespeare* (Totowa, N.J.: Barnes and Noble, 1983), 9–36; Sue-Ellen Case, *Feminism and Theatre* (London: Macmillan, 1988), 19–27; Stephen Orgel, "Nobody's Perfect: Or Why Did the English Stage Take Boys for Women?" *South Atlantic Quarterly* 88 (1989), 7–29; and Valerie Traub, *Desire and Anxiety: Circulations of Sexuality in Shakespearean Drama* (London: Routledge, 1992), esp. 91–144.

31. Traub ably summarizes the complex position of same-sex desire within Early Modern England: "The discourses of homoeroticism were neither monological nor monovocal. Most importantly, homoerotic activity—for men and for women—was not a primary means of identification of the self. Homoeroticism had little to do with any of the social roles, statuses, and hierarchies in which an early modern subject might be located and thereby define him- or herself. Early moderns simply did not essentialize homoeroticism in quite the way we do" ("Desire and the Difference It Makes," in *Desire and Anxiety,* 111). See also Alan Bray, *Homosexuality in Renaissance England* (London: Gay Men's Press, 1982), and Bruce Smith, *Homosexual Desire in Shakespeare's England* (Chicago: U of Chicago P, 1991).

32. *The Anatomie of Abuses* (London: Richard Jones, 1583).

33. Kathleen McLuskie makes a somewhat analogous argument in "The Act, the Role, and the Actor: Boy Actresses on the Elizabethan Stage," *New Theatre Quarterly* 3 (1987), 120–30.

34. The works by Winnicott most influential to my thinking are *The Maturational Processes and the Facilitating Environment* (New York: International Universities Press, 1965); *The Family and Individual Development* (New York: Tavistock, 1968); and, especially, *Through Pediatrics to Psycho-Analysis* (New York: Basic, 1975) and *Playing and Reality*. The feminist revision I adopt and deploy owes a great deal to Jane Flax's wonderful book, *Thinking Fragments: Psychoanalysis, Feminism, and Postmodernism in the Contemporary West* (Berkeley: U of California P, 1990). Flax's work has been

indispensable to my attempt to contextualize my discussion of gender and subjectivity within the feminist, psychoanalytic, and post-modern texts with which I have been grappling. My discussion of gender and subjectivity in this section owes much to Flax's extraordinarily impressive critical synthesis.

35. As Flax puts it, "Persons who have a core self find the experiences of those who lack or have lacked it almost unimaginable. Borderline patients' experiences vividly demonstrate the need for a core self and the damage done by its absence. Only when a core self begins to cohere can one enter into or use the transitional space in which the differences and boundaries between self and other, inner and outer, and reality and illusion are bracketed or elided. Postmodernist texts themselves belong in and use this space. It is grandiose and misleading to claim that no other space exists or that this one alone is sufficient" (*Thinking Fragments*, 219).

36. "When Is a Character Not a Character? Desdemona, Olivia, Lady Macbeth, and Subjectivity," in *Faultlines: Cultural Materialism and the Politics of Dissident Reading* (Berkeley: U of California P, 1992), 52–79, esp. 62–63. Sinfield's location of a space for interiority within materialist critique of character opens the door for a psychoanalytic probing of interiority that acknowledges the formative influences of cultural discourse. Emily C. Bartels similarly argues for an understanding of subjectivity in Shakespearean drama that mediates between interiority and agency on the one hand and subjugating cultural forces on the other, though she makes the familiar mistake of dismissing psychoanalytic method for its alleged "anachronistic" projection of a concept of "stabilized identity" to a culture that could scarcely conceive of it ("Shakespeare and Performance of Self," *Theatre Journal* 46 [May 1994], 171–85).

37. "When Is a Character Not a Character?" 78.

38. See Jacques Lacan, *The Four Fundamental Concepts of Psychoanalysis*, trans. Alan Sheridan (New York: Norton, 1978), 153–55.

39. See Lacan, in *Ecrits: A Selection*, trans. Alan Sheridan (New York: Norton, 1977), 281–91.

40. See Lacan, "The Mirror Stage," in *Ecrits: A Selection*, 2–4.

41. Lacan, *Four Fundamental Concepts*, 84. My understanding of the gaze and the look is heavily indebted to Kaja Silverman's accounts in "Fassbinder and Lacan: A Reconsideration of Gaze, Look, and Image," in *Male Subjectivity at the Margins* (New York: Routledge, 1992), 125–56.

42. Lacan, *Four Fundamental Concepts* 94–110; see Silverman's brilliantly lucid discussion of Lacan's concept of the screen ("Fassbinder and Lacan," 145–52).

43. See Silverman, "Fassbinder and Lacan," 130.

44. "Fassbinder and Lacan," 144.

45. "Fassbinder and Lacan," 151–52.

46. "Coldness and Cruelty," in *Masochism*, trans. Jean McNeil (New York: Zone, 1989), esp. 40–62.

47. *Seduction*, trans. Brian Singer (New York: St. Martin's, 1990).

48. "The Ecliptic of Sex," in *Seduction*, 10.

49. For a persuasive critique of Deleuze's "body-without-organs," see Alice Jardine, *Gynesis* (Ithaca, N.Y.: Cornell UP, 1985), 208–23.

50. "The Ecliptic of Sex," 14.

51. My discussion of "mimicry" and "hysteria" is heavily indebted to Diamond's essay,

"Mimesis, Mimicry, and the 'True-Real,'" in *Acting Out*, ed. Lynda Hart and Peggy Phelan (Ann Arbor: U of Michigan P, 1993), 363–82. The principal texts from which Diamond derives these models of subversive performance are Luce Irigaray, *Speculum of the Other Woman*, trans. Gillian C. Gill (Ithaca, N.Y.: Cornell UP, 1974) and Julia Kristeva, "The True-Real," in *The Kristeva Reader*, ed. Toril Moi (New York: Columbia UP, 1986), 214–37.

52. *Gender Trouble: Feminism and the Subversion of Identity* (New York: Routledge, 1990), 11.

53. "The Power of Discourse and the Subordination of the Feminine," in *This Sex Which Is Not One*, trans. Catherine Porter (Ithaca, N.Y.: Cornell UP, 1985), 76.

54. "Mimesis, Mimicry, and the 'True-Real,'" 369–76.

55. As Butler points out, drag in itself is not necessarily a subversive spectacle and may reify as well as contest gender norms. See *Bodies That Matter*, 125.

56. "Mimesis, Mimicry, and the 'True-Real,' 376–79. As Diamond points out, hysteria has been "the clamoring site of disruption" in feminist theory over the last decade (376). See also Catherine Clément, "Sorceress and Hysteric," in *The Newly Born Woman* (ed. Hélène Cixous and Catherine Clément, trans. Betsy Wing (Minneapolis: U of Minnesota P, 1986), 3–39.

57. In a fascinating essay, Jeanie Forte discusses the work of feminist performance artists who "perform the body" in much the same spirit as Cixous exhorts women to "write the body," asserting a material, nonmimetic body against subjugating modes of representation ("Focus on the Body: Pain, Praxis, and Pleasure in Feminist Performance," in *Critical Theory and Performance*, ed. Janelle G. Reinelt and Joseph P. Roach [Ann Arbor: U of Michigan P, 1992] 248–62). Yet the nonmimetic performing body is more likely to prove subversive within a contemporary Shakespearean production, which invites expectations of straightforward mimesis, than within a piece of performance art, which does not.

58. *This Sex Which Is Not One*, 164.

59. This definition is drawn from John Willett's gloss on gestus in the notes to Brecht's essay, "The Modern Theatre Is the Epic Theatre," in *Brecht on Theatre*, trans. John Willett (New York: Hill and Wang, 1957), 33–42. See also Brecht's essays, "On Gestic Music," 104–106, and "A Short Organum for the Theatre," nos. 63–67, 198–201. For some helpful explications of Brecht's concept of gestus, see Roland Barthes, "Seven Photo Models of *Mother Courage*," trans. Hella Freud Bernays, *The Drama Review* 12, no. 1 (Fall 1967), 44–55; and Patrice Pavis, "On Brecht's Notion of Gestus," in *Languages of the Stage: Essays in the Semiology of Theatre* (New York: Performing Arts Journal Publications, 1983), 39–49.

60. See "Short Description of a New Technique of Acting Which Produces an Alienation Effect" (137), and "A Short Organum for the Theatre," no. 57 (196–97), in *Brecht on Theatre*.

61. See "Alienation Effects in Chinese Acting" (91–99); "Short Description of a New Technique of Acting" (143–45); and "A Short Organum for the Theatre," nos. 42–49 (191–94), in *Brecht on Theatre*.

62. "Brechtian Theory/Feminist Theory: Toward a Gestic Feminist Criticism," *TDR* 32 (Spring 1988), 82–94.

63. Margot Heinemann, "How Brecht Read Shakespeare," in *Political Shakespeare* (Ithaca, N.Y.: Cornell UP, 1985), 206.

64. *Gender Trouble*, 30.

65. See, for instance, Sue-Ellen Case, *Feminism and Theatre*, 119–32; Janelle Reinelt, "Feminist Theory and the Problem of Performance," *Modern Drama* 32 (March 1989), 48–57; Forte, "Focus on the Body"; and the following essays by Elin Diamond: "Brechtian Theory/Feminist Theory" and "Refusing the Romance of Identity: Narrative Interventions in Churchill, Benmussa, Duras" in *Performing Feminisms*, 92–105; "The Violence of 'We': Politicizing Identification," in *Critical Theory and Performance*, 390–98; and "Mimesis, Mimicry, and the 'True-Real.'"

66. See, for instance, many of the essays in *Upstaging Big Daddy: Directing Theater as if Gender and Race Matter*, ed. Ellen Donkin and Susan Clement (Ann Arbor: U of Michigan P, 1993).

67. "Mimesis, Mimcry, and the 'True-Real,'" 368.

68. *Alice Doesn't*, 157.

69. "Writing (Shakespearean) Acting: Actor Training and the Designs of Authority," unpublished manuscript, presented to the Shakespeare Association of America, 1995.

70. I take this anecdote from G. B. Shand, "My Lives in the Gaps in My Lives," unpublished manuscript, presented to the Shakespeare Association of America, 1995.

71. Samuel Crowl, "Hamlet 'Most Royal': An Interview with Kenneth Branagh," *Shakespeare Bulletin* 12 (Fall 1994), 7.

72. See Keith Appler, "Deconstructing the Regional Theatre with 'Performance Art' Shakespeare," *Theatre Topics* 5 (March 1995), 35–51.

73. Appler, "Deconstructing the Regional Theatre," 40.

74. Appler, "Deconstructing the Regional Theatre," 49.

75. See John Rouse, "Brecht and the Contradictory Actor," in *Acting (Re)Considered*, ed. Phillip B. Zarilli (London: Routledge, 1995), 228–41, esp. 238–40.

76. "From a Letter to an Actor," in *Brecht on Theatre*, 234.

77. "The Popular, the Absurd, and the Entente Cordiale," *Tulane Drama Review* 5, 121.

78. The tendency of performance critics to textualize performance is the subject of a recent essay by Anthony B. Dawson, "The Impasse over the Stage," *English Literary Renaissance* 21, no. 3 (Autumn 1991), 309–27. Although Dawson admirably assesses the limits of this endeavor and convincingly asserts the intractability of performance to theory, I cannot agree with his conclusion that "theory and theater have very little to say to each other," which underestimates the possibility of their reciprocally enriching interaction.

79. See "Formal Problems Arising from the Theatre's New Content," in *Brecht on Theatre*, 227. Brecht even suggests that empathy is occasionally acceptable, defending the audience's tendency to identify with Kattrin in her death scene in *Mother Courage*. See "Note" to the essay "From the *Mother Courage* Model," in *Brecht on Theatre*, 221.

80. For a superb discussion of the relation of *All's Well That Ends Well* and *Measure for Measure* to the Shakespearean corpus, see Richard Wheeler, *Shakespeare's Development and the Problem Comedies: Turn and Counter-Turn* (Berkeley: U of California P, 1981).

81. For a more extended consideration of *Hamlet* as intertext for the problem comedies, see Hillman, *William Shakespeare: The Problem Plays*.

## 1. *All's Well That Ends Well*

1. *Bulletin of the Shakespeare Association of America* 16 (July 1992), 4.

2. *Shakespeare's Problem Comedies* (New York: Macmillan, 1931). Although Lawrence insists that these plays should be accepted simply as stories, requiring the same level of unsophisticated reception as the widely known traditional tales from which, by his reckoning, they were derived (73–77), folklore scholars have for some time uncovered the potent cultural and psychological dramas that such tales encode. See, for instance, Alan Dundes, "The Psychoanalytic Study of Folklore," in *Parsing through Customs: Essays by a Freudian Folklorist* (Madison: U of Wisconsin P, 1987), 3–46. *All's Well* may be considered a play that pushes the folktale's subterranean psychic drama provocatively close to the narrative surface, threatening the uncomplicated unfolding of the oedipal plot and the gender ideology it encodes. A feminist gestus aims to heighten the drama of that threatened rupture by staging the play's repressed contents.

3. See, for example, Janet Adelman, *Suffocating Mothers: Fantasies of Maternal Origin in Shakespeare's Plays, Hamlet to The Tempest* (New York: Routledge, 1992), 84–86; Barbara Hodgdon, "The Making of Virgins and Mothers: Sexual Signs, Substitution Scenes, and Doubled Presences in *All's Well That Ends Well*," *Philological Quarterly* 66 (1987) 47–55; Susan Snyder, "'The King's Not Here': Displacement and Deferral in *All's Well That Ends Well*," *Shakespeare Quarterly* 43 (Spring 1992); and "*All's Well That Ends Well* and Shakespeare's Helens: Text and Subtext, Subject and Object," *English Literary Renaissance* 18 (1988), 73–77.

4. References to *All's Well That Ends Well* are based on *The Riverside Shakespeare,* ed. G. Blakemore Evans et al. (Boston: Houghton Mifflin, 1974).

5. I italicize *feminine* and *masculine* in order to make clear that I use the terms to denote modes of desire (passive and active) while distancing myself from the Freudian view that such modes are rooted in the biological difference between male and female.

6. I borrow the resonant phrase "curled darling" from Robert Ornstein, *Shakespeare's Comedies: From Roman Farce to Romantic Mystery* (Newark: U of Delaware P, 1986), 182. Carolyn Asp, in her fascinating psychoanalytic account of the play, also notes Helena's initial embrace of masochistic femininity, "Subjectivity, Desire and Female Friendship in *All's Well That Ends Well*," *Literature and Psychology* 32 (1986), 52.

7. For an extremely helpful discussion of the paradigm of "closed femininity," see Peter Stallybrass, "Patriarchal Territories: The Body Enclosed," in *Rewriting the Renaissance: The Discourses of Sexual Difference in Early Modern England,* ed. Margaret W. Ferguson, Maureen Quilligan, and Nancy J. Vickers (U of Chicago P, 1986), 123–42.

8. "Cultural Confusion and Shakespeare's Learned Heroines: 'These Are Learned Paradoxes,'" *Shakespeare Quarterly* 38 (Spring 1987), 1–18.

9. *The Sovereign Flower: On Shakespeare as the Poet of Royalism Together with Related Essays and Indexes to Earlier Volumes* (London: Methuen, 1958), 137.

10. Knight, *The Sovereign Flower,* 138. In a sense, Knight extends Helena's (or Shakespeare's) mystification of virginity: "the love is infinite, 'a thousand loves'; it is the window to a great insight. It may be related to the state of perfect integration from which poetry is born."

11. "Blind Spot of an Old Dream of Symmetry," in *Speculum of the Other Woman,* trans. Gillian C. Gill (Ithaca, N.Y.: Cornell UP, 1985), 50.

12. Cf. Mariana in *Pericles*: "If fires be hot, knives sharp, or waters deep, / Untied I still my virgin knot will keep" (4.2.146–47).

13. See Jacques Lacan, *Feminine Sexuality*, trans. Jacqueline Rose (New York: Norton, 1985), 144–45.

14. Jardine perceives a more fundamental split in Helena's behavior: her exemplary passivity in the play's second half atones for her transgressive forwardness in the first. "[T]he sexually active Helena of the first part of the play [becomes] the virtuously knowing, ideal wife" ("Cultural Confusion and Shakespeare's Learned Heroines," 11). I would contend that Helena is consistent throughout the play in mitigating her audacity with displays of "femininity," that her recession in the play's second half simply extends her strategy—or habit—of compensatory self-effacement. Her urge to assume an exemplary femininity reflects Shakespeare's need—or, rather, a cultural need working through him—to purify and mystify female sexuality in order to neutralize its provocations. Hence, the possible value of a staged bed-trick that foregrounds and demystifies female desire.

15. As Jardine points out, the infamy that Helena courts, if realized, could "ostracize [her] from the community, recasting her wisdom as witchcraft" ("Cultural Confusion and Shakespeare's Learned Heroines," 10).

16. Some commentators believe that the young lords are indeed standoffish. See, for instance, Joseph Price, *The Unfortunate Comedy: A Study of* All's Well That Ends Well *and Its Critics* (Liverpool UP, 1968), 155–56. I find it difficult to credit this reading because of the unlikelihood of the wards' openly flouting the King's formidable demands for cooperation (2.3.56, 72–73). It is far more likely that Lafew takes a position peripheral to the proceedings and so misconstrues their meaning.

17. "Visual Pleasure and Narrative Cinema," *Screen* 16, no. 3 (1975), 11–12.

18. *The Four Fundamental Concepts of Psycho-Analysis,* trans. Alan Sheridan (New York: Norton, 1978), 75.

19. "*All's Well That Ends Well* and Shakespeare's Helens," 11.

20. While relatively few modern critics have subscribed to such an extremely negative view of Helena (see, however, Bertrand Evans, *Shakespeare's Comedies* [Oxford UP, 1960], 145–66; and Richard A. Levin, "*All's Well That Ends Well* and 'All Seems Well,'" *Shakespeare Studies* 13 [1980], 131–44), many have felt compelled, until very recently, to *judge* Helena's character in some measure, and have often found cause to indict or at least regret the duplicitous and predacious tactics that belie her celebrated virtue. See E. K. Chambers, *Shakespeare: A Survey* (London: Sidgwick and Jackson, 1925), 200–207; Clifford Leech, "The Theme of Ambition in *All's Well*," *ELH* 12 (1954), 17–29; Alexander Leggatt, *Modern Language Quarterly* 32 (1971), 22–41; W. L. Godschalk, "*All's Well* and the Morality Play," *Shakespeare Quarterly* 25 (1974), 61–70; David Scott Kastan, "*All's Well That Ends Well* and the Limits of Comedy," *ELH* 52 (1985), 575–89. Critics, of course, have also judged in Helena's favor. See my own earlier essay, "'That Your Dian / Was Both Herself and Love': Helena's Redemptive Chastity," *Essays in Literature* 17 (1990), 160–78. Judgments of Helena perhaps follow inevitably from a formalist focus on the play's "genre trouble" rather than its "gender trouble" (to borrow Judith Butler's term).

21. *Gender Trouble: Feminism and the Subversion of Identity* (New York: Routledge, 1990), 140.

22. *Ways of Seeing* (New York: Viking, 1973), 121.

23. De Lauretis discusses this contradiction in especially helpful terms in *Alice Doesn't*, 156–59.

24. See, for instance, Janelle Reinelt, "Feminist Theory and the Problem of Performance," *Modern Drama* 32 (March 1987), 48–57.

25. Stacy Wolf and Michael Peterson, review of *A Midsummer Night's Dream*, *Theatre Journal* 42 (May 1992), 228.

26. See Sigmund Freud, "Femininity," in *The Standard Edition of the Complete Psychological Works*, ed. James Strachey (London: Hogarth, 1964), 22, 112–35. According to Freud's reductive biological model, the little girl's desire shifts from wanting a penis to wanting the one who possesses it. She thus surrenders or represses the active part of her libido ("masculine" desire) in return for her father's (i.e., male) love, consenting to her condition of "lack," of passivity and dependence.

27. I am indebted to Ralph Alan Cohen for pointing out the pervasiveness of the negative in the language of *All's Well* in "The (K)notty Discourse of *All's Well That Ends Well*," unpublished manuscript, presented to the Shakespeare Association of America, 1993.

28. "Sexuality must not be thought of as a kind of natural given which power tries to hold in check, or as an obscure domain which knowledge tries gradually to uncover. It is the name that can be given to a historical construct: not a furtive reality that is difficult to grasp, but a great surface network in which the stimulation of bodies, the intensification of pleasures, the incitement to discourse, the formation of special knowledge, the strengthening of controls and resistance, are linked to one another, in accordance with a few major strategies of knowledge and power" (*The History of Sexuality, Volume I: An Introduction*, trans. Robert Hurley [New York: Random House, 1978], 105–106).

29. Although she overestimates the liberating effects of Elizabethan marriage for women, Juliet Dusinberre nonetheless gives a good account of the ideal of marital chastity with which Puritan reformers sought to displace a monastical (catholic) one (*Shakespeare and the Nature of Women* [London: Macmillan, 1975], 20–63).

30. Richard A. Levin offers the most extreme version of this view, essentially arguing—seldom with textual support—that everything that happens in the play is the direct result of her indefatigable conniving ("*All's Well That Ends Well* and 'All Seems Well'").

31. "Feminism, Marxism, Method, and the State: An Agenda for Theory," *Signs* 7 (Spring 1982), 530–31. While MacKinnon's comment offers a useful gloss on Helena's predicament, it can hardly be taken as universally true; female sexuality is surely far too powerful, multifaceted, and complex to suffer reduction to the simple task of attracting and pleasing men.

32. James Hillman suggests that Helena never gives the slightest indication that she cares whether Bertram desires her or not; she wishes to construct herself out of her construction of him and so aspires only to render him powerless to reject the image she wishes to project onto him (*William Shakespeare: The Problem Plays* [New York: Twayne, 1993], 67). Although I agree that Helena positions Bertram as self-substantiating Other, I would argue that her alliance with Diana bespeaks a need not merely to stand in for but to *become* the object of Bertram's desire, to present herself at play's end as, among other things, a body bearing physical evidence of its antecedent desirability.

33. "The statement, 'I am a man,' . . . at most can mean no more than, 'I'm like he

whom I recognize to be a man, and so recognize myself as being such.' In the last resort, these various formulas are to be understood only in reference to the truth of 'I is an other,'" Jacques Lacan, "Aggressivity in Psychoanalysis," in *Ecrits: A Selection*, trans. Alan Sheridan (New York: Norton, 1977), 23.

34. Lynda E. Boose discusses this homology in her stunning essay "Scolding Brides and Bridling Scolds: Taming the Woman's Unruly Member," *Shakespeare Quarterly* 42 (1991), 199–200; also Stallybrass, "Patriarchal Territories: The Body Enclosed," 126.

35. For a superb psychoanalytic account of Bertram's fear of Helena's engulfing maternalism, see Adelman, *Suffocating Mothers*, 79–86.

36. "But only the girl with whom one has not grown up from childhood, and become accustomed to, can ever be to us in the truly sexual sense, a real girl. That is to say, she alone can possess these powerful stimuli to the sense of sexual desirability, never developed in people one has grown unconsciously used to, which are essential to the making of a real girl," in *Sex and Marriage* (Westport, Conn.: Greenwood, 1977), 42.

37. Ruth Nevo contends that the Countess is "rather more than half in love with her son," and "since she cannot have a husband in her son, she will identify with the girl who would be his wife, and so transform her love for Bertram into a double maternal solicitude" ("Motive and Meaning in *All's Well That Ends Well*," in *"Fanned and Winnowed Opinions": Shakespearean Essays Presented to Harold Jenkins*, ed. John W. Malion and Thomas H. Pendleton [London: Methuen, 1987], 33, 35). My argument is closer to that of Adelman, who identifies a "binding maternal power" in the Countess which Helena enacts and extends (*Suffocating Mothers*, 79–80).

38. For a brilliant discussion of the oedipal conflict between Bertram and the King, see Richard P. Wheeler, *Shakespeare's Development and the Problem Comedies*, 35–45.

39. Nevo also notes the strangeness of "mother" within the menu of lovers' epithets, "Motive and Meaning in *All's Well That Ends Well*," 37–38.

40. Other critics have noted the Clown's role as Bertram's double (see, for instance, Snyder, "'The King's Not Here,'" 23–24), though none that I know of has argued that the parallel encompasses an ambivalent attitude toward Helena.

41. The way in which male initiation rites tend to exclude women and often require the reception of a wound that constitutes a male vulva has been noted by, among others, Mircea Eliade, *Rites and Symbols of Initiation: The Mysteries of Birth and Rebirth*, trans. Willard R. Trask (New York: Harper & Row, 1975), esp. 21–40; and Bruno Bettelheim, *Symbolic Wounds: Puberty Rites and the Envious Male* (Glencoe, N.Y.: Free Press, 1954; rpt. New York: Collier), esp. 90–121.

42. See, for instance, Ornstein, *Shakespeare's Comedies*, 183.

43. David Haley's recent study, *Shakespeare's Courtly Mirror: Reflexivity and Praxis in All's Well That Ends Well* (Newark: U of Delaware P, 1993), offers perhaps the most thorough defense of Bertram, arguing that his character can be understood only in the context of aristocratic "praxis" and not individual psychology. Haley argues that Bertram, like Hal, becomes the heroic nobleman he was destined to be from the outset: "[T]he playwright has fashioned the character primarily with a view to the character's heroic end. Bertram must be conceived as the nobleman he will ultimately be" (218). Haley's confidence in Bertram's maturation—and concomitant elision of his inadequacies—strikes me as problematic, as does his reification of an heroic code that the play seems to destabilize. Although Haley resists psychoanalytic interpretations, his notion

of "mirroring" lends itself to Lacanian translation: Bertram must identify with a culturally imposed image that allows him to signify within the cultural (courtly) spectacle, must fit himself to the screen that enables capture by the gaze. That such identification constitutes a *misrecognition* seems apparent from the insubstantiality of the models to which Bertram is subject: the militaristic flummery of Parolles and the nostalgically mythologized courtliness of his father, the Count.

44. Robert Smallwood, "Shakespeare at Stratford-upon-Avon, 1989, Part II," *Shakespeare Quarterly* 41 (Winter 1990), 494.

45. Steve Vineberg, "Problem Plays," *Threepenny Review* 52 (Spring 1993), 32.

46. Carol Rutter, *Clamorous Voice: Shakespeare's Women Today* (London: Women's Press, 1988), 81.

47. Rutter, *Clamorous Voices*, 88.

48. Rutter, *Clamorous Voices*, 88.

49. J. L. Styan, *All's Well That Ends Well: Shakespeare in Performance* (Manchester UP, 1984), 72.

50. See Price for an account of Houseman's staging (*The Unfortunate Comedy*, 67), and Smallwood for a description of Kyle's ("Shakespeare at Stratford-upon-Avon, 1989," 494).

51. *Pornography and Silence: Culture's Revenge against Nature* (New York: Harper, 1981), 22. Griffin offers compelling evidence of the consistent recurrence of this plot, although her association of women with nature and her affirmation of a natural sexuality seem problematically essentialist.

52. *The Uses of Enchantment: The Meaning and Importance of Fairy Tales* (New York: Random House, 1975), 308.

53. "America's Cinderella," in *Cinderella: A Folklore Casebook*, ed. Alan Dundes (New York: Garland Publishing, 1982), 298.

54. Yolen, "America's Cinderella," 296.

55. My reading of the traditional tale of "Cinderella" is indebted to that of Bettelheim (*The Uses of Enchantment*, 260–72), who regards the climactic insertion of foot into slipper as both an affirmation of female sexuality and a palliation of a male castration anxiety symbolized by the Prince's inability to observe the blood from the amputated parts of the step-sisters' feet. The limits of Bettelheim's reading reflect the limits of its Freudian predicates: to characterize Cinderella as an "uncastrated woman" whose dangled foot expresses a "desire for a penis" presupposes the embeddedness of "penis envy" in the female psyche and the experience of "lack" as a biological condition rather than a patriarchal construction. The point seems worth stressing because, shorn of its biological determinism, Bettelheim's reading of "Cinderella" applies most intriguingly to *All's Well:* through the bed-trick, Helena both affirms her sexuality and ameliorates Bertram's castration anxiety—the dread of loss and lack that accompanies his aversion to her. Helena not only gives Bertram a taste of the sexuality that Cinderella symbolically evokes but presents herself at the end as uncastrating (rather than uncastrated), one who has already had Bertram sexually without damaging him.

56. Carol Thurston, *The Romance Revolution: Erotic Novels for Women and the Quest for a New Sexual Identity* (Urbana: U of Illinois P, 1987), 8.

57. Thurston points out that the callous male who learns to be sensitive has recently been challenged by a "new hero" whose sensitivity is manifest from the outset (*The Romance Revolution*, 72).

58. Tania Modleski, *Loving with a Vengeance: Mass-Produced Fantasies for Women* (New York: Methuen, 1982), 45. As a genre of contemporary fiction written almost exclusively by and for women and, as a recent site of feminist criticism, the romance novel seems a valuable referent for a male critic/director pondering the narratives— both old and new—that intersect with *All's Well's* drama of sexual difference. For a spirited and compelling defense of linking Shakespeare to popular culture, see Harriet Hawkins, *Classics and Trash: Traditions and Taboos in High Literature and Popular Modern Genres* (U of Toronto P, 1990). For a very different critical use of the romance novel, see Linda Charnes, "What's Love Got to Do with It? Reading the Liberal Humanist Romance in Shakespeare's *Antony and Cleopatra*," *Textual Practice* 6 (Spring 1992), 1–17. Charnes discerns a romance-novel sensibility not in Shakespeare's play but in the "traditional liberal-humanist" reading of it, in which "'love' will proleptically revise and make emotional sense of all preceding experience, no matter how violent and disjunctive" (11).

59. "In both [*All's Well That Ends Well* and *Measure for Measure*], the bed-tricks are employed to cure or transform male fantasy through its apparent enactment" (Carol Thomas Neely, *Broken Nuptials in Shakespeare's Plays* [New Haven: Yale UP, 1985], 92). Although Neely sees the bed-trick as primarily humiliating for Helena (as I do not), she does acknowledge Helena's affirmation of the "sweetness of her pleasure and the growth that will ensue: 'the time will bring on summer, / When briars shall have leaves as well as thorns, / And be as sweet as sharp'" (4.4.31–33), 80.

60. *Alice Doesn't*, 99, 83.

61. See Neely, *Broken Nuptials*, 73, and Hodgdon, "The Making of Virgins and Mothers," 60.

62. *Alice Doesn't*, 153, 157.

63. For a helpful discussion of the King's fistula, see F. David Hoeniger, *Medicine and Shakespeare in the English Renaissance* (Newark: U of Delaware P, 1992), 293–98. Surveying contemporaneous medical treatises, Hoeniger concludes that Shakespeare's audience would have assumed that the King's fistula was *in ano*. Hoeniger believes that the cured King's reference to "this healthful hand, whose banished sense / Thou hast repealed" indicates that the wound might actually have been located in his hand, as though Shakespeare were playing a joke on an audience inclined to believe that the fistula was *in ano*. This single line, however, does not provide strong enough evidence that Shakespeare wished to contradict the audience's assumption. The Fisher King "had been crippled by a spear-thrust in the thighs. It seems clear that the words usually translated 'wounded through his two thighs' were intended to mean 'wounded between his two thighs.' In plain language, he was emasculated. The Fisher King is impotent and his land is threatened with ruin," Robert Cavendish, *King Arthur and the Grail: The Arthurian Legends and Their Meaning* (London: Weidenfeld and Nicolson, 1978), 140.

64. See Styan, *All's Well That Ends Well*, 25, 52.

65. Smallwood, "Shakespeare at Stratford-upon-Avon, 1989," 494.

66. Guthrie's production offered a purely mystical example of faith-healing. See Styan, *All's Well That Ends Well*, 54.

67. I am essentially paraphrasing Snyder here ("'The King's not here,'" 27).

68. See Lacan, *Four Fundamental Concepts*, 96–97. As Silverman explains, Lacan is "concerned with the process whereby the subject assumes the form of a representation, or—to state the case somewhat differently—*becomes a picture*, a process which involves

*three* rather than *two* terms: subject, screen, and gaze," in *Male Subjectivity at the Margins,* 148.

69. Smallwood, "Shakespeare at Stratford-upon-Avon, 1989," 495.

70. *Speculum of the Other Woman,* 244, 292.

71. Some critics have contended that the play itself resembles a morality play. See, for instance, Knight, *The Sovereign Flower;* Robert Grams Hunter, *Shakespeare and the Comedy of Forgiveness* (New York: Columbia UP, 1965); and William B. Toole, *Shakespeare's Problem Plays* (The Hague: Mouton, 1966), 130–51.

72. de Lauretis, *Alice Doesn't,* 133.

73. For an excellent discussion of the implications of the word "kind" for Shakespeare's audience, see Arthur Kirsch, *Shakespeare and the Experience of Love* (Cambridge UP, 1981), 142.

74. Asp also identifies Helena's veiled sadism: "I would go so far as to say that lurking behind Helena's apparent psychological masochism of her initial attitude towards Bertram lies its opposite, i.e., anger or rage at having been denied subjectivity by him and a willingness to inflict pain, a psychological form of sadism" ("Subjectivity, Desire, and Female Friendship," 58). Asp, however, sees Helena as more unequivocally altered and triumphant than I do, arguing that she decisively shifts from a deluded idolization to a realistic assessment of Bertram, giving up an obsessive desire for otherness rooted in the Imaginary for structural coherence as wife and mother within the Symbolic. In my reading, neither of these shifts is clear-cut: Helena's desire continues unabated, implicating Bertram as Other and exceeding the maternal and wifely roles she claims.

75. G. K. Hunter speaks for many critics: "[T]he mere substitution of Bertram's cryptic fustian . . . for the elaborate recognitions of the earlier comedies does not remove from our minds the desire for some expression of what is being resolved," Introduction to *All's Well That Ends Well,* in *The Arden Shakespeare* (London: Methuen, 1959), lv.

76. In Susan Snyder's Lacanian reading of *All's Well,* Helena's goal eludes her because it is essentially illusory: "'the bright particular star' she pursues is her own fantasy, a far cry from the increasingly soiled and compromised actuality of Bertram. . . . The whole shape of the story thus enacts desire in Lacanian terms: at best you get a flawed, imperfect substitute for the image that drives you" ("'The King's Not Here,'" 30). I see more ambivalence and ambiguity in the play's ending, owing to Bertram's possible awakening to Helena's difference which, while not redeeming his demonstrable inadequacies, nevertheless points him to a new and enabling knowledge.

77. It seems clear that Helena must be *visibly* pregnant in the play's final scene, not simply because Diana's testimony that she "feels her young one kick" places the pregnancy in its advanced stages but because Helena's claim to have fulfilled Bertram's conditions would otherwise lack substance. The claim is still problematic, of course, given that Bertram actually requested a child (in the source, Giletta presents Beltramo with twin boys) and that Helena could be carrying another man's baby. Still, it seems unlikely that Helena would claim fulfillment without visual corroboration. I am also intrigued by the possibility that, if Helena is indeed visibly pregnant, her line "When I was like this maid" could be heard as "when I was like this made."

78. See Adelman, *Suffocating Mothers,* 85; Nevo, "Motive and Meaning," 44; and Kay Stockholder, *Dream Works: Lovers and Families in Shakespeare's Plays* (U of Toronto P, 1987), 75–76 for corroborative readings of the wish-fulfillment fantasy encoded in Bertram's impossible conditions.

79. See Thomas Laqueur, *Making Sex: Body and Gender from the Greeks to Freud* (Cambridge, Mass: Harvard UP, 1990), 1–9.

80. Helen Wilcox, "'Help of Heaven' or 'Act of (Wo)Man'?: Sacred and Secular in *All's Well That Ends Well,*" unpublished manuscript, presented to the Shakespeare Association of America, 1993.

## 2. Measure for Measure

1. See J. W. Lever for an excellent summary of Shakespeare's use of his sources in *Measure for Measure,* in *The Arden Shakespeare* (London: Methuen, 1965), xxxv–lv.

2. Carolyn Brown also considers the sadomasochistic dimensions of the play in her important essay, "Erotic Religious Flagellation and Shakespeare's *Measure for Measure,*" *English Literary Renaissance* 16 (1986), 139–65. Brown traces the play's excoriative imagery to the monastical practice of flagellation, which was celebrated as the most efficacious agency of penitence, breeding in anchorites a capacity for deriving pleasure from the infliction or reception of pain. I ultimately find the play's sadomasochistic dynamics more complex than her conclusion allows: "[T]he Duke subliminally enjoys observing brutal acts, Angelo inflicting them, Isabella receiving them" (165).

3. As discussed in the introduction, my principal source for formulating a definition of sadism and masochism is Gilles Deleuze's "Coldness and Cruelty" in *Masochism* trans. Jean McNeil (New York: Zone, 1989). Deleuze's principal contribution to the study of these "perversions" was to declare them utterly distinct. The sadist wishes to elicit involuntary suffering from an unwilling victim and could therefore never tolerate a true masochist. The masochist constructs and controls a scenario of voluntary suffering in which his partner acts the part of sadistic tormentor. The masochist could therefore never tolerate a true sadist (40–41). As Angelo, Isabella, and the Duke are not true sadists or masochists, and as I argue that Angelo and Isabella vacillate between the two positions, I use the word "sadomasochism" for the sake of convenience, despite finding Deleuze's case for separating them wholly persuasive.

Another of Deleuze's contributions—another respect in which his study of masochism differs from Freud's—was to identify the mother as central to male masochism. In Freud's view, the one who wields the whip is always an image of the father (see "A Child Is Being Beaten," in *The Standard Edition of the Complete Psychological Works,* trans. James Strachey [London: Hogarth, 1953], 175–204). Deleuze asserts that, while the sadist does indeed assume the figure of the punishing father, specifically aiming, by punishing a "feminine" image of himself, to obliterate any likeness to the mother, the masochist invests the mother with the power of law specifically in order to obliterate likeness to the father—and to remove the oedipal prohibitions he imposes. The masochist resolves oedipal guilt by constructing his female tormentor as an image of the desired mother. Deleuze calls the tormentor the "oral mother," who mediates between the roles of the oedipal (bad) mother and the uterine (good) mother. As the oedipal mother, she punishes the masochist's forbidden desires but only in order to allow him to experience a nongenital sexual pleasure that returns him to an approximation of the preoedipal dyad with a uterine mother (63–68).

Although Deleuze says nothing of female masochism (or sadism, for that matter), his view, by analogy, would seem to be close to Freud's: the female masochist simultaneously overcomes and fulfills her forbidden desire for the father by submitting to the punishments of a father-figure and thereby regressing to a presexual access to him. See Kaja Silverman's assessment of Freud's, Reik's, and Deleuze's accounts of masochism in her brilliant essay, "Masochism and Male Subjectivity," in *Male Subjectivity at the Margins* (New York: Routledge, 1992), 185–213.

4. Recent productions have, in fact, boldly engaged the play's erotic, sadomasochistic dynamics. Jerry Turner's 1976 production for the Oregon Shakespeare Festival opened with the image of a hooded, well-muscled male figure, nude to the waist, whipping a topless woman hung up by her hands. The Duke sat at a desk center stage while the torture scene unfolded behind an upstage scrim, as though he were fantasizing it.

Michael Bogdanov's 1985 production for the Stratford, Ontario, festival began with a half-hour preshow cabaret in which the actors, including three leather-clad transvestites, lounged and danced decadently, and which culminated in a curtain speech by a "master of ceremonies" who admonished the crowd that "gentlemen may not remove their trousers. Ladies may remove anything they like" (See Herbert S. Weil, Jr., "Stratford Festival Canada," *Shakespeare Quarterly* 37 [Summer 1986], 246–49).

In Robert Egan's 1983 production for the Mark Taper Forum, the preshow presented the Duke kneeling in prayer downstage of a massive crucifix to the accompaniment of heavily amplified Latin prayers. At the "shadowy corridor" upstage center "a ghostly punk-like androgynous figure" beckoned to him, "while on either side, behind the glass wall and lit in lurid red, punk-style couples writhed lasciviously" (Martha Andresen, "*Measure for Measure* at the Mark Taper Forum," *Shakespeare Quarterly* 37 [Winter 1986], 507).

Charles Marowitz, directing his own Artaudian adaptation of the play, boldly isolated the play's erotic subdrama. The sexually repressed Isabella actually desires Angelo and becomes palpably excited at the thought of sleeping with him. Informed of her decision, Claudio embraces her lasciviously and leads her to Angelo, who strips her naked and takes her to his bed. In the morning, she discovers, to her horror, Claudio's severed head atop Angelo's desk. In Marowitz's version, the Duke does not assume a disguise and tidily resolve all the play's conflicts. At the play's end, Isabella is scorned, arrested, and dismissed (see Michael Scott, *Renaissance Drama and a Modern Audience* [London: Macmillan, 1982], 63–65).

5. The fact that the play debuted during the first year of James's reign has led many New Historicist critics to read the "return-of-the patriarch" narrative as a device for addressing cultural anxiety surrounding the monarchical transition. See, for instance, Leonard Tennenhouse, "Representing Power: *Measure for Measure* in Its Time," in *The Forms of Power and of Power of Forms in the Renaissance,* ed. Stephen Greenblatt (Norman, Okla.: 1982), 139–56; Jonathan Goldberg, *James I and the Politics of Literature: Jonson, Shakespeare, Donne, and Their Contemporaries* (Baltimore: Johns Hopkins UP, 1983), 230–39; Jonathan Dollimore, "Transgression and Surveillance in *Measure for Measure,*" in *Political Shakespeare: New Essays in Cultural Materialism,* ed. Jonathan Dollimore and Alan Sinfield (Manchester UP, 1985), 72–87; Steven Mullaney, *The Place of the Stage: License, Play, and Power in Renaissance England* (U of Chicago P, 1988), 103–15; Stephen Greenblatt, "Martial Law in the Land of Cockaigne," in *Shakespearean Negotiations: The Circulation of Social Energy in Renaissance England* (Berkeley: U of California P, 1988), 129–42.

6. For a definition of liminality, see Victor Turner, *The Ritual Process: Structure and Anti-Structure* (Chicago: Aldine, 1969), 95–107. Turner describes liminality as a condi-

tion of statuslessness—permanent in the case of shamans and prophets, temporary in the case of those undergoing a rite of passage—from which one experiences the *communitas* underlying and sustaining the social structure. Although only temporarily liminal, the Duke assumes some of the power associated with the permanently liminal: he achieves a "statusless status, external to the secular social structure, which gives him the right to criticize all structure-bound personae in terms of a moral order binding on all, and also to mediate between all segments or components of the structured system" (116–17). The problem is that it is virtually impossible to dissociate the Duke's shamanism from his political ambition. It is never entirely clear whether *communitas* or self-interest propels his liminal mission.

7. Graham Nicholls provides a succinct account of Pennington's portrayal in *Measure for Measure: Text and Performance* (London: Macmillan, 1986), 89–90.

8. In G. Wilson Knight's famous essay, the Duke is indeed a figure of Christ, the Word incarnate, bringing a new dispensation to sinners condemned by the old law, "*Measure for Measure* and the Gospels," in *The Wheel of Fire* [Oxford UP, 1930; rpt. London: Methuen, 1949]). This allegorical reading of the Duke heavily influenced productions, particularly in the early 1960s. See Ralph Berry, *Changing Styles in Shakespeare* (London: Allen and Unwin, 1981), 39–40. More recent criticism, manifesting increased distrust of authority, has tended to portray the Duke not as allegorically representing God but as capriciously "playing god," implementing a dangerously imperfect and self-interested worldly power. In his recent, highly illuminating essay, Robert Watson suggests that the Duke functions "not simply as *imitatio dei*, but as *imitatio dei absconditi*" ("False Immortality in *Measure for Measure*: Comic Means, Tragic Ends," *Shakespeare Quarterly* 41 [1990], 432).

9. "Fassbinder and Lacan: A Reconsideration of Gaze, Look, and Image," in *Male Subjectivity at the Margins*, 135–36.

10. "Sex was taken charge of, tracked down, as it were, by a discourse that allowed it no obscurity, no respite. . . . One could plot a line going straight from the seventeenth-century pastoral to what became its projection in literature, 'scandalous literature' at that" (*The History of Sexuality, Volume I: An Introduction*, trans. Robert Hurley [New York: Vintage, 1980], 19–21).

11. See Brown, "Erotic Religious Flagellation," 147.

12. See Roland Barthes, *Sade Fourier Loyola*, trans. Richard Miller (New York: Hill and Wang, 1976), 145.

13. Scott, *Renaissance Drama and a Modern Audience*, 65.

14. See Richard Paul Knowles, "Robin Phillips Measures Up: 'Measure for Measure' at Stratford, Ontario, 1975–76," *Essays in Theatre* 8 (1989), 45–46.

15. Nicholas Shrimpton, "Shakespeare Performances in Stratford-upon-Avon and London," in *Shakespeare Survey* 38 (Cambridge UP, 1985), 204. Penny Gay goes further in describing the closeness that the Duke and Isabella achieved in Noble's production: "[I]t was the only production, in my experience, in which it becomes clear during the course of the play that this extraordinary couple have fallen in love" (*As She Likes It: Shakespeare's Unruly Women* [London: Routledge, 1994], 136).

16. See Anthony B. Dawson, "*Measure for Measure*, New Historicism, and Theatrical Power," *Shakespeare Quarterly* 39 (Fall 1988), 339. Such intimate gestures do not necessarily rob the Duke's marriage proposal of its surprise or provocation. Nor did all the productions featuring them end with Isabella's acceptance. These intimacies may

even sharpen the surprise and provocation of the Duke's proposal—or at least sharpen Isabella's sense of bewilderment and betrayal when she learns the extent to which the Duke has deceived and manipulated her. In my own production, audiences emitted audible gasps of surprise when the Duke proposed to Isabella, despite the warmth and rapport—and physical comfortableness—of their relationship. The director and actors, unlike the reader, must develop a specific relationship between the Duke and Isabella that has kinetic consequences, that demands translation into a body language of some kind, one capable of registering—however subtly and subliminally—the emotional and even erotic undercurrents of their encounters. Such a body language is necessarily ambiguous, however. In this play, bodies cannot be trusted.

17. Many critics note the extent to which Angelo functions as the Duke's double. See, for instance, Nancy S. Leonard, "Substitution in Shakespeare's Problem Comedies," *English Literary Renaissance* 9 (1979), 296–97; David Sundelson, *Shakespeare's Restoration of the Father* (New Brunswick, N.J.: Rutgers UP, 1983), 90; Alexander Leggatt, "Substitution in *Measure for Measure*," *Shakespeare Quarterly* 39 (1988), 345–46; and Ruth Nevo, "*Measure for Measure:* Mirror for Mirror," *Shakespeare Survey* 40 (Cambridge UP: 1988), 111–12. My reading differs from theirs in portraying Angelo not simply as surrogate or scapegoat but as a projection of the Duke's self.

18. Nevo suggests that Escalus functions as "a part of himself which [the Duke] now repudiates" ("*Measure for Measure:* Mirror for Mirror," 111).

19. Freud uses the terms "ego ideal" and "superego" more or less interchangeably in *The Ego and the Id,* trans. Joan Riviere (New York: Norton, 1960), 18–29. I am drawing on Kaja Silverman's differentiation of the terms in accordance with Freud's distinction between that aspect of the ego which identifies with the id's object-choice (ego ideal) and that aspect which delimits identification (superego). See "Masochism and Male Subjectivity," 193–95.

20. Freud, *The Ego and the Id,* 24.

21. This parallel, often noted by the play's commentators, was emphasized in Egan's production: the two were "paired, likened, played off against each other to heighten the special kinship just behind the verbal animosity . . . the recognition thus teased at in these scenes was not the Duke behind the friar but the Lucio within the Duke" (Andresen, "*Measure for Measure* at the Mark Taper Forum," 508).

22. See Michel Foucault, *Discipline and Punish: The Birth of the Prison,* trans. Alan Sheridan (New York: Vintage, 1979), 48: "The public execution, then, has a juridico-political function. It is a ceremonial by which a momentarily injured sovereignty is reconstituted. It restores that sovereignty by manifesting it at its most spectacular . . . over and above the crime that has placed the sovereign in contempt, it deploys before all eyes an invincible force."

23. "The gaze is 'unapprehensible,' i.e., impossible to seize or get hold of. The relationship between eye and gaze is thus analogous in certain ways to that which links penis and phallus; the former can stand in for the latter, but can never approximate it" (Silverman, "Fassbinder and Lacan: A Reconsideration of Gaze, Look, and Image," 130).

24. For a description of the theatrics of public confession, see Karin S. Coddon, "'Suche Strange Desygns': Madness, Subjectivity, and Treason in *Hamlet* and Elizabethan Culture," in *Renaissance Drama,* n.s. 20 (1990), 51–75.

25. Deleuze, "Coldness and Cruelty," 29. In an undergraduate Shakespeare class, I

screened several versions of the eye-gouging scene from *King Lear.* The students unanimously agreed that the cruelest Cornwall was Peter Brook's Patrick Magee (who, fittingly, also played Sade in Brook's *Marat/Sade*) because he was so inhumanly passionless.

26. Deleuze's account of sadism coalesces with the feminist reading of pornography as an intrinsically sadistic mode of representation through which men indulge fantasies of mastering women who embody their own discarded sexual selves. See, for instance, Susan Griffin, *Pornography and Silence* (New York: Harper, 1981) and Andrea Dworkin, *Pornography: Men Possessing Women* (London: Women's Press, 1982).

Pornography is an exceptionally complex subject. Even within feminist ranks attitudes toward it differ sharply. For instance, Linda Williams, who calls herself an "anti-censorship feminist," finds the attitude of Griffin and Dworkin and other "anti-pornography" feminists to be needlessly prosecutorial and untenably utopian, arguing that "a whole and natural sexuality that stands outside history and free of power" is purely mythical, and that power is an ineradicable part of human sexuality. See the opening chapter of her fascinating study of pornographic films, *Hard Core: Power, Pleasure, and the "Frenzy of the Visible"* (Berkeley: U of California P, 1989).

27. In the monasteries, as Brown points out, while monks and nuns frequently flayed themselves in private for bodily trespasses, they also regularly submitted to public beatings from their superiors, which "promoted both active sadism in the flogger and vicarious sadism in the spectators"—turning the punishment of sinning flesh into public spectacle ("Erotic Religious Flagellation and Shakespeare's *Measure for Measure,*" 144).

28. See L. A. Parry, *The History of Torture in England* (London: Sampson Low Marston, 1934; rpt. Montclair, N.J.: Patterson Smith, 1975), 41.

29. As Foucault puts it, "the punishment is carried out in such a way as to give a spectacle not of measure, but of imbalance and excess; in this liturgy of punishment, there must be an emphatic affirmation of power and its intrinsic superiority" *(Discipline and Punish,* 49). Angelo's public degradation of Claudio becomes the visible sign of the "excess(iveness)" of executing a man for having enjoyed conjugal relations with his common-law wife. The absence of "measure" in Angelo's sentence is particularly telling given the play's title and recasts the Duke's threatened retribution at the end as "excess for excess."

30. "Coldness and Cruelty," 55.

31. Dawson writes insightfully of the way the play's sexual politics are "imaged as a form of inscription, men writing on women" (*"Measure for Measure,* New Historicism, and Theatrical Power," 336).

32. Brown relates the "proneness" urged on Isabella to the flagellant's position and therefore to Isabella's pledge to "strip [her]self to death" ("Erotic Religious Flagellation," 163–65). I cannot agree, however, that Isabella is a masochist. For one thing, there is no evidence that she wishes to enact the fantasy she projects. For another, her treatment of Claudio—and even of Angelo in the play's final scene—brings her much closer to sadism, to mortifying an abjected image of the sexual self.

33. The image recalls Angelo's characterization of Claudio's crime: putting "mettle" in "restrained means" to make "a false [life]" (2.4.48–49)—impregnating an unmarried woman and engendering an "unlawful" child. It also anticipates Isabella's later dread of giving "unlawful birth" (3.1.189–91).

34. Nevo sees Juliet as "Isabella's alter ego . . . the woman in Isabella which Isabella, choosing chastity to God, has not chosen to be" (*"Measure for Measure:* Mirror for Mirror," 115). Janet Adelman considers the splitting of the two characters a product of the play's psychic landscape: "[I]n effect, Isabella is imagined—by Claudio and by the play—as a response to Juliet" (*Suffocating Mothers: Fantasies of Maternal Origin in Shakespeare's Plays, Hamlet to The Tempest* [New York: Routledge, 1992], 90).

35. For the first view, see Brown, "Erotic Religious Flagellation," 153; for the second, see Marvin Rosenberg, "Shakespeare's Fantastic Trick: *Measure for Measure,*" *The Sewanee Review* 70 (1972), 54.

36. Juliet Stevenson, who played Isabella for Adrian Noble in 1983, contends that Isabella, although not afraid of or surprised by her sexuality, nevertheless wants to dominate it, and so selects the St. Clares: "[T]he severity of the order is, I believe, commensurate with the scale of those latent passions in her, which she feels must be harnessed, controlled" (quoted in Carol Rutter, *Clamorous Voices: Shakespeare's Women Today* [London: Women's Press, 1988], 41).

37. See William Empson's discussion of the multifarious meanings of "sense" in this play: "Sense in *Measure for Measure,*" in *The Structure of Complex Words* (London: Chatto and Windus, 1951), 270–88. Adrian Noble physicalized this "breeding of sense" by having Isabella actually touch Angelo on the phrase "go to your bosom" and elicit an erotically charged reaction (see Steve Vineberg, "Problem Plays," *The Threepenny Review* 52 [1993], 34).

38. "Isabella in *Measure for Measure,*" *Shakespeare Studies* 15 (1982), 143.

39. Peter Stallybrass gives a thorough account of this paradigm in "Patriarchal Territories: The Body Enclosed," in *Rewriting the Renaissance: The Discourses of Sexual Difference in Early Modern Europe,* ed. Margaret W. Ferguson, Maureen Quilligan, and Nancy J. Vickers (U of Chicago P, 1986), 123–42, esp. 126–29.

40. Quoted in Ralph Berry, *On Directing Shakespeare: Interviews with Contemporary Directors* (London: Croom Helm, 1977), 94.

41. Isabella's specularity in this scene is a key point in Kathleen McLuskie's important essay, "The Patriarchal Bard: Feminist Criticism and Shakespeare: *King Lear* and *Measure for Measure,*" in *Political Shakespeare,* 88–108, esp. 95–97. McLuskie contends that "the theatrical strategies which present the action to be judged resist feminist manipulation by denying an autonomous position for the female viewer of the action" (95). I would say instead that "the theatrical strategies which present the action to be judged" do not inhere in the text but grow out of it and are therefore multiple and inclusive of feminist tactics.

42. My portrayal of Isabella as an actress is anticipated somewhat by Marcia Riefer, "'Instruments of Some More Mightier Member': The Constriction of Female Power in *Measure for Measure,*" in *Modern Critical Interpretations: William Shakespeare's* Measure for Measure, ed. Harold Bloom (New York: Chelsea House, 1987), 140–41; and Charles R. Lyons, "Silent Women and Shrews: Eroticism and Convention in *Epicoene* and *Measure for Measure,*" *Comparative Drama* 22 (1990), 123–40, especially 129–30—though neither discusses Isabella's performance as specifically an enforced feminine masquerade.

43. "Coldness and Cruelty," 63.

44. "Coldness and Cruelty," 31–32, 76, 88–89, 104.

45. Wheeler suggests that Angelo is "responsible to a severe but insufficiently

internalized superego; he is secure only so long as he remains in subordinate relation to a readily available figure of paternal authority" (*Shakespeare's Development and the Problem Comedies* [Berkeley: U of California P, 1981], 94). In my reading, Angelo transfers allegiance to an image of maternal authority, before whom he abases himself—thus assuming the masochist's position, however temporarily.

46. See Watson's fascinating discussion of the many ways the play evokes the Virgin Mary as a shadow for both Isabella and Angelo ("False Immortality in *Measure for Measure*," 425–26).

47. *Suffocating Mothers*, 93. Wheeler also notes that Angelo, unlike Hamlet, Iago, or Othello, internalizes the split between the ideal and the sexual rather than projecting it onto a woman (*Shakespeare's Development and the Problem Comedies*, 99).

48. See Lacan, "A Love Letter," in *Feminine Sexuality*, 153–54.

49. Griffin sees this scenario as the underlying theme of all pornography. See *Pornography and Silence*, 29–35.

50. Adelman anticipates this point in *Suffocating Mothers*, 91.

51. Although, to my mind, she simplifies Angelo by calling him a sadist, Brown offers helpful commentary on the sadism intrinsic to Angelo's threats ("Erotic Religious Flagellation," 158).

52. "Theory and Practice: Pornography and Rape," in *Take Back the Night: Women on Pornography*, ed. Laura Lederer (New York: William Morrow, 1980), 139.

53. "False Immortality in *Measure for Measure*," 425.

54. For Harriet Hawkins, these lines seem "deliberately designed by Shakespeare to arouse Angelo as saint, sensualist, and as a sadist. And so, of course, they do" ("'The Devil's Party': Virtues and Vices in *Measure for Measure*," in *Modern Critical Interpretations*, 85).

55. "Masochism and Male Subjectivity," 197.

56. The persecuted, feminized sensualist Claudio may also call to mind the persecuted god of Euripides' *The Bacchae*, Dionysos, who, disguised as a mysterious, effeminate stranger, is likewise placed in chains and paraded through the city, forced to submit to the chastisements of the Angelo-like governor, Pentheus, who ridicules his unmanliness. Pentheus' pose as omnipotent male authority, however, proves as shaky as Angelo's. Both men decide to give their sensual race the rein, Pentheus involuntarily enacting a version of the masochist's scenario, wearing women's clothes and suffering the brutalizations of the very women he vowed to punish, and Angelo turning sadist and punishing the "feminine" forces that excite the urge to lose "masculine" control.

57. Hannah Tillich, *From Time to Time* (New York: Stein and Day, 1973), 14.

58. Griffin asserts, "the metaphysics of Christianity and the metaphysics of pornography are the same. . . . All the elements of sadomasochistic ritual are present in the crucifixion of Christ" (*Pornography and Silence*, 14, 68). Beatrice Faust argues that Christianity's effect on the visual arts was to drive erotica underground and replace it with sadomasochism (*Women, Sex, and Pornography* [New York: Macmillan, 1980], 86).

59. Although he does not explicitly relate Isabella's "rubies" speech to the dynamics of sadomasochism, Wheeler discusses it in terms that anticipate mine: as a re-sexualization of her desexualized gift of virginity to God (*Shakespeare's Development and the Problem Comedies*, 112).

60. See Freud's account of female beating fantasies as manifestations of oedipal guilt in "A Child Is Being Beaten," 184–99.

61. My reading of Isabella's father-fixation is indebted to Adelman's account in *Suffocating Mothers*, 96–98.

62. See Nevo's discussion of Mariana as Isabella's "deeply wished-for double" (*"Measure for Measure:* Mirror for Mirror," 118–19).

63. McLuskie suggests that a feminist performance of *Measure for Measure* is not really possible, for it "would require a radical rewriting both of the narrative and of the way the scenes are constructed" (97). Yet earlier in the same essay she specifies elements of an hypothetical feminist production that seem neither radical nor difficult to realize: "celebrat[ing] Isabella's chastity as a feminist resistance" and "making her plea for Angelo's life a gesture of solidarity to a heterosexual sister" (94). Her other suggestion—"deny[ing] the lively energy of the pimps and bawds" in order to "foreground their exploitation of female sexuality" is somewhat more problematic. One may certainly endeavor to depict the exploitation of female sexuality, as my production did, but turning Pompey into a villain is quite another matter. Still, one could achieve considerable tension by underlining the link between the irrepressible, disarming pimp and the exploitation he enables. In any case, McLuskie underestimates the deconstructive capacities of contemporary performance.

64. Quoted in Rutter, *Clamorous Voices*, 41.

65. Because Hillman does not contextualize Isabella's chastity within a rapacious phallocentric order, he reads it as a self-diminishing defense against sexual turmoil rather than a self-sustaining defense against sexual violation. In Hillman's account, what Isabella protects is not a personal integrity but an impossible ideal of purity (see *William Shakespeare: The Problem Plays*, 124).

66. Nicholls, *Measure for Measure*, 81.

67. See Weil, "Stratford Festival, Canada," 247–48.

68. Gay, *As She Likes It*, 142. According to Gay, this choice achieved precisely the effect I claim for it: "Her 'To whom should I complain?' had a frighteningly contemporary resonance in the context of this overt sexual violence."

69. Robert Smallwood, "Shakespeare at Stratford-upon-Avon, 1991," *Shakespeare Quarterly* 43 (1992), 355.

70. Before being led off, Lucio turned to one of the hooded executioners standing nearby and appealed for help; the headsman then pulled off his hood (another unveiling) and revealed himself to be Pompey, who then emitted a retributive dog-like growl, the same derisive sound with which Lucio had accompanied his earlier admonition that Lucio "go to kennel" (3.2.85).

71. One may speak of a female "lack" within the world of *Measure for Measure* simply on the basis of the marginalization and absence of female characters. Kate Keepdown and Elbow's wife, both of whom are mentioned repeatedly, do not appear in the play. In addition, the women in the play are mostly estranged from one another. There is no nurturing mother-daughter relationship such as Helena enjoys with the Countess and no female alliance such as she enjoys with Diana and the Widow. Isabella teams up with Mariana in order to entrap Angelo, but both are "instruments of some more mightier member." Isabella and Juliet are close friends, yet they never meet in the play. Juliet and Mariana share a common fate—common-law wives plagued by dowry problems who "stealthily" consummate their marriages—yet they remain unacquainted.

72. Martha Henry, who played the role for Phillips in his 1975 production, offered a particularly arresting portrayal of Isabella as pathologically repressed. At the conclu-

sion of her second interview with Angelo, left alone to contemplate his shocking proposition, she splashed cold water onto her flushed face: "[T]he image that the glacial, white-dressed pure virgin is *hot* is a crystallization of what the scene is about," explains Phillips (quoted in Berry, *On Directing Shakespeare*, 103). When telling Claudio of Angelo's lecherous advances, Isabella obsessively ran her hands over her brother's body (Knowles, "Robin Phillips Measures Up," 44). In Nunn's production, Isabella's repugnance to sexuality suggested "some abhorrent past experience" (Small-wood, "Shakespeare in England," 354). Kyle's production portrayed Isabella as over-coming her repression to such an extent that she leapt into the Duke's arms on his first proposal:

> His response "but fitter time for that" to this passionate young woman carried the knowing smile which suggested a cooling-off period before enthusiastic love-making. (Nicholls, *Measure for Measure*, 80)

In all three instances, it could be argued, reducing Isabella's chastity to a symptom of repression simplifies her complex sexuality. Helen Mirren's portrayal (for Peter Gill's production, 1979) seems to have anticipated Stevenson's in defining chastity as an act of resistance against a normative femininity synonymous with sexual availability on male terms. Neither Mirren nor Stevenson wore the traditional nun's outfit, as though underlining their secularizations of chastity (see Scott, *Renaissance Drama and a Modern Audience*, 69). Stevenson fully intended this costuming choice to be defamiliarizing:

> I didn't want the audience to be looking at a nun all night. I wanted to break down what they would invariably have associated with that image. I wanted to say to them, "Look at this person. *Listen* to this person. Don't judge her from the image. Listen afresh." (Quoted in Gay, *As She Likes It*, 138)

Critical accounts of the play suggest that Stevenson's efforts to rehabilitate Isabella's image were largely successful. See Gay's discussion of these favorable reviews, along with her own laudatory reading of Stevenson's portrayal as successfully feminist: "Stevenson's Isabella was an embodiment of late twentieth-century feminism come of age and accepted into mainstream thinking; her performance enabled audiences to see that a woman's claim for control of her own body is reasonable and normal, and that such autonomy can be a positive force in society" (*As She Likes It*, 139). That this effect was achieved *without* recourse to a gestus of rape underlines the benefit to a director of an extraordinarily gifted actor.

73. See Lyons for a fascinating account of Isabella's resemblance to a shrew ("Silent Women and Shrews," 136–38). The notion of a female "openness" that invites "enclo-sure" I borrow from Stallybrass ("Patriarchal Territories," 126–29).

74. He also enters the play at approximately the same point as Parolles and similarly initiates a ribald dialogue that takes the play into a lower, sexual register. Unlike Parolles, who constructs a fixed persona, Lucio projects varying personae. But both are essentially theatrical beings.

75. Hillman sees Lucio not simply as as a rival exhibitionist but a rival creator, playing Lucifer to the Duke's God (*William Shakespeare: The Problem Plays*, 108).

76. In Wheeler's account the Duke's shaming and rescuing of Isabella answers a psychological need to effect Isabella's transformation from sexually provocative woman to safely desexualized wife (*Shakespeare's Development*, 129–30).

77. For an illuminating discussion of the different ways directors have staged this final moment, see Philip C. McGuire, *Speechless Dialect: Shakespeare's Open Silences* (Berkeley: U of California P, 1985), 63–93. For other helpful accounts of the play in performance, see Nicholls, *Measure for Measure*; Berry, *Changing Styles in Shakespeare*; Scott, *Renaissance Drama and a Modern Audience*; Jane Williamson, "The Duke and Isabella on the Modern Stage," in *The Triple Bond: Plays, Mainly Shakespearean, in Performance*, ed. Joseph Price (University Park: Pennsylvania State UP, 1975), 149–69; and Knowles, "Robin Phillips Measures Up." For a provocative discussion of the play's resistance to feminist performance, see McLuskie, "The Patriarchal Bard." For a discussion of the possibilities of feminist intervention in performance, see Rutter, *Clamorous Voices*, 27–42. Hillman regards Isabella's silence as a kind of red herring, arguing that the Duke *imposes* silence on her in order to preclude any possibility of resistance. Both times the Duke proposes marriage, says Hillman, he denies her the opportunity to speak, "the first time by announcing a change of subject, later by imposing on her the role of listener" (*William Shakespeare: The Problem Plays*, 92). Hillman's reading is characteristically sensitive and suggests a way of staging the ending of the play that, to my knowledge, has never been attempted. Still, his interpretation presupposes that the Duke expects Isabella to resist, which is arguable, to say the least. In addition, even if, as Hillman implies, the Duke defers his second marriage proposal to the future, his request that Isabella accompany him to the palace still empowers her with choice; her silence may confound his request for accompaniment as much as it obstructs his proposal of marriage. Her answer to the first implies an answer to the second.

78. "'Instruments of Some More Mightier Member,'" 142.

79. Kliman argues that Claudio's dependence on Juliet's dowry suggests that there is no family fortune, and that Isabella is therefore dowerless. She speculates that Isabella's dowerlessness may well have compelled her to enter a convent ("Isabella in *Measure for Measure*," 138). Lyons observes that the Duke's disinterest in Isabella's dowry stands out in a play that gives such great attention to the dowries of Juliet and Mariana ("Silent Women and Shrews," 137).

80. "One can see *Measure for Measure* as a play that opens with the law being invoked to punish fornication by death and that closes with the law being utilized to punish fornication by marriage" (McGuire, *Speechless Dialect*, 71).

### 3. *Troilus and Cressida*

1. Carol Cook also notes the way in which Helen serves as "the empty marker of value in the economy of masculine desire," the "black hole which draws all things to it" ("Unbodied Figures of Desire," in *Performing Feminisms: Feminist Critical Theory and Practice*, ed. Sue-Ellen Case [Baltimore: Johns Hopkins UP, 1990], 182). See also Linda Charnes's insightful discussion of Helen as a "curiously inadequate" phallic signifier ("'So Unsecret to Ourselves': Notorious Identity and the Material Subject in *Troilus and Cressida*," in *Notorious Identity: Materializing the Subject in Shakespeare* [Cambridge, Mass.: Harvard UP, 1993], 83. These two brilliant essays offer especially powerful accounts of the way subjectivity and gender are constructed within the world of the play.

Cook's essay examines the play in relation to Lacan's critique of desire and anticipates my argument in her assertion that the play illustrates that the female subject cannot sustain male desire unless suffering transformation from a materially present subject to a symbolically lacking object—whose lack may be either (as the play demonstrates) fetishistically disavowed or sadistically reviled.

The phrase "notorious identity," which I use repeatedly, comes from Charnes. Her central claim is that *Troilus and Cressida* "represent[s] neurosis in the form of subjectivity crippled by cultural inscription" (72). In her emphasis on the play's destabilizing mimesis—the gap it opens up between the play's characters and their celebrated originals—and her discussion of a male homosociality mediated by the exchange of women's bodies, Charnes's argument is close to mine. My central disagreement with her essay is the prohibitive power it affords textual precedent, ironically affirming, in the context of literary influence, a myth of origins that her essay so skillfully discredits in the context of subjectivity. Although she acknowledges that "the brilliance of this play resides in the way it at once pays its legendary 'debt' and prods us to anticipate" a new ending to the story ("this time, maybe, Troilus will 'stand up' for Cressida and . . . she will 'hold out' for him" [101]), she ultimately affirms the unalterability of the original conclusion. Not only Troilus but the play itself forces Cressida to assume the figure of legendary traitress. Cressida not only meets her preordained end but is constantly, painfully aware of its inevitability. "Cressida must bear the awareness that every step she takes toward Troilus seals her 'fate' as an artifact, and secures her signification as the 'heart of falsehood'" (79).

I argue, by contrast, that by failing to dramatize Cressida's infamous betrayal, by lending her scene with Diomedes so much silence, equivocation, and ambiguity, and by allowing Cressida an attempt to represent herself beyond this scene—an attempt that Troilus defeats—the play does *not* deliver Cressida to her notorious identity. Moreover, I argue that Cressida is aware not of a specific textual identity she must necessarily enact but of a generalized gender image that she is seduced into nearly enacting.

2. My discussion of seduction is heavily indebted to Jean Baudrillard's fascinating treatise, *Seduction,* trans. Brian Singer (New York: St. Martin's, 1990). See the Introduction of this book for my critique of Baudrillard's reification of phallocentric gender ideology. His case for the superiority of feminine seduction to masculine production presupposes the unalterability of a "phallocratic" order and glosses over the effects of disenfranchising women from the productive, discursive agencies that he reserves for the masculine. In the political realm, the culturally imposed lack for which Baudrillard's theory of seduction compensates remains a formidable mechanism for marginalizing women.

3. In Keith Hack's 1974 OUDS production, Helen was suspended above the action for the entire play—another way of conveying her status as veiled gaze: "Helen, swinging langourously and preening herself in a looking-glass, was the constant reminder that the war was fought for *this*" (Ralph Berry, *Changing Styles in Shakespeare* [London: Allen and Unwin, 1981], 61–62).

4. This video could mimic the *Star Search* "photoshoot" competition, in which rivals for "spokesmodel" salaciously display themselves in simulated modeling sessions. The similarity might provoke laughter from the audience, which is fine.

5. The assembling of the Trojan army that I describe does not accord with the action of "sperring up," which evokes a locking of the city's gates. One could, however, easily substitute the folio's "stir up" for "sperr up," as Kenneth Palmer does in the Arden edition (*Troilus and Cressida* [London: Methuen, 1982], 98), which conveys an image of the Trojan troops preparing for battle in a manner congruent with the staging I envision.

6. In addition to Charnes ("So Unsecret to Ourselves," 72), Elizabeth Freund also writes insightfully on the play's characters' displacement from their legendary models ("'Ariachne's Broken Woof': The Rhetoric of Citation in *Troilus and Cressida,*" in *Shakespeare and the Question of Theory,* ed. Patricia Parker and Geoffrey Hartman [New York: Methuen, 1985], 19–36).

7. In Sam Mendes's 1990 RSC production, the stage picture contradicted Pandarus' words. "Displaced from the centre of the stage to the side gallery," Pandarus mediated not a processional but a ritual of purification—"an integral part of the serious fact of [the warriors'] having survived a day's battle, washing the blood from their swords and then washing their faces or drinking" (Peter Holland, "Shakespearean Performances in England, 1989–90," *Shakespeare Survey* 44 [1992], 172). In a wonderful essay, Barbara Hodgdon discusses four different stagings of this scene. Her conclusion is that, by making Cressida the object of the soldiers' (and spectators') look, most directors exploit and disempower her, depriving her of an autonomous look. Hodgdon argues that Howard Davies's 1985 RSC production restores priority to Cressida's look by positioning her and Pandarus far downstage, viewing the (absent) soldiers from a distance ("He Do Cressida in Different Voices," *English Literary Renaissance* 20 [Spring 1990], 254–86). I would argue that one captures the play's looking relations more precisely if Cressida's autonomous look is trained on exhibitionistic warriors who are more covetous of one another's admiring glances than of hers.

8. See Berry, *Changing Styles in Shakespeare,* 59.

9. See Berry, *Changing Styles in Shakespeare,* 59.

10. Gary Spear similarly traces the connection between virile display and effeminacy in his fine essay, "Shakespeare's 'Manly' Parts: Masculinity and Effeminacy in *Troilus and Cressida,*" *Shakespeare Quarterly* 44 (Winter 1993), 409–22, esp. 414–16. As Spear aptly puts it, "how do you know when someone is acting like a man or only *acting* like a man?" (415).

11. For an analysis of the homoerotic dimensions of the passage's procreative imagery, see Spear, "Shakespeare's 'Manly' Parts," 416.

12. For a corroborative account of Achilles' constructedness, see Rene Girard, "The Politics of Desire in *Troilus and Cressida,*" *Shakespeare and the Question of Theory,* 207.

13. Charnes also analyzes these phrases as aspersions of the generals' masculinity ("'So Unsecret to Ourselves,'" 93–94).

14. For an account of the perplexed and mostly negative reactions to Barton's cross-dressing Achilles, see Berry, *Changing Styles in Shakespeare,* 59. Barton himself comments on the controversy: "We were attacked for presenting Achilles as an effeminate homosexual, which was something that had never entered our minds" ("John Barton Talks to Gareth Lloyd Evans," *Shakespeare Survey* 25 [1972], 70).

For representative criticism of this iconoclastic choice, see Richard David, *Shakespeare in the Theatre* (Cambridge UP, 1978), 121. Although Barton, upon reviving the play in 1976, dropped the characterization of Achilles as cross-dresser, David and other reviewers still saw him as perversely effeminate: "[T]he memory of the earlier production inclined one to see, in Achilles' wig, dress, and bangles (no doubt Trojan male attire assumed in compliment to his Trojan lady-love), a wholly feminine apparel" (123). Roger Warren also found the 1976 Achilles a "showily effeminate" retread of the original transvestite ("Theory and Practice: Stratford 1975," *Shakespeare Survey* 30 [1977], 174).

15. "John Barton Talks to Gareth Lloyd Evans," 70.

16. Leo Bersani connects the catamitical position with femininity and castration in his essay, "Is the Rectum a Grave?" (*October* 43 [1987]), which Silverman discusses in her extraordinary essay, "A Woman's Soul Enclosed in a Man's Body: Femininity in Male Homosexuality" (in *Male Subjectivity at the Margins*, 339–88). For an alternative view of Patroclus, see Gregory W. Bredbeck, *Sodomy and Interpretation: Marlowe to Milton* (Ithaca, N.Y.: Cornell UP, 1991), 33–48, esp. 39. Bredbeck argues that "there is nothing in the play to substantiate Thersites' bitter condemnations as more then mere possibilities," that Patroclus "transcends the base labels applied to him" (39). Yet, inasmuch as Patroclus identifies himself as Achilles' lover (3.3.219–25), Thersites' labels, stripped of their "baseness," may be considered essentially accurate. Patroclus' status as "boy," his "little stomach" for the war, even his penchant for acting destabilize his "masculinity" far more than his inclusion in Agamemnon's listing of dead warriors (which Bredbeck sees as evidence of his nobility) upholds it.

17. See Spear's objection to the characterization of Patroclus as a drag queen in the Yale Repertory Theatre production in 1990 ("Shakespeare's 'Manly Parts,'" 412, note 8). My point is simply that Patroclus' effeminacy derives not from mannerism or sartorial habit but from his refusal of phallic masculinity, signaled by his lack of appetite for the war and his role in prolonging Achilles' absence from it. He is effeminate for eschewing the power that defines masculinity, not for looking or acting "feminine." Hence the conundrum caused by his cross-dressing.

18. My understanding of Troilus' fantasy of maternal plenitude is indebted to Janet Adelman's brilliant essay on *Troilus and Cressida* in *Suffocating Mothers: Fantasies of Maternal Origin in Shakespeare's Plays*, Hamlet to The Tempest (New York: Routledge, 1992), 38–63, esp. 52–55. Ultimately, I see this fantasy as subordinate to another: the fantasy of female lack that foreordains Cressida's failure as (m)other. Troilus' image of maternal nurturance is, from the beginning, less a sustaining fantasy than a disabling fiction, an impossible dream. Troilus is less interested in realizing a fantasy of recovered maternal plenitude than in seducing Cressida into demonstrating its unrecoverability.

19. See Jacques Lacan, "The Agency of the Letter in the Unconscious or Reason since Freud," in *Ecrits: A Selection*, trans. Alan Sheridan (New York: Norton, 1977), 146–78, esp. 160–64.

20. For many critics, the separation that follows sexuality is the key aspect of the lovers' relationship. See, for instance, Derek Traversi, *An Approach to Shakespeare* (Garden City, N.Y.: Doubleday, 1956), 325–37; L. C. Knights, "The Theme of Appearance and Reality in Shakespeare's *Troilus and Cressida*," in *Some Shakespearean Themes* (Stanford UP, 1959), 67; Charles R. Lyons, "Cressida, Achilles, and the Finite Deed," *Etudes Anglaises* 20 (1967), 233; and Barbara Everett, "The Inaction of *Troilus and Cressida*," *Essays in Criticism* 32 (1982), 126. Stephen A. Reid provides a Freudian reading of this separateness ("A Psychoanalytic Reading of *Troilus and Cressida* and *Measure for Measure*," *Psychoanalytic Review* 57 [1970], 263–82), emphasizing the temporal limitations of the sexual act. Adelman provides an interpretation grounded in object-relations psychology, in which, "from the first, Troilus' desire for Cressida is invested with the power of a nostalgic longing for, and fear of, union with an overpoweringly maternal figure" (*Suffocating Mothers*, 52). And Cook offers a Lacanian reading, in which "the desired object does not satisfy desire but kindles it" ("Unbodied Figures of Desire," 184).

21. See Lacan, "Sexuality in the Defiles of the Signifier," in *The Four Fundamental Concepts of Psycho-Analysis* (New York: Norton, 1978), 153–55. See also Alan Sheridan's

note on desire as Lacan conceives it: "[D]esire (fundamentally in the singular) is a perpetual effect of symbolic articulation. It is not an appetite: it is essentially excentric and insatiable. That is why Lacan coordinates it not with the object that would seem to satisfy it, but with the object that causes it" ("Translator's Note," in *Four Fundamental Concepts*, 278). I should like to reiterate that I regard such desire not as normative but as narcissistic.

22. Troilus' recoil from Cressida also calls to mind Pandarus' song about the honey bee, which offers an image of male sexual experience as not only frustrating but defeating. Instead of imbibing nectar, one loses honey:

> Full merrily the humble-bee doth sing,
> Till he hath lost his honey and his sting;
> And being once subdu'd in armed tail,
> Sweet honey and sweet notes together fail.

(5.10.41–44)

Typically the song omits reference to the desired female object, but her presence is strongly implied. It is she who takes the honey and removes the sting, who "subdues" the desiring male. Kenneth Palmer believes that Pandarus describes himself in this verse—that the songless humble bee is the disprized pimp rather than the disaffected lover—even while pointing out that "he appeals, in effect, to the sexual pattern: expectation, attainment, revulsion" (the Arden *Troilus and Cressida*, 302). Considering that Pandarus evokes "the sexual pattern" in order to answer the question, "why should our endeavor be so lov'd and the performance so loath'd?" (5.10.38–39), the verse more likely addresses the sexual disillusionment that causes Troilus to rebuff Pandarus rather than the implications of the rebuff itself.

23. Julia Kristeva, "Woman Can Never Be Defined," in *New French Feminisms*, ed. Elaine Marks and Isabella De Courtivron (Amherst: U of Massachusetts P, 1980), 137.

24. *Jouissance* "transgresses" the "law of homeostasis that Freud evokes in *Beyond the Pleasure Principle,* whereby, through discharge, the psyche seeks the lowest possible level of tension. . . . in that respect, it is *beyond* the pleasure principle" (Sheridan, "Translator's Note," in Lacan, *Four Fundamental Concepts,* 281). See also Lacan, "God and the *Jouissance* of the Woman" and "A Love Letter," in *Feminine Sexuality,* ed. Juliet Mitchell and Jacqueline Rose (New York: Norton, 1985), 137–61.

25. "The law of seduction takes the form of an uninterrupted ritual exchange where seducer and seduced constantly raise the stakes in a game that never ends" (Baudrillard, *Seduction,* 22).

26. Many critics have made this point, of course. What I take to be unique in my argument is the idea that Troilus tries, from the beginning, to seduce (in Baudrillard's sense of the word) Cressida into the betrayal that will substantiate his cherished self-image. Subsequent to finishing my work on this play, I was fortunate enough to encounter Richard Hillman's essay, which offers a parallel discussion of Troilus as a "non-Machiavellian manipulator," improvisationally constructing himself through the construction of Cressida (*William Shakespeare: The Problem Plays* [New York: Twayne, 1993], 26).

27. Even critics sympathetic to Cressida believe that she ultimately plays the role of traitress traditionally assigned her. Knights, for instance, while noting the sincerity with which Cressida confesses her love to Troilus, nonetheless observes, "so far as she is presented directly, she is the wanton of tradition" ("The Theme of Appearance and Reality in Shakespeare's *Troilus and Cressida,*" 68). Freund, while employing a strikingly

different methodology, reaches virtually the same conclusion: "Even as—indeed, precisely because—we are persuaded that her love is stronger than her craft, we are made to realize that in being her rhetorical self (and there is surely no other) she can never be herself" ("'Ariachne's Broken Woof,'" 24). To have no other self but her rhetorical self is to be the wanton of tradition. Even Charnes, who argues that Cressida's subjectivity exists precisely in the gap between her notorious identity and her attempts to escape it, asserts that Cressida is "constituted to be false" ("'So Unsecret to Ourselves,'" 77).

28. *Seduction*, 13.

29. When that strategy fails, he spins a yarn for Cressida meant to prove that Helen finds Troilus desirable, a tactic ostensibly aimed at stirring jealousy but which also has the effect of reinforcing Helen's status as Cressida's mirror (1.2.92–176).

30. I draw this image quite directly from Fassbinder's film, *Gods of the Plague*, which Silverman discusses in "Fassbinder and Lacan," 134–36. "Pinned on the wall over Margarethe's bed is an enormous poster of a blonde woman's face, presumably a blown-up advertisement. The face bears a sufficiently close resemblance to Margarethe as to make evident even to the casual viewer that the poster represents the mirror in which that character sees herself. However, whenever Margarethe appears in the same frame as the larger-than-life woman, she is not only dwarfed, but diminished by the comparison" (134).

31. Catherine Belsey points out the ambiguity of this speech. The "unkind self" may not be synonymous with the "kind of self" that resides with Troilus, as I have taken it, but an alternative to it, "already determined to leave Troilus and become another's fool" ("Desire's Excess: *Edward II, Troilus and Cressida, Othello*," in *Erotic Politics: Desire on the Renaissance Stage*, ed. Susan Zimmerman [New York: Routledge, 1992], 95). Charnes takes this latter view, arguing that Cressida, overburdened by her notorious identity, knows that she will, in fact, betray Troilus. ("'So Unsecret to Ourselves,'" 78). Such a reading seems to me to reduce Cressida's subjectivity to an effect of textuality and to minimize Cressida's *difference* from her notorious identity.

32. *Seduction*, 69.

33. See note 28.

34. *Disowning Knowledge in Six Plays of Shakespeare* (Cambridge UP, 1987), 35.

35. Girard contends that Troilus loses his desire for Cressida after sleeping with her and retrieves it only when her reference to herself as "a woeful Cressid 'mongst the merry Greeks!" (4.4.56) conjures the presence of male rivals ("The Politics of Desire in *Troilus and Cressida*," 188–98). Girard contends that Troilus' rivalry with the Greeks—his "mimetic desire"—revives his desire for Cressida. While I would agree that, within the world of the play, "it always takes other men to make an erotic or military conquest truly valuable in the eyes of the conqueror himself" (193), I would argue that Troilus' desire—his desire for *satisfaction*—remains intact after sleeping with Cressida, and that her assignment to the Greek camp enables precisely the *symbolic* satisfaction for which he ostensibly longs.

36. See Adelman's incisive analysis of Cressida's characterization. The problem is not her "inconsistency" but her "opacity" once she leaves Troilus. She ceases to be a character in her own right: "[T]he play makes her status as subject contingent on her relationship with Troilus: separated from him, she becomes irreducibly other; and her sexual betrayal is the sign of her status as opaque object" (*Suffocating Mothers*, 52). I would certainly agree that Cressida recedes as a subject once she leaves Troilus, that the

spectator has less access to her interiority, but the continuity in her characterization is more important than the discontinuity. Cressida has difficulty representing herself and appears "irreducibly other" *throughout* the play. Her "opacity" once leaving Troilus only intensifies her essential unrepresentability. I would agree with Freund's assertion that "Cressida always exists only as a sign to be recontextualized" ("'Ariachne's Broken Woof,'" 31)—so long as one strikes the words "always" and "only." In the play's phallocentric world, she exists as a sign to be recontextualized, all right, but also as a desiring woman aspiring to a coherent subjectivity. The feminist gestus I have devised is designed to capture the tension between the two.

37. Adelman astutely points out that Cressida's behavior in the "kissing scene" revives the defensive sexual wit she displayed in 1.2 (*Suffocating Mothers,* 51). Inasmuch as that witty persona turned out to be fraudulent, however, one could say that she offers, in the kissing scene, the performance of a performance.

38. I have substituted the Arden "accosting" for the Riverside (and quarto and folio) "a coasting" in order to clarify the image: Cressida welcomes accosting; she incites amorous overtures; she *seduces.* See Kenneth Palmer's note on this line (*Troilus and Cressida,* 247).

39. Geoffrey Aggeler, "Utah Shakespeare Festival," *Shakespeare Quarterly* 36 (Summer 1985), 231.

40. Roger Warren, "Shakespeare in Britain," *Shakespeare Quarterly* 37 (Spring 1986), 117.

41. As Barbara Bowen observes, "In this context, Cressida's choice of Diomedes becomes an understandable reaction to the need for a guardian and her 'betrayal' of Troilus appears guiltless and inevitable" (*Gender in the Theater of War* [New York: Garland, 1993], 56).

42. This problem of unengagement arose at Shakespeare Santa Cruz's 1994 production of *The Merchant of Venice,* in which the character of Portia was essentially fragmented into three separate personae: an empty-headed princess in a silly wig and frilly gown; an insecure, cross-dressed girl over-matched by her self-appointed mission, and a powerful, charismatic woman. Portia became an aggregate of three unassimilated images, lacking the underlying sense of character with which to make them signify dramatically or provide a stable base for the director's intended gestus of female empowerment.

43. Lorraine Helms discusses the difficulties of acting Cressida in her essay, "Playing the Woman's Part: Feminist Criticism and Shakespearean Performance," in *Performing Feminisms,* 196–203. Helms raises some important issues, but I would disagree that the "calculated artificiality" of rhymed couplets in Cressida's soliloquy in 1.2 "serve[s] mimetically to represent the coquetry which patriarchal criticism attributes to Cressida" (200). Skilled actors can minimize the artificiality of rhymed couplets through arhythmic readings and strong subtextual dynamics. Because Cressida, left alone, is unburdening herself of her deepest anxieties, her speech need not seem calculated or artificial.

44. Helms discusses the way in which this scene was staged in the 1987 Stratford, Ontario, production: "Diomedes subjected Cressida to relentless symbolic violence, intermittently underscored by physical menace. He left Cressida so near hysteria that, when she came to her soliloquy, the words were virtually unintelligible. The text of Cressida's collusion gave way before an image which represented the terror of rape as

forcefully as Gloucester's on-stage blinding represents the horror of mutilation." Helms suggests that this staging achieved a feminist gestus, not simply because it "deconstructed the patriarchal representation of a vain and shallow coquette," but because it also deconstructed Troilus' vilifying of her: "[T]he audience had just seen a rape; they now saw patriarchal ideology at work as Troilus bustled about blaming the victim" ("Playing the Woman's Part," 202–203). This staging, like the gestus of gang-rape in the kissing scene, employs the imagery of male brutality not only to create sympathy for Cressida but to explain otherwise inexplicable behavior and thus preserve the character's continuity and integrity. I would argue that a more equivocal treatment of the scene and a less violent dislocation between Cressida's conduct and Troilus' interpretation more ably renders her position as a fragmented female subject. Judging from Barbara Hodgdon's account, Davies's production seems closer to the mark: Juliet Stevenson's moody, anxious Cressida bestowed affections on Diomedes in a manner that, according to Hodgdon, could be read as strategic rather than sincere, rendering the male spectators' pejorative commentary explicitly erroneous. Moreover, the scene was set in semi-darkness, shifting focus from Cressida's and Diomedes' bodies to the male onlookers' voices, underscoring their ability "to control the meaning of the spectacle" ("He Do Cressida in Different Voices," 282–83).

45. Adelman implicitly finds this speech inadequate as an explanation of Cressida's action, arguing that, "after 4.4, the play gives us no place to ground our speculation" about her motives; "exactly when we most need to understand what Cressida is doing, we are given no enlightenment" (*Suffocating Mothers,* 51). Helms asserts, "these lines make sense from Troilus' perspective, from Ulysses' or Thersites', but not from Cressida's. Such decentering renders this speech among the most difficult to perform in the Shakespearean canon; it also presents perhaps the greatest challenge to a feminist performance" ("Playing the Woman's Part," 202). I believe the speech, albeit sketchy and recessive, does contain clues for both the textual exegete and the actress. Assuming that Cressida actually does find herself attracted to Diomedes, as their scene together suggests, she resolves her conflicted feelings by submitting them to the patriarchal notion of female wantonness: "The error of our sex" is the received myth through which she manages an otherwise unmanageable sexuality. Taking her attraction to Diomedes as evidence of her unredeemable depravity, she consents—at least within the scene—to the act that would confirm it.

46. Joel Fineman contends that Cressida's faithlessness threatens Troilus with "No difference," with a denial of his necessary distinction from Diomedes and all other men ("Fratricide and Cuckoldry: Shakespeare's Doubles," in *Representing Shakespeare: New Psychoanalytic Essays,* ed. Murray M. Schwartz and Coppélia Kahn [Baltimore: Johns Hopkins UP], 99). Fineman's argument coalesces somewhat with mine: the "distinction" that Troilus wishes for depends, I would say, upon Cressida's demonstrating her satisfaction by him.

47. *Seduction,* 22.

48. In Libby Appel's 1984 production for the Utah Shakespeare Festival, Cassandra "spoke the prologue and remained on the balcony above the main stage during much of the action to function as a chorus. In the play's concluding scene, she was joined by Thersites and Pandarus to utter in a choric chant Pandarus' bitter farewell to the audience" (Geoffrey Aggeler, "Utah Shakespearean Festival," 230).

49. In Barton's 1976 revival, Diomedes entered the scene of his encounter with

Cressida with a "Helen doll" slung over his shoulder, which he retrieved after exiting, triumphant, with the sleeve that Cressida gave him (see Hodgdon, "He Do Cressida in Different Voices," 278). At the end of the play, after Pandarus' final speech, Thersites could be seen in an underground vault fondling a life-size female doll (see Bowen, *Gender in the Theater of War*, 53). These dolls, like my mannequins, situate Cressida's downfall within a phallocratic culture that objectifies and fetishizes the female body. As Bowen puts it, "it seems clear that Barton was suggesting that Cressida's self-division . . . is inevitable in a world that turns women into icons. Barton's final image, then, of Thersites holding a doll becomes a bitter parody of Paris and Helen, Troilus and Cressida, Cressida and Diomedes; in fact, of the whole Trojan conflict over sexuality as possession" (*Gender in the Theater of War*, 53).

Bowen also credits Barton with two other choices conducive to feminist subtext: "Helen appeared bound to Paris by a golden chain, with which she was led about the stage; Cressida in the betrayal scene was given a courtesan's mask to wear on the back of her head, revealing it only as she turned to exit with Diomedes" (*Gender in the Theater of War*, 53).

Some reviewers saw the mask not as a gestic signifier of Cressida's subjection to text, however, but as a reductive, unironic confirmation of her descent into harlotry (see Warren, "Theory and Practice: Stratford 1976," 175). Interestingly, the mask later was dropped in favor of Cressida's emitting a brazen cackle as she accompanied Diomedes offstage. By transforming Cressida from sign (mask) to agent (cackle) this choice becomes a more straightforward signifier of her corruption, making her not the hapless recipient of a notorious identity but the active embodiment of it.

50. As Adelman observes, "in its treatment of Troilus as a warrior . . . the play here conflates a developmental narrative (in which young Troilus emerges into fierce manhood) with a narrative of escape from emasculation (in which love has disarmed an already accomplished warrior)" (*Suffocating Mothers*, 61).

51. In Sam Mendes's 1990 RSC production, Thersites was a "white-faced" hunchback, "with eyes red with rheum, his hands covered in surgical gloves to hide his eczema" (Peter Holland, "Shakespeare Performances in England, 1989–90," 173). Certainly Thersites' own bodily corruption could help account not simply for his disease-ridden language but for his snarling misanthropy, perhaps even his status as "privileged man"—a man forced into marginalization by his physical repulsiveness.

52. I theorize these homosocial dynamics with help from Eve Kosofsky Sedgwick's seminal study, *Between Men: English Literature and Male Homosocial Desire* (New York: Columbia UP, 1985), esp. 1–27.

53. See Spear's extended discussion of the play's evocation of the penetrable male body ("Shakespeare's 'Manly Parts,'" 418–19).

54. Berry, *Changing Styles in Shakespeare*, 59.

55. Robert Speaight, quoted in Berry, *Changing Styles in Shakespeare*, 59.

56. See Alan C. Dessen, "Price-Tags and Trade-Offs: Chivalry and the Shakespearean Hero in 1985," *Shakespeare Quarterly* 37 (Spring 1986), 104.

57. In Davies's production, Pandarus was devastated by the separation of the lovers: "[H]e broke down, and ended up a wreck in dark glasses, obsessively playing the piano throughout the final battle sequences while the set collapsed around him" (Roger Warren, "Shakespeare in Britain, 1985," 118).

# INDEX

DAVID MCCANDLESS is Associate Professor of Theatre and English at Carleton College.